SO LONG UNTIL TOMORROW

So Long Until Tomorrow

*From Quaker Hill
to Kathmandu*

by LOWELL THOMAS

WILLIAM MORROW AND COMPANY, INC.
NEW YORK   1977

Printed in the United States of America.

1   2   3   4   5   6   7   8   9   10

Library of Congress Cataloging in Publication Data

Thomas, Lowell Jackson (date)
   So long until tomorrow.

   Continues Good evening everybody.
   Autobiographical.
   1. Thomas, Lowell Jackson.   2. United
States—Biography.   I. Title.
CT275.T554A35   070'.92'4   [A]   77-10541
ISBN 0-688-03236-2

BOOK DESIGN   CARL WEISS

To L.T. Jr. and Tay,
who share many
of these adventures

Contents

I pity the man who can travel from Dan to Beersheba, and cry, 'tis all barren.

—LAURENCE STERNE, 1713–1768

Foreword: Catching Up with Myself

"You are old, Father William," the young man said,
  "And your hair has become very white;
And yet you incessantly stand on your head—
  Do you think, at your age, it is right?"
                                        —Lewis Carroll

"Sure."

                                        —L.T.

Two years ago, when I had written 100,000 words of this memoir and had only gotten myself to the year 1941 and the Japanese attack on Pearl Harbor, my publisher urged me to continue the story in a second volume. As usual I have been on the move both here at home and around the world, and everywhere I have been asked, "When will you tell us the rest of it?" At my age nearly everything reminds you of something else and so, here I am, writing this introduction to the rest of the story.

The fact is that the coming of World War II was a logical place to take a breather. It marked the end of an era. For a fabulous half-century before, the world had been treated to an astonishing array of new marvels—the telephone, automobile, airplane, motion pictures, radio and television, to mention only the obvious. It is true that we had also been through a world war and a catastrophic depression, but words like "Buchenwald" and "nuclear bomb" and "ecological disaster" had not yet become part

11

of the language; nothing seemed irrevocable and hope was more than a Sunday sermon.

It was in that buoyant and sometimes half-mad period that I was young. In the first book of this ongoing saga, I told how growing up on a mountain in Colorado's Cripple Creek gold camp with mining men who had roamed the world had imbued me with a zest for far horizons, and how I began reaching for them when I was just past twenty and took my first trip to Alaska. Now, looking back over that long stretch of years, it seems that thereafter I was always on my way to catch a ship, train or plane.

In 1917, there came the unexpected, thoroughly incredible experiences with the armies in Europe and the Near East. In Italy, I heard that a new commander, a certain General Allenby of cavalry fame, was being sent to Egypt, and I played a hunch into the great adventure that changed my life. Pulling strings from Rome to London and back, I got myself assigned to Allenby's command—the only foreign journalist so accredited. Arriving to report the fall of Jerusalem to Allenby's army, I stayed to join a mysterious, almost mystical young English archeologist who was leading the Arabs in battle against their Turkish occupiers, a blue-eyed anomaly named T. E. Lawrence. Ben Hecht once said that I half-invented Lawrence, but no one could have even partially invented that moody and tragic genius. I simply told what I had seen—and it turned out to be the first time the outside world had heard anything of Lawrence's brilliant desert campaign.

After the war, following a season in New York at the Century Theater and at Madison Square Garden, in a sort of command performance I told the Allenby-Lawrence story for a long run in London's Covent Garden and at huge Royal Albert Hall, then took my picture-and-word production around the world. This only heightened my taste for travel, and I spent another year in Malaya, Burma, India, and on into Afghanistan, then a forbidden kingdom, where I filmed the ruler, Amir Amanullah, and his exotic people.

By the year 1930 I was settled into what might have seemed a routine way of life. My wife and I had taken over a farm in the hills of Dutchess County north of New York City and I was writing books, filling more platform engagements in the U.S.A. and Canada and making my first appearance on the new medium, radio, while trying to adjust to the good life of a country squire. Then one day swashbuckling Floyd Gibbons got in trouble with his radio sponsor and the next thing I knew I was on in his place, saying, "Good evening, everybody," and telling the day's news. I stayed at that for the next forty-six years, longer than anyone or any program in the history of the broadcast medium.

One of the things the Second World War ended was the first regular television program, actually a simulcast of my news broadcast. Washington said it couldn't spare the critical equipment in wartime, but I don't think I would have stuck with a regular TV program anyway—it would have tied me to a New York studio. So, as those of you who pick up the story here will see, I was off again, this time covering the European and Pacific war fronts and, afterward, roaming the wide world in search of high adventure to record on film for TV and screen.

In this volume, as in the first, I have tried to live up to a promise I made the reader: no pronouncements, no pontification. I want to tell about some of the fun I've had these eighty-five or so years, some of the fascinating people I've been lucky enough to meet and some of the good friends I've made. There is a little about golf and skiing, two of my enthusiasms, but again, no advice.

Before I began this autobiography, I wondered whether I really wanted to take the time to sit down and write about my life instead of actually living it. As it turned out, I've gone right on doing what I have always done—which may be why the writing of these books has taken so long, with events sometimes outpacing the writing. For example, at the end of this volume, I tell about my marriage and 50,000-mile honeymoon, events that were definitely not on the schedule when the writing began. And so if the reader finds the story ending somewhat abruptly, well, that's how life is. It isn't really the end, just the place where I've finally caught up with myself. Maybe I'll have more to tell at a later date. At age eighty-five, I wonder. Of course, I hope so.

L.T.

Quaker Hill,
Pawling, N.Y.

SO LONG UNTIL TOMORROW

I. The Rover Boys at War

The mission of this Allied Force was fulfilled
at 0241 local time, May 7, 1945.
—General of the Army Dwight D. Eisenhower

One day early in 1940, Niles Trammell, soon to retire as president of NBC, telephoned me to report that the network was going to launch a television news program. "Lowell," he said, "you put us in the news business with radio and now we want you to be the one to do it with TV. How about it?"

To be asked to take on history's first regular television news program was a distinct honor, and I told him so, but I had some reservations. Not everyone in the broadcast industry was fervent about television's future. Trammell's own boss, David Sarnoff, founder and chairman of NBC's omnific parent company, Radio Corporation of America, had recently warned me never to invest a nickel in TV. Its insatiable lust for talent would be impossible to satisfy, he said. Besides, the coaxial cable would cost too much, and the screen was too small. Talk about clouded crystal balls!

What really bothered me, though, was that television would tie me to a New York studio. Radio imposed no such limitation. In fact, for the last six years of the decade during which I had been doing the news, I was rarely seen at Radio City, broadcasting instead from near my home at Quaker Hill, seventy miles north of New York—the first remote studio in the business—or from wherever I had been lured by a ski slope or some other intriguing aspect of the globe's farther reaches.

Still, TV was another "first," maybe a more important one, and I could not turn down the challenge. "Okay, Niles," I said, and at 6:45 P.M., February 21, 1940, I went on the air with these words:

> Good evening, everybody. For the first time this nightly program is being televised as well as broadcast. In fact, Major Lenox Lohr, our new president of NBC, who is here with me on this historic occasion, has just remarked that this actually is the first sponsored program ever to go out by television.

What I now was doing was called a simulcast in those early days of the tube—broadcasting for radio and a TV camera at the same time. It was a far cry from today's massive productions, which involve hundreds of specialists and show business types every time Walter Cronkite, John Chancellor, Barbara Walters or David Brinkley goes on the air. I couldn't take a breather by passing the ball to a Charles Collingwood or a Garrick Utley in London. We old radio hands—who in 1940 included men like H. V. Kaltenborn, Raymond Gram Swing, Gabriel Heatter, Boake Carter and many others—were strictly on our own, and when I first brought the news to television, it was no different.

Oh, I did have a makeup man, but as Mark Twain once said about being ridden out of town on a rail, except for the honor of the thing I'd just as soon have passed it up. I hated to waste time at the studio, and usually arrived at the last split second. This turned the makeup man into a nervous wreck. There he'd be, quivering by the door when I walked in, with barely enough time to slap me in the face with a powder puff before the red light on the camera blinked to indicate that it was air time. Once I started the broadcast with a goodly coating of powder on my upper lip; I don't know how it looked to the people watching, but the cameraman broke up. After twitching and struggling for an agonizing sixty seconds, I finally let loose a gargantuan sneeze. Another first!

For a year or so, my wife Fran and I lived in an apartment at the Waldorf Towers, spending our weekends at Quaker Hill. The guns were already booming in Europe by then and the news was grim. One after another, Denmark, Norway, Holland and

Belgium fell to the Nazi blitzkrieg. In May, Neville Chamberlain, the symbol of appeasement, resigned and Winston Churchill became Britain's Prime Minister, offering his people nothing but "blood, toil, tears and sweat." Less than a month later, with France tottering, he defied Hitler to do his worst.

On June 4, I opened the news with this account of the disastrous Battle of Flanders.

> He did not gloss over the Allied defeat . . . the charge of complacency can no longer be brought against the London government. Britain will fight on. The Prime Minister made that pledge. He put it in these vivid phrases: "We shall fight in France, on oceans, on landing grounds, in fields, and in the streets. We shall never surrender."

Then French resistance collapsed altogether and the valiant British people stood alone. In the United States, President Roosevelt signed into law the first peacetime draft in American history. Peace had become a luxury for us, and a tenuous one at that. As the Japanese acted out their aggressive dreams of mastery in the Pacific, the United States embargoed shipments of scrap iron and cut back on the use of critical materials. Among the victims: the infant television industry.

I was just as happy. After a year, the spirit of wanderlust with which I seem to have been born was in full rebellion against enslavement to the TV camera. With the flames of war spreading across the world, I wanted to be free to move about, to do something more than walk from the Waldorf to Radio City and back again. Years later, with the war over and TV ready to boom, when asked to take on a nightly broadcast again I said no. I didn't want to live in New York City, I didn't want to be married to a camera. Over the next three decades, I would do several television series and a good many specials, and I still continued the daily news broadcast—but for radio only. Radio could go wherever I went—or nearly everywhere.

In the beginning, it felt good just to be back in the country. In 1926, when Fran and I bought a farm on Quaker Hill in the Lower Berkshires of New York State, the entire community consisted for the most part of a dozen or so farming families. Time worked its inevitable changes. The population grew, and to our regret the roads were paved; city families seeking the solace of the countryside built graceful new homes or remodeled old ones overlooking the long meadows where, two hundred years before, the Quaker settlers had flourishing farms.

I had worked a few changes myself. I had built a baseball field for our team, the Nine Old Men, where we played Sunday afternoon games against teams of celebrities such as Robert Ripley's Believe-It-Or-Nots, the New York Artists and Models Guild and President Roosevelt's improbable conglomeration of F.D.R.'s sons, government leaders and reporters called the Roosevelt Packers. And though the enthusiasm of all hands usually exceeded our skill, the crowds in the bleachers loved every uproarious minute of it, F.D.R. more than anyone.

We had over a hundred miles of bridle paths cleared. Robert Trent Jones laid out a golf course for us and Fran and I built a community clubhouse. By moving a couple of buildings and installing a tow, we had our own ski chalet, slope and trails, so everyone could enjoy skiing, a top priority enthusiasm of mine, right here at home. From a sleepy little country crossroad Quaker Hill had become a lively half-rural area with like-minded neighbors enjoying the blessings of peaceful, unspoiled surroundings and good company.

But one day in the autumn of 1942, as I ambled along the trails and winding roads on horseback, I was suddenly struck with the realization that the war, into which Pearl Harbor had plunged us less than a year before, had wrought its own changes on the Hill, and they were drastic. A strange new quiet had overtaken us. Not a young face was to be seen; the boys were off to the fighting and the younger women were backing them up in defense jobs. Those who remained stayed close to home, preoccupied with work and with the dark thoughts we all shared in that troubled time. In the spring, F.D.R. had sent me a poignant note—"Dear Lowell, I am afraid Hitler has ended our ball games for the duration"—and the ball field sat deserted all summer, as did the ski slopes in winter.

And somehow that all troubled me. Surely this wonderful place with its fine facilities could be put to use, even in wartime— especially in wartime! All over the country there were young men waiting to head out for the war fronts, or those already returned with psychic and physical scars; mightn't some of them find here a place to recover a sense of themselves and the country they were giving up so much to defend?

In Pawling, one of the nearby towns adjacent to our twelve-mile-long hill, others shared the same vague unease that we weren't doing more. For a time, the Army ran a cryptographic training center at Dr. Frederick L. Gamage's once-prestigious Pawling Boys' School, but then they combined it with an older code-cracking center at Rantoul, Illinois. So now we had an empty prep school as well as a nearby cottage-lined lake which Consolidated Edison had used as a rest and recreation center in happier days. But no G.I.'s.

Then I was approached by Ralph Lankler, a most unusual young divine who had come to Quaker Hill in 1934 as a visiting minister and is still with us today. He and others suggested that I go down to Washington and do some scouting. "Surely among all the important people you've met, Lowell, you'll find someone who is willing to let us get into the war."

I packed a bag and went, although two days in Washington for me usually was good for a handful of aspirins; some lobbyist or government official or the head of one national organization or another was always after me to say something on the air about his pet project. As for important people, the only ones who came to mind were my Dutchess County neighbors President Franklin D. Roosevelt and Henry Morgenthau, and somehow I doubted Pawling and Quaker Hill, which were not famous for electing Democrats, would be high on their list of concerns.

But as the train clacked south and I got to thinking how an airplane would have had me in my hotel room by then, someone else, who was important indeed, occurred to me—General Henry H. Arnold, Commander in Chief of the U.S. Army air forces throughout the world. Nearly twenty years had passed since "Hap" Arnold and I first crossed paths, but the circumstances were such that we had remained friends; after all, when two men get up and walk away from an airplane accident together, their fate is somehow linked and it is hardly surprising they'd stay in touch.

Arnold had been in official exile for some time when we first met, an airman relegated to the cavalry post at Fort Riley, Kansas, for his zealous support of the inspired but ill-starred pioneer of American air power, General Billy Mitchell. One day in 1923 I was at Fort Riley, presenting my Allenby-Lawrence film and my personal account of the Near East war. Arnold, fascinated by the subject, invited me to his quarters and kept me up half the night talking. In the morning, so that I would avoid a long, roundabout train journey, he had volunteered to fly me to Oklahoma City, next stop on my tour.

In a small, open-cockpit Jenny we took off on a memorable flight. Somewhere over Kansas, near Coffeyville, the OX-5 motor began coming apart, pieces flying out through the exhaust stack and threatening to behead me, but "Hap" sat right up there wrestling our wounded bird to earth, bringing it in with several bone-crunching bounces, but in one piece. Gazing around the potato field where we'd finally come to rest, I said, as soon as my breath came freely, "This isn't exactly the place I had in mind!"

To which Arnold replied, "You know, I've been meaning for a month to have that motor overhauled."

For years after, whenever "Hap" attended a function where I happened to be a speaker, he heard me retell the story. But when he became chief of the greatest air force in the history of aviation, with two and a half million men in his command, I decided it was no longer fitting.

Now, pressed as he must have been by more important matters, he made time to see me almost at once. And as soon as I told him the nature of my mission, he slapped his desk and said, "Lowell, you have come to the right place." For months, his top medical officers had been planning a whole series of rehabilitation centers across the country; now they—and he—were anxious to set one up as a pilot program and try out their ideas. Pawling, with its prep school and the Con Edison lake, assembly room, dining area and cottages, and the Quaker Hill facilities nearby, sounded perfect.

Within a few days of my return home, General David N. W. Grant, the Army Air Corps Surgeon General, and his colleague, Colonel Howard Rusk, who was to become the world's ranking authority on medical therapy and rehabilitation, arrived for a tour of our area. They must have liked what they saw, for barely a month later the Air Corps moved in doctors, nurses and administrative staff, followed by many wounded and exhausted airmen. U.S. Army Air Corps Rehabilitation Center No. 1 was in business, and a rewarding and exciting project it turned out to be—for all of us.

It put Pawling on the map, and the locals were much pleased. Apart from making the trails and ski slopes available with a "man without a country," the Marquis Nicolas degli Albizzi, as instructor, I arranged for a different guest speaker every Saturday morning, men like Eddie Rickenbacker, whose experiences would thrill and inspire any audience. But the recuperating airmen themselves had many a fantastic tale to tell, for they were among the first of our men to have been involved in combat. Many had rows of decorations attesting to their valor in battle, including a few Congressional Medals of Honor. In those early days of the war, no community had a better opportunity to hear such firsthand accounts of the fighting from the participants.

Some had already made quite a name for themselves, like Colonel Phil Cochran, the dashing fighter pilot who inspired cartoonist Milton Caniff's famous character Flip Corkin. General Jimmy Doolittle, not long returned from the hair-raising bomb run over Tokyo, also rested up at one of the cottages on the lake. But most were unsung heroes, and one, I decided, a jittery flyer just in from the South Pacific, had a story worthy of a book.

His name was Gordon Manuel, and he had been a guide in the Maine woods. The war had given him plenty of cause to be jittery. As he was returning from a night mission his B-24 bomber had been shot down off enemy-held New Britain, where he swam ashore with a broken leg, the only survivor. Somehow he managed to set it, subsisting on shellfish and eluding the Japanese until he'd recovered his strength. Then he joined the local tribesmen and organized them into a guerrilla force that harassed the Japanese garrison day and night. He told us how he once even crept into the city of Rabaul and, by the light of an erupting volcano, made sketches of the fortifications. Eventually he contacted the men of General George Kenney's New Guinea air headquarters and was rescued, decorated, promoted and eventually sent to Pawling to further recuperate.

I was all set to write Manuel's saga when I made two serious mistakes. First, I invited author Quentin Reynolds to give one of those Saturday morning talks, on a weekend when

I had to be away. When I returned, I found the enterprising Quent had whisked my man off to a New York apartment, and there kept him until he had the whole story, first published as a serial by *Collier's* Magazine, then as a book, *Seventy Thousand Against One*.

The ski area Fran and I had put on a nearby slope had turned out to be quite a success, and during the war was used by many of our country's top skiers, such as Fritz Wiessner of Himalayan fame; Steve Bradley, co-captain of a championship Dartmouth team; Art Devlin, an Olympic star; and many others who were temporarily or permanently marooned in New York City, or assigned to some war duty there. Luckily for us there was an international ski pro available who had been turned down by all the Allied armies because he had an Italian title. In those days we were jittery and suspicious of nearly everyone. During World War I, when I spent a short time with the Italian mountain troops, I had met one of their commanders, a marquis, who although his title was of Italian origin was also of English and Russian blood—an unusual athlete who had trained with both the Italian and the Czar's cavalry. We had met in the Alps, when I visited his *Arditi* on Monte Rosa. After the First World War he had come to North America and had spent a number of years as a winter sports director at the Lake Placid Club in the Adirondacks, and later, with his Norwegian friend Erling Strom, had established a camp for skiers, hikers and mountain climbers for the CPR, near Banff in British Columbia.

He had been wounded a number of times, and had become something of a hero in Italy. After the war he married an American nurse; she drowned at Lake Garda when they were on their honeymoon. Wanting to report to her parents in Denver, he applied for a leave of absence, but was turned down; thereupon he went AWOL and left Italy, never to return. This meant that when World War II came along, he was a man without a country. As a nobleman it would have been suicide for him to have returned to Russia.

In 1942 both Canada and the United States were unwilling to make use of his military talent. If there ever was a man ideally suited for a military career, it was the Marquis Albizzi. His pal Erling Strom once wrote of him:

The West was not for him. Neither was the East, for that matter. He belonged to another world and another time. His background and bringing-up made him unfit to cope with the trials and tribulations of present-day life. Tremendously powerful and with an almost cruel streak, absolutely fearless and impervious to pain, he would have done well with Attila, king of the Huns, or with Genghis Khan, or maybe Cortez could have used him in Mexico. Later than that he should not have lived.

Erling also went on to say that no one had influenced his life to the degree the Marquis had.

When I heard he might be available I lured him from Canada and put him in charge of our ski area, which for the duration was used by the airmen at the local rehabilitation center. The fliers who came to Strawberry Hill for ski instruction with the "Markee," as they called him, all said it did more for them than any other activity. No doubt this was because when you ski it's almost impossible to think of anything else. Also Albizzi had a tonic effect on them.

By the time General Jimmy Doolittle came to the Pawling Air Force Center for a brief visit, I had already been keeping tabs on his remarkable career for a decade or more. Then it took another thirty-five years to finish the book—mainly because Jimmy kept piling one fantastic exploit on another.

Ask any ten men in the world of aviation to name the top airman in history and nine of them will say Doolittle. Some think he doesn't look it. I disagree. He is short, nearly bald now and so diffident about his legend that you might easily mistake him for a retired bank clerk. But what a mistake that would be.

He grew up in Alaska, where his father was panning for gold on the beach at Nome. At school he was the smallest in his class and, as is often the case, became the butt of huskier classmates. This lasted until, one by one, he had "convinced" them. By the time he completed high school in California, he was amateur bantamweight champion of the Pacific Coast. At the University of California at Berkeley, someone talked him into taking on the school's three ranking light heavyweights and when he disposed of them in a total of four rounds, the boxing coach announced, "Doolittle, you may weigh only one hundred thirty pounds, but from now on you're the team light heavy-weight!"

Soon after, at the traditional meet between Cal and Stanford, he climbed into the ring with Stanford's highly-touted light heavyweight. The crowd, presuming they were to see a comedy act prior to the final bout, laughed appreciatively. A minute and a half later, the fight was over and the Stanford boxer, felled by a right-hand haymaker to the jaw, had to be dragged to his corner.

For a time Doolittle considered the ring as a career, but Jo, his lovely bride—who was to share so many of his adventures—persuaded him otherwise. Boxing's loss was aviation's gain. By the 1920s, Jimmy Doolittle had become one of the most spectacular flyers in the world, our number one test pilot and speed record-breaker. He made the first solo flight across the continent, from Florida to California; was first to do the supposedly impossible "outside loop"; first, at Massachusetts Institute of Technology, to earn the degree of Doctor of Aeronautical Engineering; and, backed by millionaire Harry Guggenheim, was the first ever to fly blind (all outside visibility cut off by a hood that made him absolutely dependent on instruments)—one of the most important steps in the advancement of aviation.

While doing research for the Guggenheim Foundation, Lindbergh and Doolittle were invited to spend the weekend at the Guggenheim home on Long Island. At a nearby estate, where they were taken to a party, they were introduced to the special guest of honor who had become famous as one of America's top polo stars. This tall, striking athlete, when introduced to the two, looked down at the shorter man and said: "So you're Jimmy Doolittle! I saw you only once before, and then only for a moment!" It was the Leland Stanford champion, the man Jimmy had knocked out. His name, Eric Pedley.

By the 1930s, with several South American countries in the market for military aircraft, most European and American plane builders, hoping to land fat contracts, were sending their fighter planes and their crack pilots to Colombia, Venezuela, Peru, Bolivia, Chile, Argentina and Brazil. Curtiss-Wright asked the Army Air Corps for the loan of one, Lieutenant James H. Doolittle, and sent him, along with a mechanic to do the maintenance and a vice president to do the selling. When he flew his

Curtiss Hawk to Chile he arrived at Santiago a bit ahead of his rivals.

As it turned out, Doolittle was to do some selling, too. After all, Jimmy's winning ways were not confined to the air; he also had—and still has—a flair for making friends. One evening, at a party with a group of Chilean airmen, he applauded their guitar-playing and Latin dances, then decided that diplomacy called for him to reciprocate. Unequipped to sing or dance, he entertained them with some acrobatics learned in his undergraduate days, climaxing his act with a handstand on a second-story window ledge. Unhappily, something gave—whether Jimmy or the ledge is unclear. But, making the best of it, he somersaulted in midair, landed on his heels and broke both legs. The mending job performed in a Santiago hospital was not the best. Jimmy's legs were always more than a little distorted after that, but it inhibited neither his flying nor his enormous zest for physical conditioning and today, in his eighties, he can still out-hike or out-run men half his age.

Jimmy was always a little reluctant to tell about that episode—"Yes, it happened," was about as far as he'd go. But many years later, when I was flying on a wartime tour with Sam Pryor of Pan American Airways and two generals, looking for sites for emergency airfields, I ran into a flyer who had been there that night and he corroborated every detail, including what happened next. Jimmy knew that occupying a hospital bed was no way to win an air meet.

The German air ace had arrived and was reported to have implied that his American rival was overstaying his time in the hospital, since his plane wasn't much to boast about. The stakes were already high, and now the feeling between the airmen mounted. When the President of Chile proposed an aerial circus for the edification of his Parliament, Jimmy and his mechanic devised some unusual splints using part of a lady's corset, and on the morning of the air circus they took him out to the airfield in an ambulance.

The German had already taken off. Doolittle was lifted into the cockpit of his plane, broken legs clamped to the rudder bar. Off he shot, heading straight for the German plane. Both men were combat pilots, both familiar with every aerial maneuver. But few could match Jimmy's skill in the sky. He kept diving at the other plane with his little Curtiss Hawk, coming closer and closer, finally driving the German so low over the field that he was forced to land.

He bounded out of his plane, full of fury. Had the Chilean officials seen what the insane American had done to him? Indeed they had—and Curtiss-Wright landed the order. A few days later, just for good measure, Jimmy again had himself hoisted into the cockpit and locked to the rudder bar. This time he took off to make the first solo flight across South America, over the towering Andes from Chile to Argentina.

Meanwhile I kept gathering biographical data on Doolittle, and Doolittle kept adding spectacular chapters to the story almost faster than I could record them. Then came the well-known climax, in April, 1942, when he led sixteen twin-engine B-25s off the heaving deck of the carrier *Hornet*, blasted Tokyo and gave American morale its greatest boost since the start of the war. The New York *Daily News* proposed that he should be named *Doomuch*. The Japanese, stunned, fell for F.D.R.'s little joke that the raiders had come from a secret base called Shangri-La.

Doolittle flew on and on. Soon he was in command of our air forces in North Africa, then later he was made head of the Eighth Air Force in England, playing a major role in Hitler's defeat. In peacetime, he became an adviser to presidents, a leader in the aerospace industry and a member of innumerable government boards and agencies.

The stormy day the B-25s took off from the pitching *Hornet*, one of the naval officers took out his watch. As Jimmy led the way the commander said: "Lieutenant Colonel Doolittle is on his way to Japan." Some minutes later he said: "Colonel Doolittle is now over Tokyo." And later still he said: "General Doolittle has landed in China." His prophecy was indeed accurate.

He returned from the Tokyo Raid as General Doolittle, and at the White House he received his Congressional Medal. Then he and his almost equally famous wife, Jo, came to visit us at Clover Brook. Fortunately we had time to take down the story of the flight which now had so greatly added to his fame. At 2:00 A.M. one morning the phone rang. It was General Arnold calling from Washington. He simply said: "Lowell, get him up, put him on the phone!"

After an early breakfast he kissed Jo good-bye and I drove him to Mitchel Field, on Long Island. He didn't tell any of us, including his wife, where he was going. On the way to Long Island, I suggested that he was bound for North Africa, which proved to be the case.

Then followed the next series of Doolittle adventures and experiences, his command of airmen who would play a major role in winning the war. In fact when we next met, underground, at his headquarters just outside London, two more stars had been added to his shoulders.

I am glad our book about Jimmy Doolittle is finally out, for there is no telling what he may do next.

It was in the early summer of 1943 that Sam Pryor, one of the heads of Pan American World Airways, had invited me to join him and an Air Corps survey team on a flight along South America's long northeast coast. More and more of our bombers and fighter planes were being ferried to the war fronts via the narrowest stretch of the South Atlantic, from Natal on the bulge of Brazil to Dakar in West Africa. But the hazards of the flight from the United States to Natal, over Brazil and the Guiana jungle, soon demonstrated the need for emergency airfields along the coast. Pinpointing likely sites was the mission of Sam Pryor and the Air Corps generals. Mine was to have a look at a little-publicized aspect of the war and do some broadcasts from the Caribbean, the Guianas and on down to Rio.

In Havana we were met by Colonel Leigh Wade, one of the pilots on the historic first flight around the world twenty years before. Leigh had quit the service between the wars and stories had it that he'd busied himself selling arms, and I mean airplanes and warships, in Latin America. As I didn't press him about it, we spent most of our brief time together reminiscing about the epochal first world flight, for which I had been the official historian.

In Dutch Guiana, we stayed at an airfield not far from where a bomber had crashed some days before. Military personnel had been scouring the terrain from the air and on foot and eventually found Tom Harmon, the pilot, who had ridden his plane into the forest. After landing in the treetops he had made his way to a river. But the other crew members, who had taken to their parachutes, were never heard from again. This was not an uncommon story in the untracked wilderness along the shoulder of South America, but the great airlift went on.

When we reached Natal, jumping-off point for the 2,000-mile flight across the Atlantic, hundreds of airmen were encamped along the beach, ready to take off shortly before dawn. The C.O. asked me if I would address them, and though I could hardly say no, I was at a loss for something appropriate to say. I am not much for such exhortations—nor did I think these fine young men needed me to urge them to do their best. As I climbed up on a box in the full moonlight and looked over all those khaki uniforms, I fell back on a subject obviously close to their hearts and one I never tire of: flying.

"Most of you men will be taking off from this beach in a few hours, headed for Africa. I wonder if any of you knows who was first to fly this ocean, the South Atlantic."

No one did—including me, until later, when I looked it up and learned it had been a Major Ramón Franco, brother of the Spanish dictator—but it started me off on a ramble through some of the major landmarks in aviation history. Lindbergh, I reminded them, had not been first to fly the North Atlantic. He had been the seventy-seventh. But he had been the first to do it alone. The honor of linking Europe and North America by air belonged to John Alcock, an Englishman, and his American co-pilot, Arthur Whitten Brown (both later knighted), who had done it in 1919, preceding Lindbergh by eight years. A barnstorming American named Clyde Pangborn deserves to be remembered as the first to fly the Pacific non-stop, dropping his landing gear after taking off from the coast of Japan and skidding to earth at his hometown, Wenatchee, Washington, a little over forty-one hours later. The greatest air race of all had been the race to see which nation's plane or planes would be the first to fly all the way around the globe. We had won this one. When I asked if any of the airmen there at Natal knew the names of our Army fliers who had been involved, only their commanding general answered.

At any rate this impromptu talk, in the dark there on the beach in Brazil, may have been responsible for what happened twenty-five years later when Lowell, Jr., and I produced a book, *Great Flights That Changed History*—a volume that included the most recent aerial first. He had taken part in the first flight around the world over both poles—the only time it has ever been done.

But as I spoke to those young airmen at Natal, I wondered how many would make it across to Dakar in West Africa. Early the next morning I heard their engines sputter to life, and then the lasting drone as they flew off in the gray light of dawn, and I wished them all a silent but fervent happy landing.

In the morning, I followed them partway out over the Atlantic. General Bob Walsh, the C.O. at Natal, had asked me if I wanted to fly out to the island of Fernando de Noronha, several hundred miles offshore, where U.S. forces were building an emergency landing strip. We flew in between two of the volcanoes that made up that rocky isle, a squeeze that probably wasn't as tight as it seemed at the time, and stayed to have lunch with the hearty, full-bearded men who were working on the field. Suddenly one of them, a young man with a particularly handsome growth of red whiskers, came up and said, "I'd like to shake your hand. I worked for you for two years, but this is the first time we've met." It turned out he had been a well-digger on the Quaker Hill property I had developed some years back, so we had a bit of a reunion on the Isle of Murderers—so named because it had once been the Brazilian government's equivalent of Devil's Island—4,000 miles from home.

When Sam Pryor and his party flew back north, I went on to Buenos Aires, crossing the Andes in a non-pressurized Panagra DC-3. At 17,000 feet, pilot Warren Smith invited me to join him in the cockpit and from time to time we each took a whiff from his oxygen bottle. When I asked him how many times he'd flown over the Andes, he casually remarked that this happened to be his one-thousandth crossing. I was impressed enough to mention this remarkable record to the President of Chile when we landed in Santiago. Next day there were front page stories about it in the Chilean press, and soon after Warren Smith was decorated by President Juan Antonio Ríos himself.

On I flew to Lima—where, for a formal dinner at the Presidential palace, I had to borrow a formal outfit. A tall Panagra executive was the one who came to my rescue. The sleeves were so long that every time I unlocked my elbows, my hands disappeared. Across from me at dinner was a red-headed Irishman, a member of the cabinet named Gallagher, who spoke not a word of English. His grandfather had been the engineer on Darwin's ship, the *Beagle*. Enamored of Peru, he had returned with a hundred or more Irish, who settled there at the foot of the Andes.

At Panama, I expressed a mild interest in the Canal defenses. The C.O. was Lieutenant General George H. Brett, who some months before had been General MacArthur's air commander. Brett hadn't gotten on too well with MacArthur and, as was the case with some other subordinate commanders in the South Pacific, before and after, he was assigned to an area where there was no action. General Ralph Royce later told me how his relations with the Supreme Commander in the Pacific had gotten to where they communicated only through memos.

General Brett, a pioneer in military aviation, onetime Chief of the Army Air Corps and now head of the Caribbean Defense Command, did not appear to be grieving at his ouster. He volunteered to fly me for a look at the Canal in his own B-17, and as we walked down the flight line, he told me something of its checkered past. Spanking new, it had been sent to the Philippines just before the Japanese made their surprise attack on Manila, catching most of our planes on the ground at Clark Field. The *Swoose*, as it came to be lovingly named, had been in the air and so escaped destruction. She was one of only a few and had gone on to serve valiantly in the Pacific war, her exploits featured in William L. White's best seller, *Queens Die Proudly*. Now she was pastured out in Panama, still in shabby battle dress, still full of bullet holes.

Making certain my flight aboard the *Swoose* would be unforgettable, General Brett flew her right down on the deck, bare yards above the Canal locks. I saw only a blur of ships, steel and water as we hedgehopped along, banked sharply and sped back. Once, though, I did chance to look around at the general's crew— a colonel, a lieutenant colonel and a major. All three seemed a little unhappy; the colonel was shaking his head in disbelief and the major had his eyes closed. It was clear they shared the feeling that, at fifty-seven, General Brett might be a little far along for that kind of hot-dog flying. But once again both the general and the *Swoose* came through, just as they had so many, many times before.

For most Americans past the age of forty, those war years are now a kaleidoscopic parade of memories, highlighted, perhaps, by a recollective flash that stops the action at the place they were and whatever they were doing on D-Day, or the moment they heard F.D.R. was dead. My kaleidoscope is elaborated by the broadcasts I did. To this day, whenever I leaf through the bound volumes of scripts lining the walls of my New York office, I feel again the tensions of a world at war, see faces that moved through my life during those moments in history, hear the voices of generals and the battle-weary G.I.s who might have been checked here, even thrown back there, but pressed relentlessly forward, tightening their stranglehold on Germany and Japan. Remember?

November 2, 1942. The United States invasion of North Africa so far is a complete success. General Eisenhower's advance guard is rolling toward Tunis at breakneck speed.

May 14, 1943. Tonight our soldiers are fighting in a nightmare of a place, Attu, one of the islands out at the end of the long Aleutian chain.

July 26, 1943. Well, the inevitable has happened—Italian fascism crashed in ruins, Mussolini fallen. In Sicily the Canadian Army has carved its way twelve miles nearer to Catania.

June 5, 1944. Rome has been captured! Columns of American tanks, armored cars and infantry moved down the broad Via dell'Impero, which seven years ago Benito Mussolini pointed out to me, as we stood on the balcony of the Palazzo di Venezia, as one of his proudest achievements.

June 6, 1944. Tonight's communiqué just in from D-Day invasion headquarters summarizes the news. "Allied forces," it says, "have succeeded in their initial landings in France." Our troops are battling in the streets of the Norman city of Caen, nine and a half miles inland.

January 3, 1945. The estimate from Allied headquarters is that Von Rundstedt has thrown in 200,000 troops—units of infantry and armor—to hold the Bulge.

The war was far from over, but everyone—including Hitler—knew it had entered its final, decisive phase. Fran and I were in Washington around this time and decided to salute General Arnold and his wife Bea with a dinner at the Mayflower Hotel. It seemed singularly appropriate to invite those pioneer airmen who, like "Hap" Arnold, had laid their careers on the line in support of Billy Mitchell. Mitchell, so far ahead of his time that he had been cashiered from the service, was long gone, but a handful of his disciples had persevered. Scorned in peace, they proved in the crucible of war the absolute clarity of Billy Mitchell's vision. Now they were back from exile, to the enemy's everlasting regret, commanding the world's most powerful air force. A great many of them were my friends, and I toasted them and their leader "Hap" Arnold: "Gentlemen, I think the War Department and the admirals believe you now. I'm sure Hitler does."

Among the guests at our Mayflower "Hap" Arnold party was Jack Frye, president of the newly organized Trans World Airlines. Frye had telephoned to ask if he might bring a friend. And so for the first time we met Howard Hughes, a tall, cold-eyed, rather strange young man, in formal dinner attire—except for his white tennis shoes. Howard Hughes, even then, looked solemn enough to have been at a funeral, haunted eyes staring at you out of a deadpan expressionless face. He said practically nothing, was hardly the life of the party, and left little impression on any of us.

But the evening turned out to be not exactly a total loss for Hughes. Some time later, he borrowed my NBC engineer, Dick Stoddard, for his record flight around the top of the world. Dick never did come back to us. He became a millionaire manufacturer of electronic gadgets—presumably backed by Hughes.

A few weeks later, General Arnold telephoned me: "Lowell, some of your radio and newspaper colleagues seem to have a secondhand idea of this war. I'd like to set it up for you to take a planeload over and show them what's going on. How about it?"

Although I laughed and wondered if he was pulling my leg, actually nothing could have pleased me more than to spend some time with our fighting men in France, Germany and Italy. But newsmen are a notoriously—even fanatically—individualistic lot and the thought of riding herd on a planeload of them! Ho! Ho! Oh, no! But I assumed my real responsibility would be to get them over to Europe and start them off, so I said, "Sure, 'Hap,' I'll do it." Thus began the saga of the Rover Boys Abroad, a film we made that no one had originally planned.

The group that General Arnold's Public Information office rounded up for the trip ran the gamut. Among them were left-leaning Johannes Steel, and a right-wing Republican, former Congressman George Hamilton Combs; nose-to-the-grindstone types, exceptionally able reporters like Quincy Howe, Cesar Searchinger, and John Vandercook, all radio commentators. The term "newscaster" hadn't yet been invented. New York *Herald Tribune* drama critic Howard Barnes may have been the most popular man aboard, a two-fisted drinker who put in considerable time sleeping it off. We were, as someone put it, quite a cross-section of American journalism.

After a night flight across the Atlantic, we landed at London's Croydon Airfield, to be met by Chris Young, an old skiing buddy of mine. I had tapped Chris to serve as my cameraman and there probably wasn't a happier guy in the European Theater of Operations. A surrealist artist and poet, poor Chris had been relegated to an underground darkroom and—until I asked "Hap" Arnold to assign him to me—was resigned to spending the war in his "black hole of Calcutta."

The others were all for an inspection of the London pubs, but after an evening with General Jimmy Doolittle in his subterranean headquarters I shooed them aboard the DC-3 assigned to us and off we went to make the rounds of our bomber and fighter bases in Europe. Then, confident my charges had gotten into the swing of things, I said "so long" and took off on my own. Without any precise idea of what I wanted to see first, I inquired about some of our farthest advanced units and learned that the 30th Division with Simpson's (Lieut. Gen. William H.) Ninth Army had reached the Weser River in northern Germany and had just taken historic Hameln. An Air Force one star general in a single-engine unarmed plane offered to take me there, and two hours later, flames from the burning city and the smoke of the continuing battle signaled our arrival.

I really had a brief panorama of what it was like up there as our lead elements went slicing through Germany. As it happened, I had a neighbor in the 30th, Les Ward, brother of my longtime secretary Electra. As I moved forward trying to find him, the impact of war, the selfless heroism it called forth in some men and the toll it exacted from all, struck as forcibly as it had more than a quarter of a century before when I covered the battlefronts of World War I. The commanding officer of the 30th, Major General Leland S. Hobbs, had his temporary headquarters in a large school building west of the Weser. There he sat composing letters to the next of kin of those recently killed in battle. He said his officers and men had the situation under control, so there he was calmly dictating, with a city in flames just across the river. Where were the children who once came to learn in this school? Hiding somewhere, hungry and afraid, as children in Poland, Holland, Belgium and France had hidden when the Nazi armies bestrode Europe—as though any of them, Allied or German, had any responsibility for the acts of the power-mad dictator who had called forth this holocaust.

The general directed me to a regimental headquarters inside the burning city. There a colonel assigned one of his officers to take me to the front where only an hour before the G.I.'s had been engaged in hand-to-hand combat. There is where I found Les. He had just taken two Nazi prisoners.

"Hi, Les. How're you doing?"

He peered under my steel helmet, obviously unconvinced by his first look. "Lowell Thomas!" he exclaimed. "Well, they always said you got around."

We had a chat. He gave me messages for Electra and the rest of his family. With a wave, he disappeared with his companions, and I started back. Les was lucky; he came through the war, raised a fine family and is one of Pawling's solid citizens.

When I returned to headquarters, the colonel (who had said, "*If* you come back, there is something here in Hameln you ought to see") took me into the still burning center of the city, to the *rathaus*. Hameln, of course, was known the world over as the city of the Pied Piper. The legend of how he led the children away forever is based on historic fact, one of those eternally fascinating puzzles of the past, for no one knows where they went or why. But the tale had been immortalized in one of the most famous of all clocks, the clock on the *rathaus* tower, from behind whose iron doors the Pied Piper emerged every hour, playing his alluring flute and followed by the children of Hameln. In happier days, streams of tourists came to marvel at it; alas, now the *rathaus*, Hameln's city hall, was a bombed-out ruin, the clock tower, the Pied Piper and the children all smashed and scattered in the heaps of burned and smoldering timbers.

But that wasn't what the colonel had brought me to see. He led me into some caverns they had discovered beneath the old building and his flashlight, cutting the darkness, lit up walls lined with rows and rows of dusty wine bottles. It was a genuine treasure trove, and as the captain and I walked along, we stopped now and then to inspect a bottle. We also liberated a few.

Suddenly we heard laughter in the blackness. Following the flashlight beam down a side grotto, we came on an unlikely detachment, two G.I.s accompanied by a Scot, his tam-o'-shanter well down over one ear, engaged in some spirited—if I may be forgiven the word—inter-Allied celebrating. The colonel was a good sort and gladly accepted the G.I.s' offer of a drink. The whole scene cheered me up enormously.

I was certain I had a story, and began interviewing the Scot. He turned out to be one of Montgomery's lads from the Fifth Army, well to the north. How had he gotten here? He wouldn't say. "Well, what's your name?" I persisted. "Who are you?"

He took another belt from his bottle, grinned and said, "I'm not the Pied Piper, I'm the pie-eyed Piper of Hameln."

Early in April, I rejoined the Rover Boys in Luxembourg, the little Grand Duchy which had been overrun by the Germans in 1940, retaken by Patton in 1944 and was now the headquarters of Omar Bradley, head of the Twelfth Army Group, described as "the greatest single striking force ever assembled under a single field commander." Here we had an opportunity to interview General Bradley, as down-to-earth and solid a leader as our army had produced. That night all of us broadcast to America by short wave from a mobile radio unit set up in a field near the city. We took turns, one man at the mike and the rest of us waiting outside, just sitting around on the grass and enjoying the soft spring evening. When our arch-liberal Johannes Steel went in to take his turn, we heard him defer to the censor by beginning, "I am somewhere in the center of Europe."

Whereupon John Vandercook sat up and in a voice easily picked up by the microphone, sang out, "Wrong, Johannes. You are, as always, to the left of center!"

We were still in Luxembourg on April 12 when the news that would stun the world reached us: President Roosevelt had died of a massive cerebral hemorrhage at his retreat in Warm Springs, Georgia. Next day, I talked about our new president in my broadcast:

> It has been noted that Harry Truman is a plain and modest Midwesterner, whom surprising circumstance carried from ward politics back in Missouri to the Presidency of the United States. And today with the newsmen he certainly was in character. Talking to them, he said: "Boys, when they told me yesterday what had happened, I felt like the moon and stars and all the planets had fallen on me."
>
> Meanwhile the race for Berlin goes on, with five American armored columns on their way to the Nazi capital.

Next day I took off on my own again. I had seen a bulletin to the effect that the city of Halle, then confronted by Major General Terry Allen's 104th Timberwolf Division, was one of the few places in Germany almost untouched by the Allied bombing. The name of Halle rang an immediate bell: I remembered it as the home of Count Felix von Luckner's mother, and if the city was still in one piece, there was a chance von Luckner would be there. And if there was one man in all Germany I wanted to see, it was the old Sea Devil.

I had known him by reputation even before we met, as who hadn't in those devil-may-care days after World War I. Von Luckner fit that madcap era perfectly, a huge, rollicking man who had paid his dues and now meant to enjoy every day of the rest of his life. "You know, Tommy," he told me once, "we all came into this world crying while everyone else was laughing. By Joe, I mean to go out laughing—let the others do the crying!"

During World War I, he commanded the legendary sailing ship, the *Seeadler—Sea Eagle*—a heavily-armed raider disguised as a Norwegian merchantman. In a few incredible months at sea, this amiable buccaneer sank $25 million worth of Allied shipping in two oceans without taking a single life or harming even one human. Captured, while in an open boat after leaving the coral

atoll of Mopelia in the South Pacific, he escaped from prison in
New Zealand, was captured again, escaped and was captured still
again. He was planning his third escape when the war ended.
Afterward, he traveled the length and breadth of defeated Germany, urging his discouraged countrymen—especially the younger
generation—to "stay with the pumps; do not abandon the ship!"

Felix and I became close friends when he and his beautiful Swedish countess came to Clover Brook so I could do a book
about his adventures, *Count Luckner, The Sea Devil*, and a se-
quel, *The Sea Devil's Fo'c'sle*. Then, in 1929, Chicago millionaire
Burt Massee chartered the count's luxurious, four-masted schooner
for a Caribbean honeymoon cruise with twenty-six guests including Fran and me, and von Luckner as skipper. Some say our
fantastic voyage might have gone on indefinitely if Massee hadn't
gotten a cable saying he'd been wiped out in the stock market
crash.

Felix and I stayed in touch until World War II broke over
Europe and, with it, his troubles with the Nazis. He had no use
for them, continued to praise the Americans—he had even written
a book glowingly describing his experiences in the United States—
and refused to give up the honorary citizenship granted him by
Britain and several American cities. Hitler, afraid to liquidate the
popular Sea Devil, a German national hero, had to content himself with a public burning of his books and the destruction of
von Luckner's four-masted yacht, the *Mopelia*. Meanwhile the
count himself was kept under house arrest in Berlin, appearing,
whenever he did, in the company of a pair of SS men. The only
time he could shake them was when he took them to the barroom at the Adlon Hotel and drank them under the table.

All this I'd learned from returned war correspondents
whom I queried for news of von Luckner; Glen Stadler of the
United Press supplied most of my information on von Luckner.
Then, with America's entry into the war, I lost track of him. But
now I thought I had a clue to the whereabouts of my old friend
and that I might even be able to help him and his countess.
Within a couple of days, I'd managed to catch a plane and a jeep
headed in the right direction and arrived at Terry Allen's headquarters outside Halle only hours after his troops had taken the
city. I and the general in command of the 104th Division had
had a mutual friend, General Ted Roosevelt, President Theodore

Roosevelt's oldest son, who had died on a Normandy beach after splashing ashore with his division in the great invasion, and Allen received me warmly. Almost too warmly—after dinner they gave me quite an initiation and at 2:00 A.M. proclaimed me a member of their Timberwolf Division: uniform, shoulder insignia and all. When I asked Terry Allen whether he had any word about Count von Luckner, he laughed and said he certainly did. The old Sea Devil was indeed in Halle; when things had begun to fall apart in Berlin, he'd given his guards the slip and, with his wife, made his way here to be with his mother, who was nearly a hundred years old.

How did General Allen know all this? Because von Luckner had been at this headquarters only two days before, sitting in the same chair I now occupied.

Then he went on to tell me the story, and it was in the truest von Luckner tradition. Allen said when the 104th Division closed on Halle, his intelligence reported that die-hard SS troops still held the city and were resolved to fight to the last man. Allen ordered leaflets dropped with a no-nonsense ultimatum: if there was any resistance, the American artillery was prepared to reduce Halle to rubble.

The results were dramatic. Everyone in the city knew von Luckner; now, facing disaster, the civilian population turned to him for help. Women and aging men came and pleaded with him to save Halle. Believing his friendship with the Americans was worth something, the count tucked the scrapbooks of his triumphant American tour under his arm and made straight for the 104th lines. Luckily the scouts didn't shoot him down—presumably, gigantic as he was, he did not look particularly menacing armed only with a bundle of books. But his bearing was such that when he demanded to be taken to their commanding general, they looked at each other, shrugged and complied.

Telling the story, Terry Allen laughed again. He said he had never heard of von Luckner, but after looking through the scrapbooks and listening to the jovial count's tale, he was convinced he was indeed in the presence of a kindred spirit. When von Luckner asked that the bombardment be postponed for forty-eight hours to give him a chance to get the SS to leave, Allen agreed.

He had not seen von Luckner since. He did not know what he had said to the SS commander, but it could not have been an easy thing. For not until moments before the deadline, only a few hours before I'd arrived, had the SS fanatics slunk away to the east leaving Halle open to the American advance. The city was saved; once again Count Felix von Luckner had rendered an incalculable service to his beleaguered countrymen.

Next morning, Colonel Ralph Willey, one of Terry Allen's staff officers, went with me into Halle to find him. Ironically, von Luckner's ancestral home had been one of the few buildings in all the city to have been bombed out. He was staying, we learned, with a doctor in the next street. It was still early when we knocked on the door. The von Luckners, the astonished doctor replied to my inquiry, were still in bed. I asked if we might come in and wait, and as he was hardly in a position to refuse, he invited us to step inside.

It wasn't long before von Luckner, an imposing six feet four, appeared at the top of the stairs. He didn't see me at once, as I stepped behind the colonel and the doctor. When he came down, I put my arm around his shoulder and gently said, "Hello, Felix. How are you?"

He looked at me sharply, the shock of recognition spanning the years in a flash. Then he burst into tears. As soon as he could speak, he bellowed up the stairs in English, "Ingeborg! Ingeborg! Look who's here, by Joe! It's Tommy!"

We had a marvelous reunion, laughing, crying, drinking heartily from the bottle Terry Allen's staff colonel had brought along. But Felix's troubles were not over. The Russians were due to take over Halle, and about all they'd be likely to provide for an aristocratic former officer of the Kaiser's navy was a firing squad.

Lieutenant General George Patton's Third Army headquarters were then at nearby Leipzig and, as it happened, the Rover Boys were about to pay him a visit. I rejoined them at once and we were warmly welcomed by America's most colorful World War II commander. Fortunately General Patton had read my book about von Luckner—appreciatively, he said, as only one flamboyant personality can appreciate another—and promptly dispatched one of his officers to bring the von Luckners from Halle.

Next morning, I happened to be downstairs ahead of the

rest of our group. As Patton came striding up I noticed he was wearing the four stars of a full general on his collar. "Sir," I said, "I wonder if I am the first to congratulate you?"

"Ssh," he said, grinning. "It isn't official. I've been nominated but not yet confirmed by the Senate!"

We shared a secret laugh and I knew the irrepressible George Patton and freewheeling Felix von Luckner were, by Joe, really going to enjoy one another. And they did. Patton kept the von Luckners at his headquarters for a lively week or more, Felix entertaining the Third Army general and staff with his tales and the same uninhibited zest he had displayed for the Kaiser, the Czar and endless audiences over the years. Then Patton had the von Luckners spirited off to safety in Sweden.

By that time I was long gone. I had a rendezvous over Berlin.

First there was a rumor that Berlin had fallen to the Russians, and the Rover Boys persuaded Colonel Bill Nuckle, our liaison officer, to fly us straight into Tempelhof, the airfield in the heart of Berlin. Had we survived, it could have been quite a coup. Luckily, though, we didn't stake our lives on the chance to be the first Allied journalists to reach the capital of the crumbling Third Reich. As we were boarding our plane, one of Nuckle's aides came speeding out in a jeep and convinced us to change our plans. The fact was, he had learned, that far from having surrendered the city, Nazi troops were clinging to it desperately and at that moment were fighting a fierce block-by-block battle against the advancing Russians. Furthermore, their anti-aircraft batteries were still blazing away. It would have been, to say the least, highly embarrassing had we tried landing in their midst.

The Rover Boys decided to head back to Paris. Once again I detached myself, flying forward to an advanced American air base where our planes were making periodic reconnaissance flights over the front line and beyond. When I asked the C.O., Colonel Dick Leghorn, whether I could hitch a ride with one of his pilots, he volunteered to fly me himself—if I didn't mind riding piggyback. His plane was a single-seat Mustang P-51, but if I really was set on flying over Berlin, he would remove the radio equipment and maybe I could squeeze into the small space behind the cockpit.

"Sure," I said blithely, and I don't think I've ever been so cramped in my life, folded over so my chin rested on my knees and the top of my head pressed against the canopy. On the other hand, what non-combatant had such an overview of one of the war's climactic moments?

We took off with a lieutenant colonel, his second-in-command, flying wing cover in another Mustang. Soon enough black, billowing smoke clouds on the German plain clearly outlined the doomed city. As we zoomed over at a thousand feet, it looked as though it had been devastated by a massive earthquake. Mountains of smoldering rubble lined the streets; whole blocks consisted of nothing but the battered and scooped-out shells of office buildings and apartments, some of them crashing to dust even as we circled above. Erupting water mains spewed fountains into the streets while, yards away, fires burned out of control.

This was the city on which, boasted Hermann Goering, not an enemy bomb would ever fall; if even one did, he once taunted some British visitors, "you can call me Meyer." Now, hidden in the rubble below, the people who believed him, the haunted remains of Berlin's 4,500,000 population, crouched in their self-inflicted darkness and waited for the invader.

Down there, too, Adolf Hitler stalked through his bunker beneath the Reichschancellery, sending fantasy orders to non-existent armies, then falling into paroxysms of rage when no counterattacks developed. A few days later, on April 30, 1945, he would be dead by his own hand, forced at last to face the bitter truth that he had brought his vaunted Thousand Year Reich to ruin. It had lasted a bit more than twelve years.

Meanwhile, the Soviet forces pressed on inexorably. On the eastern outskirts of the city, their tanks and rocket trucks could be seen clambering over the debris, pushing toward the heart of the city—the once glorious Unter den Linden, the Potsdamerplatz and the Tiergarten. Watching, I tried to reconstruct the Berlin I remembered from those chaotic days just after World War I, when the Kaiser had fled and the forces of revolution battled a tottering government for control. There were machine-gun battles in the streets then, snipers in or on every building, danger everywhere. But Berlin endured. Now, in its World War II death spasm, it was unrecognizable; the Berlin I knew was gone forever.

Back at the base, I caught a ride to Paris, again flying

piggyback, this time in a twin-engine P-38. I had no difficulty communicating with the pilot—I was doubled up on his shoulders, my face about three inches from his ear. It was quite a flight. Halfway to Paris he announced his intention of demonstrating for me the virtues of the P-38. I assured him he didn't need to bother. No bother, he insisted; he was that proud of his airplane. Why, even with my extra weight it had enough power to fly on a single engine. Whereupon he feathered the port engine and we slowed dramatically and began to lose altitude.

"Listen," I said, "you don't have to put on a show for me. I'm glad to take your word for the plane's capabilities."

"No, no, you've got to see this for yourself. No other fighter plane would stay in the air, overloaded as we are and with one engine out."

And he went on about the P-38 with the intimate tone a man usually reserves for the girl he loves, while I watched the green fields moving up and even closer to us. Occasionally he gave the operating engine a spurt of power and we leveled off, or even climbed a bit, but by the time we approached Orly, a military field outside Paris, there was no need for us to go into a descent pattern; we were barely a hundred feet off the deck.

As a pilot he also was quite an actor. As soon as we hopped out, he told me the port engine had conked out all on its own. Grinning with relief, he said if he hadn't feathered it when he did, it probably would have caught fire in midair. So over the last two hundred miles, putting on a little show for my benefit, he had struggled to keep the crippled plane aloft.

"You certainly had me fooled," I said, happy to have had this news with both feet planted on the ground. "Were you worried?"

"Only about what I might tell you if the other engine gave out."

I had a lot to report on my broadcast—the flight over a Berlin in flame and ruin; a description of the beaten German armies I'd seen fleeing west in milling disorder; and my own encounter with a P-38 and its wing-and-a-prayer pilot—also finding Count von Luckner, the Sea Devil. Afterward, my colleague John Vandercook congratulated me on having come back with so much material. Although I was the veteran of our group, he said, I'd been the only one with the energy and resourcefulness to go off on my own and find the war. The rest of the Rover Boys, he noted glumly, had passed much of their time sitting around the Hotel Scribe, venturing forth only far enough to buttonhole some staff officer or politician, and were now reduced to reporting each other's conjectures.

I laughed, and then kept moving. I'm not exactly a loner by nature, but I figured I had the rest of my life to drape myself over a hotel bar if I chose to do it. Meanwhile there were dramatic stories breaking all over Europe and I meant to get as close as I could to them. This time I flew off to Italy, landing at Caserta, near Naples, where Colonel Tex McCrary, an old friend, invited me to share his Quonset hut.

Tex, a savvy New York public relations man wearing the silver leaf of a lieutenant colonel, was then in the throes of his spectacular pursuit of actress Jinx Falkenburg. She had come through Caserta with a USO troupe not long before and suave, worldly Tex McCrary was now no better off than a fifteen-year-old schoolboy suffering through his first crush. The walls of his quarters were plastered with pictures of the alluring Jinx; there wasn't much else he cared to talk about, and he sighed a lot. He had already followed her across half of Europe and, next day, was glad to fly me to General Mark Clark's headquarters outside Florence in hopes of a scrap of news of her troupe's whereabouts. Fortunately for Tex's sanity, he and Jinx were married less than two months later. After the war they launched their long-running network radio show, raised a fine family and, in the best romantic tradition, lived happily ever after.

General Clark invited me to stay for luncheon. It was a momentous day; not far from Lake Como near the Swiss border, Benito Mussolini had been captured and Clark looked forward to interrogating him within the next few hours. But as we sat at the table, a staff officer came in and silently gave him a slip of paper. That night, April 30th, I broadcast the news:

When I talked with General Mark Clark, word had come from Italian partisans that Mussolini had been picked up. That was all, at first. But as we sat at lunch a penciled note was handed to the general. It read: "Mussolini, his mistress and a group of his close associates—eighteen in all—have been shot, and their bodies are now on exhibition in a public square in Milan."

I flew on to Rome, where I hoped to interview the Pope. Thanks to the intercession of Acting Ambassador Harold Tittmann, barely an hour after my arrival I was being led through the maze of marble loggias at the Vatican, a contingent of the colorful Swiss Guard bringing their maces to the floor with a crash as I passed. I was ushered through an anteroom swarming with cardinals and bishops, their cassocks swirling as they turned to watch me go by, enviously perhaps, as I was shown straight through. And then, all at once, I was alone in a huge tapestried chamber with a frail, ascetic-looking man who took my arm in greeting and led me to a chair. It had all happened so quickly that not until we sat facing each other was I fully aware I was chatting with His Holiness, Pope Pius XII.

We talked for half an hour or more, of the war years when he had been a virtual prisoner in this little enclave, of his prayers that the coming peace would forever end the scourge of militarism and killing, his hope for America to use her great strength to lead the world toward reconciliation and justice, and about his travels in America when he was the Papal Nuncio.

A few minutes before noon, His Holiness told me how each day, on the stroke of twelve, he met to pray with soldiers of the Allied armies. There would be many Americans today, he said, and perhaps I would like to join them now; and he would follow in a few moments. Whereupon he showed me to a door opening into a crowded chapel. It was jammed with a thousand or more soldiers, more than half of them G.I.'s, obviously waiting in some suspense for His Holiness. And as I closed the door behind me and looked out at the sea of men, all of them staring straight back at me, one voice, in unmistakably New York accents, sang out to register their joint disappointment: "Hell, he ain't no Pope!"

Berlin fell on May 2nd, and it all went quickly after that. While isolated fragments of the *Wehrmacht* battled on in deepening futility, shattered units and hundreds of thousands of men fled westward in an effort to elude the Russians by surrendering to the Allies. Grand Admiral Karl Doenitz, anointed Hitler's successor, cabled back, "My Führer! My loyalty to you will be unconditional." By then—as nobody bothered to tell Doenitz—Hitler had already killed himself in the Reichschancellery bunker.

On May 5th, Field Marshal Alfred Jodl and Admiral Hans

von Friedeburg made their way to Eisenhower's headquarters in a Reims schoolhouse seeking something less than unconditional surrender—an eleventh hour deal, a delay to enable still more German troops and refugees to flee west beyond the reach of the Russians. Ike's reply was characteristic: "I told General Smith to inform Jodl that unless they instantly ceased all pretense and delay I would close the entire Allied front and would, by force, prevent any more German refugees from entering our lines. I would brook no further delay."

On May 7, Jodl and Friedeburg capitulated and signed the agreement of unconditional surrender. Eisenhower asked Jodl if he understood the terms. The reply was, "Ja." Jodl said, "With this signature, the German people and armed forces are, for better or worse, delivered into the victor's hands." He saluted, left the modest Reims schoolhouse and went to inform Doenitz that the Third Reich was gone.

Meanwhile Ike was cabling the Joint Chiefs of Staff in Washington: "The mission of this Allied force was fulfilled at 0241 local time, May 7, 1945."

It seemed my mission was over, too. I requested space on an Air Transport flight home and was awaiting orders when Jimmy Doolittle, who had flown over from England, said: "Lowell, I've lost my job and have been ordered to Washington."

This was pure Doolittle. Actually the devastating strategic bombing by his Eighth Air Force had played a major role in Germany's defeat. Now he was being called home to help speed the end of the war against Japan, and on the way was to have a quick look at the war in the Pacific. He would be returning to Washington via North Africa, southern Asia and the Pacific islands. "I'm taking General Spaatz's stripped-down B-17 for the flight," he told me, "getting rid of as much weight as possible so we can take two crews and keep moving. But we have room for one more and I'm holding the space for you."

"Jimmy," I came back, "you must be joking. I'm just about to go home and catch up with all the things I should have been doing, and here you are inviting me to fly with you around the world the other way. Am I right?"

"Right! And here's the way to handle it: when you get back to New York, stall off your creditors, kiss your wife good-bye, grab your hat and fly right back here. There'll be just enough time for you to make it before we take off. What do you say?"

II. "Blest by the Suns of Home"

> We're losing the starboard engine, Dad,
> and I think it's your fault.
> —L.T., Jr., *2,000 feet over Cape Hatteras*

By the second week in May, just after the German surrender, I was back home again to take up the routine of my
regular news broadcast from our Quaker Hill studio. That lasted
about a week. On May 17, when "The Evening News With
Lowell Thomas" came on the air at 6:45 P.M., explorer Roy Chapman Andrews was at the microphone pinch-hitting for me:

> Although Lowell returned only a few days ago from the war in
> Europe, here he is off again. Evidently he got up so much
> momentum he couldn't stop, and tonight he's on his way around
> the world. I'll be sitting in for him until he returns.

Actually, I was able to get through by shortwave from
many of the way stations on that long, hectic trip—North Africa,
India, China, the Philippines, and eventually to Iwo Jima and
Okinawa, where the Japanese still fought ferociously for the
last outposts of their shrinking empire. I had no idea when I set
out what broadcasting facilities there might be in those far-flung
regions, but I did not mean to let that stop me. I had gotten to
musing about Jimmy Doolittle's invitation to fly back to Europe
and go on around the globe with him—surely an opportunity of
a lifetime. So I wired him in England to ask if the offer was still
open. Back came a radio message saying he was leaving ahead

48

of schedule, but if I'd hurry I could join him at Casablanca.

I was bushed after those memorable three months with our armies and airmen in Europe, and had every reason to stay home for a while. But when you are young—I was in my fifties then—you assume you are indestructible. So I took Doolittle's advice, paid off my creditors, kissed Fran good-bye, grabbed my hat and was off on a thrilling round-the-world chase.

When I arrived in Casablanca, Doolittle was already gone, leaving a message for me to hurry on to Cairo. In Cairo, Air Force General Benny Giles told me as we sat in his apartment overlooking the Nile that Doolittle had had to fly on, but I was to follow— this time for a rendezvous at Aden on the Arabian Sea. "But, Lowell, I'll bet you a magnum of champagne you don't catch up with that guy until Washington!"

We shook hands on it and I took off again. From Cairo I made a night flight the length of the Red Sea, along the Arabian coast with its memories of my days with T. E. Lawrence more than twenty-five years before. Of course Doolittle had already left Aden by the time I arrived. Stretched out on a mountain of mail, this time aboard a C-46, I slept through the skies over the Arabian Sea to Karachi, then on to New Delhi. On May 24, I made my first broadcast from India:

> It's a bit awkward to start off with my usual, "Good evening, everybody." It's dawn out here, and since my last broadcast from Cairo I have flown over Palestine, Arabia, ancient Mesopotamia, Persia, Baluchistan and half of India. This puts me some 9,500 miles from New York.

I went on to tell something of the brief stop we'd made in Iraq, the Biblical land of Adam and Eve, the fabled Garden of Eden. In the time of the Assyrians and the Chaldeans, in the days when Nebuchadnezzar was ruler in Babylon, it was the richest and most powerful country in the world, and Baghdad was its shining metropolis. Since then, history had largely passed it by, until now, when, with the war ending and the still-undiscovered sea of oil under the Middle Eastern sands, the great nations had begun paying slightly more attention to the sheiks and potentates who held sway there.

Baghdad was in a state of high excitement when we came in, for the Regent, Abdul Ullah, and a group of young King

Feisal's ministers were about to fly off to America. The visit was an unparalleled event in the capital city of the Arabian Nights. Not only had no member of the Hashemite family, descendants of the Prophet, ever visited America before, but many in the party had never even been in an airplane.

At that moment, the Moslem world was much concerned because the French were pouring troops into neighboring Syria. In fact, an anti-French demonstration had been about to take place when the C-54 sent by the U.S. government for the Iraqi leaders—the largest aircraft ever seen in Baghdad—flew over the Great Mosque and the bazaar. Seeing this apparition in the sky, hearing the great roaring of the motors, the pashas and sa'ids and rug merchants of the city were overcome with awe and the demonstration was forgotten—for there is an old Arabic saying that a man cannot talk of two things at once.

A few days later I arrived at Dum Dum airport near Calcutta. Here, on an inside page of the *Statesman,* then the best-known English language newspaper in southern Asia, I saw a four-line item to the effect that General James H. Doolittle had just arrived in Washington, D.C. So I had lost my bet. But I would never begrudge Benny Giles that champagne—for now I was on the middle leg of one of the most exciting trips I was ever to make.

Since there was no longer any chance of overtaking Doolittle, I decided to slow down and see something of the war in Asia. At our main air base some miles up the Hooghly River at Barrackpore, I told my story to Lieutenant General George Stratemeyer. "Well," he said, "I can't produce Doolittle, but if you want to fly the Hump, I'll let General Chennault at Kunming know you're coming, and then you can go on to Chungking for a visit with General Al Wedemeyer and Chiang Kai-shek." So it was that the following morning I was off again, this time aboard a fully loaded DC-4 that practically scraped its way over the Himalayas.

The Hump was aptly named. Between embattled China and the Allied supply bases in India, there rose the 20,000-foot— and then some—Himalayas, the most awesome mountain range on our planet. There were no emergency landing fields below, only the desolation of rocky slopes, glaciers and ice-covered peaks.

To abandon a crippled plane and bail out was only to court a lingering death in the endless mountains or the trackless Burmese jungle beyond. Nearly a thousand airmen had already lost their lives flying the Hump, but the lumbering old C-47s of the Air Transport Command flew on, carrying everything from trucks to K-rations at the rate of 45,000 tons a month, keeping China alive and in the war. Thirty years later at their annual convention in Florida, the airmen who had flown the Hump made me a member of their organization, an honor I prize indeed.

My fellow passengers made a disparate group. Among them was an erudite and charming Virginian, Assistant Secretary of State Walter Robertson, who had been sent to China for the express purpose of lending a voice of reason to Ambassador Patrick Hurley's efforts to resolve the bitter differences between Generalissimo Chiang Kai-shek and a potent new force in Chinese affairs, the Communists under a new leader, Mao Tse-tung, of whom we then knew little. In the bucket seat next to me was a U.S. cavalry colonel, assigned to help solve Chiang's eternal supply problems in an age-old way. Given the acute shortage of trucks and the primitive road network, he had been handed the mission of journeying into Sinkiang in far western China and rounding up some of the thousands of horses known to run wild there.

Most of the others aboard were G.I.'s on their way to join General Claire Chennault's Fourteenth Air Force, still popularly known as the Flying Tigers. There was something spectacularly American about them. At an altitude of 20,000 feet plus whatever it took to clear the towering Himalayan peaks, we were all forced to wear oxygen masks. Just beneath our wings lay some of the most enthralling spectacles you could hope to see. But none of this inhibited the young airmen from the pursuit of their chosen happiness—sprawling on the vibrating deck of the plane and shooting craps. In their oxygen masks they looked like men from Mars.

The Chinese called General Chennault "Old Leather Face," with good reason. But they revered him. Long before Pearl Harbor he had been serving as an "adviser" to Chiang Kai-shek, and his celebrated Flying Tigers had taught the Japanese air force many a painful lesson. It had always been Chennault's belief that the Japanese could be bombed out of Burma, out of

China and out of the war. But the ground commander, General Joseph W. Stilwell, who had walked his beaten, battered army out of Burma to India in 1942 and fought his way back in 1944, was convinced that the path to victory was overland. Churchill thought this madness and said so with customary vivacity: "Going into the jungles to fight the Japanese is like going into the water to fight a shark," he told his commanders.

Meanwhile, Vinegar Joe Stilwell, as resourceful a general as we had, was losing out on the political front, too. Embittered by Chiang's zest for fighting Communists in north China but not the Japanese, their common enemy, he made no attempt to hide his disdain for the Generalissimo and was finally relieved by President Roosevelt. But though the war was almost over when I arrived in Kunming, conflicts of purpose and strategy still racked the China-Burma-India theater of operations, and China seemed to be serving the Allies less as a path to victory than as a great swamp in which armies of Japanese were hopelessly bogged down.

Claire Chennault talked of some of these things when I saw him. He now believed the sun was irrevocably setting for Imperial Japan, but that the death blows would be struck westward from the Pacific. Then he abruptly changed the subject, suggesting I take advantage of an opportunity to fly into remote western China—Sinkiang—with veteran Captain R. L. Pottschmidt. It turned out that Potty, as everyone in Kunming called him, was flying the cavalry colonel west to meet the Tibetans who were bringing in horses for Chiang's army.

We took off at dawn and flew northwest for three hours, landing in the open country—we hadn't seen the semblance of an airfield anywhere in the vast, empty expanse below. But now we were near the city of Sichang, where a young Chinese prince, son of a warlord, feted us, and where the cavalryman paid off the Tibetans and arranged to have the horses driven on east. He still had several stops to make, but when the Tibetans asked if we would fly them home, Potty said, "Why not?"

They would have cause to regret their boldness and his generosity. Central Asia is a wild land. To the west were Tibet and the main range of the Himalayas; below us were the snaking gorges of the great rivers that flow down from the roof of the world: the Chindwin, the Irrawaddy, the Salween, the Mekong and the Yangtze Kiang. And as we were approaching the craggy heights of Minya Konka, fourth highest mountain in the world, we ran head-on into a storm that gave our DC-3 a thorough going-over. While the Tibetans huddled in their bucket seats, Potty checked the parachutes and announced that we were two short.

"Are we jumping?" I asked.

"It won't be the first time," he answered cheerfully.

"But if we're short two chutes . . . ?"

"No problem. I'll open the door for a couple of the Tibetans and say there's your home down there; but look out for that first step!"

Of course, he was joking, and fortunately it never came to the test. Rather than risk running into massive Minya Konka somewhere there in the soup, Potty turned northeast and landed at the walled city of Chengtu. There we spent the night, and after arranging another flight for the Tibetans, we flew on to Chungking on the upper Yangtze, the city where Generalissimo Chiang Kai-shek then made his headquarters, as did the U.S. commander-in-chief in China, Lieutenant General Albert C. Wedemeyer.

General Wedemeyer invited me to stay with him, and the next day took me to meet Chiang Kai-shek. It was a long and relatively private meeting, considering the Generalissimo's station and the fact that he understood English but could speak the language hardly at all. General Wedemeyer was present, as was the Vice Minister of Information, who interpreted for us. Hollington Tong, a graduate of our Columbia University, and three officers, two Chinese and one American, sat silently taking notes.

It was no secret that the Allies were of two minds about Chiang's leadership and China's role in the war. Churchill found the significance American minds attached to the Chinese land battle "strangely out of proportion":

> I was conscious of a standard of values which accorded China almost an equal fighting power with the British Empire, and rated the Chinese armies as a factor to be mentioned in the same breath as the armies of Russia. I told the President how much I felt American opinion overestimated the contributions which China could make to the general war.

But F.D.R. was firm in his support of the Generalissimo and of his persuasive wife, the eloquent and glamorous Madame Chiang. There were 500,000,000 people in China, he said to Churchill, and he was determined to keep them on our side; otherwise, when they developed economically and militarily, as they were bound to do, they would be a formidable foe. His vision was partly flawed. China did, indeed, develop economically and militarily; but the new China, the wakening giant, was far from the China Roosevelt had imagined—and it would be ruled by another man of destiny, Mao Tse-tung.

Our meeting with the Generalissimo took place in his home on the south bank of the Chia-ling River, which flows into the Yangtze. We went out to the gardens, where Chiang spoke of his hope to visit the United States, to see the wonders he had heard about all these years. It was, of course, a wish never to be fulfilled, although Madame Chiang was almost a commuter, asking for and getting great sums from us.

I asked if he was making provision for a peaceful continuation of his leadership. Although only in his middle fifties then, he had already been head of the Nationalist government for twenty years. His answer was that he was "channelizing" the government as rapidly as possible, so it would soon be well enough organized and on a sufficiently solid democratic foundation to survive regardless of who the future leaders might be.

He pointed out how for over 3,000 years, China had been an absolute monarchy; how he himself had joined Sun Yat-sen and the revolutionary movement in 1907, when he was nineteen years old; and how in only five years an ancient monarchy had been overthrown and the Chinese Republic firmly established. There was, of course, debris to be cleared away from the wreckage. Hence for twenty-five years he had been engaged in carrying out what he called the Destructive Phase of the great revolution, eliminating the warlords, blocking attempts to restore the monarchy—and waging interminable war in defense of China.

Much constructive work had already been done "against overwhelming odds." He told me how only ten years before, a traveler making a journey of a hundred miles in the province of Szechwan had to pay tribute to three warlords. Going from Chungking to Kunming in those days, perhaps a hundred and fifty miles, meant traveling twenty-four days. Now the warlords no longer ruled; there were roads, of which the Burma Road had been the most difficult to build, but it was built.

Far from the cold, austere ruler pictured by the press, I found Chiang to be a warm, animated and articulate human being when he spoke of his land and his people. When he had come to Szechwan, he recalled, the inhabitants were like walking skeletons, malnutrition and the scourge of opium having enfeebled whole populations. Now the deadly spread of opium had been halted and there was food, though not yet as much as China's millions needed. "Look around at the faces to be seen in this city," he said. "You will see the difference."

Considering the age of China and the state of decay into which it had fallen, he believed thirty years not an unreasonable period of time to complete the Destructive Phase and the elimination of reactionary elements. Then, he said, it would be possible to announce the beginning of a new period in Chinese history.

He sounded resolute, convinced of where he was going and of the inevitable victory. But when I asked the question on everyone's mind—What about Mao and his Communist armies?—he replied, "We are all Chinese. We will solve that problem."

History was to decree otherwise.

I tried many times to get through to the United States from Chungking by shortwave, but the Chinese international broadcasting beam was more a boast than an actuality and I wondered whether its signal ever got out of China. The report of my interview with Chiang Kai-shek would have to wait. Meanwhile I went off on the track of another story. The ranking American officer in the field, Major General Bob McClure, a stocky, ruddy-faced veteran of the Solomon Islands fighting, at General Wedemeyer's suggestion invited me to go with him on a trip by jeep and munitions carrier into the mountains of Kwangsi where the Chinese had given a good account of themselves in some recent fighting. With us, too, went General Ho Yin-chin, Chief of Staff of the Chinese armies, and General Yu Fei-peng, Minister of Communications, a former warlord of enormous physical proportions.

We assembled at Kweiyang, capital of the province of Kweichow, where the local general gave us a send-off banquet, a spartan wartime meal of only ten courses, rich yellow Chinese wine with each, and of course only chopsticks. It was what could be called a *ganbay* dinner because someone was always shouting, *"Ganbay!"*, meaning "bottoms up," as I learned to my subsequent regret. It was no way to get in shape for a jeep journey over some of the world's bumpiest mountain roads. Nor was I comforted by the presence of dozens of Chinese soldiers standing behind us as we ate, each holding a revolver at the ready in his hand.

The sun was already blazing hot when our convoy, a dozen jeeps and a long trail of munitions carriers, left in early morning. General Yu fanned himself furiously as we bounced along. Every time the jeeps were held up by pack trains or water buffalo, his aide would race to a stream or to the nearest rice paddy and would fill a basin with water so the great man could refresh himself and get ready for the next lap of dust clouds and bumps.

I had been riding in a jeep, sitting beside an Air Force officer whose face seemed familiar. He bore a striking resemblance to my CBS colleague and Quaker Hill neighbor, Edward R. Murrow. "Did anybody ever tell you that you look like Ed Murrow?" I asked him.

He laughed. "Our mother," he said. He was Ed's older brother, Colonel Lacey Murrow, assigned to General McClure's staff as engineering officer.

At Mah-Chang-Ping we found a detachment of American troops living in an ancient Chinese temple. Farther on, Chinese infantry and artillery outfits were scattered among the bomb-battered towns, and all along our route were clutterings of knocked-out vehicles, masses of abandoned equipment. And everywhere we saw the flimsy huts of the refugees, the hundreds of thousands, maybe millions, who had fled the coast and come straggling up this road in search of food and safety.

Several times we stopped at military hospitals which General McClure insisted on inspecting. This did not make the Chinese generals happy. Yu Fei-peng would stride through, still fanning himself vigorously, without looking left or right. Ho Yin-chin waited for us at the door. Once, McClure marched us through a long building filled with sick Chinese soldiers, old men and physical wrecks who should never have been called up, and many of whom, after brief but bitterly harsh army service, were now on their deathbeds. McClure's face turned angry red and General Yu Fei-peng fanned himself more furiously than ever.

By now we were in a country of chocolate-drop mountains, hundreds of peaks strewn across the landscape like rice croquettes on a vast platter, tranquil paddies between. At our most advanced air base, only a few miles from the Japanese at Nanning, we crawled into tents, sore from the endless jouncing, exhausted and ready for sleep. But in came squadrons of mosquitoes so ferociously determined to have a go at us that even though there were nets over our cots, a mosquito patrol had to come every few hours to spray. One of these made the mistake of squirting the spray into the face of our sleeping general, who let out a roar.

It didn't help much. I lay there listening to the drone, occasionally fighting off a *kamikaze* which had gotten through spray, netting and all, and I thought about China. And in spite of Chiang's brave words and high hopes, I thought mostly about the elaborate banquet at Kweiyang and the hungry refugees by the side of the road; and about Yu Fei-peng, Ho Yin-chin and the other warlord-generals who were among Chiang's right-hand men, and the dying recruits in that long hospital building. And somehow I came to believe that victory over Japan would only set the stage in China for an even more bitter conflict.

At the most advanced American air base, there was no gas for the fighter planes. The young flyers, psychologically geared up for combat but grounded by the difficulties of logistics in that far-flung theater of operations, did what they could to while away the time. One of the things they did was to party it up well into the night, singing and drinking—somehow their booze always got through—so that, again, General McClure's sleep was disturbed. He let out a roar for them to shut up and, though they did, he was unappeased. Next day, flying back to Kunming in a DC-3 warhorse, I was surprised to find the pilots' C.O. accompanying us: McClure had put him under arrest. That was a mistake. When General Claire Chennault, organizer of the famed Flying Tigers and now head of all U.S. airmen in China, heard about the arrest, he sent for McClure and dressed him down in no uncertain terms. His flyers, declared Chennault, were responsible to no commander but him and McClure was neither to interfere with them nor to give them any orders.

Back in Chungking, I reported to General Wedemeyer. My timing was excellent: for the first time, the Air Force was about to make a flight from the Chinese interior directly out to the Pacific, over Japanese-held territory, and there was room for me.

Until then, aircraft headed for our Pacific bases between Okinawa and the Philippines had to fly all the way over the Hump to India, across the Indian Ocean to Australia and finally north through Indonesia to the Marianas—a distance almost equal to a flight around the world. The time had come, General Wedemeyer said, to try it the direct way, although it would be hazardous, crossing enemy-held territory and mountains by night, a coast infested by Japanese small craft and a sea through which the foe's submarines were on the prowl. Was I interested in going along?

"Whom do I report to?" I said.

A few days later I was in the remote walled city of Lu-liang, where a Colonel Skii Skrilling welcomed me to his quarters and spent the next six hours telling me what a lousy assignment he had as the commandant. The colonel was a veteran Eastern Airlines pilot, and had been given an executive post in one of the most remote parts of Chiang Kai-shek's domain. With purple language he described the city, its inhabitants, his job, and the war in general. There, in a hut at the edge of an unused B-29 bomber strip, some thirty of us were called together for briefing before taking off. Twelve were young airmen who had been shot down by the Japanese and, like some of Doolittle's men on the first Tokyo raid, had been rescued by Chinese guerrillas. Another was a brawny major from Texas who had been on a most dangerous mission behind enemy lines, stealing along the China coast and gleaning invaluable details of Japanese planes shot down there—new motor designs, instrumentation and armament. He was, he said, now due for a leave, and he hoped this would prove to be the quick way to get the information to our island air bases in the Marianas.

A young lieutenant from Harvard did the briefing and took the job quite seriously, with good reason. And we listened raptly as he gave us pointers on surviving in the jungle and discussed the wide coastal area still in Japanese hands. He brought out cloth maps for each of us to carry in a special jungle vest, which also contained a revolver, ammunition, waterproof matchboxes and cigarettes, concentrated food, a compass, a knife and a "pointee-talkee" book with essential phrases in Chinese. To cheer us up there was also mosquito repellent, atabrine for malaria, sulfa drugs for open wounds and morphine "in case it really hurts."

He said the cigarettes could be worth their weight in gold, but we mustn't shake one loose in the American way and offer it from the pack. To a Chinese, that would be an insult. "You take it out and hand it to him—ceremoniously. Then it's a gift."

If we were captured by the enemy, we were to be cooperative but we were to offer no information except name, rank and serial number. If we went down in the South China Sea, our Mae Wests would keep us afloat and we were to use the mirror provided to flash at passing planes. Thus heartened, we were marched directly from the briefing to a waiting DC-4. A few moments after I was shown to a front seat just behind the cockpit a major leaned over my shoulder and said: "Did you ever hear of the name Wenrick?" It took me several minutes to give him an answer, and then it dawned on me that the Wenrick family in Darke County, Ohio, had been in some way distantly related to my mother. When I told him this he said: "Yes, I'm one of your many cousins! And I happen to be the number one pilot on this flight to take you over the Japanese army on out to the Philippines." He also said there were two other pilots and all three were under orders to stay awake, on the alert. He said they had a bunk in the cockpit and suggested I come up and use it. I did. Before I left home, Fran had given me some sleeping pills and this seemed an appropriate time to take one. When someone shook me awake the next morning, we had flown all the way out of China and across the South China Sea. Below us was Corregidor, the fortress island off Bataan. Manila Bay was littered with wrecked ships.

So much for the excitement of the night flight out of China. Many years later when I was speaking in the N.C.R. auditorium in Dayton, Ohio, there was Wenrick in the front row, now a retired colonel. Whereupon I used him as an important part of my speech. His father, Noah Wenrick, had been one of the best known citizens of Greenville, Ohio, the metropolis of the county from which nearly all of my people had come.

If you get around a great deal, when a war is on, you inevitably meet many people you know. But it usually is quite a surprise, and often seems incredible. When I climbed down from the plane after this unusual flight, there at the bottom of the steps stood Colonel Joe Dawson from Denver, one of Fran's old beaux and her classmate at East Denver High School and later at the university. Joe took me off to his quarters, where he proudly showed me the largest bed I had ever seen. It was more than king size, and could have accommodated four or five persons. The colonel said he had been told it had belonged to a wealthy Danish merchant and exporter, and Joe Dawson had a rather vivid description of the frolicking that had gone on in the huge bed which he was now using.

I knew of another young officer, one of my Dutchess County neighbors, who was attached to MacArthur's staff. In no time at all I had located him, Major Chester ("Red") Ray, younger brother of a legendary Dartmouth football star, Carl ("Mutt") Ray, who gained near-immortality by making two touchdowns in a football game when the Hanover Indians defeated the Elis in the Yale Bowl for the first time. One of MacArthur's generals told me there was no reason why they couldn't spare "Red" for a few days. One of the first things I did was make a date for a rather important interview. When we started off in the carriage I didn't tell Major Ray where we were going. I thought it would be fun to give him a surprise. Maybe twenty minutes later, as we came down a wide boulevard, he said: "By the way, L.T., isn't this the *bulevar* that leads to the president's palace?" I replied: "You're right. I thought we just might drop in!"

When we got to the palace we were ushered down a long corridor, past scores of people who were waiting, hopefully, to see the president. Without delay we were ushered inside, and almost my opening remark was: "President Osmeña, I want you to meet my old friend Major Chester Ray!" "Red" was flabbergasted, and even more so when a cameraman came and took a picture of the young officer with the Philippine president.

Osmeña, who had returned to the Philippines with the American invasion fleet less than a year before, told us his people were not waiting for the war's end to rebuild their shattered country. In fact, he said, one of his top planners, imprisoned by the Japanese for three years, had passed the time working on plans for a new and greater Manila. His secret drawings were completed by the time MacArthur landed, and now work had already begun.

In a broadcast from Manila, I reported on an interview with General Walter Krueger, MacArthur's field commander on the island-hopping advance all the way from New Guinea to the last days of this campaign on Luzon.

> Here, in the first solid building General Krueger has had for a headquarters since leaving Australia, he told me his story of the Southwest Pacific war, a most remarkable part of which is that never once from the time MacArthur started north from Australia did the Japanese win a victory. But they have fought hard, and there are still between 60,000 and 100,000 of them here in the Philippines, most of them cornered in northern Luzon, and remaining to be subdued.

The 20,000 Americans captured on Bataan and Corregidor in those first disheartening months of the war had been avenged two hundred times over, for more than 400,000 of Japan's best remaining troops had been annihilated in the Philippines by Krueger's Sixth Army. The commanding general still had one personal objective. "I'd like to take Yamashita alive," Krueger said to me with considerable feeling.

Which he did. And General Tomoyuki Yamashita, known as the Butcher of Bataan for his inhuman treatment of American prisoners of war, was in due course tried as a war criminal and hanged.

The day after my broadcast, I boarded a plane for another night flight, this time north to Guam in the Marianas. When we taxied in, I spotted a plane with a familiar name, *Argonaut IV*. I had known the first three *Argonauts*, as General "Hap" Arnold always named his command planes, and went looking for him. I found him at Admiral Nimitz's headquarters. Arnold, bound on a tour of our Pacific bases, now invited me to join him. First we flew to nearby Saipan and Tinian, the islands from which our men were punishing the Japanese homeland with massive air raids, then on to Iwo Jima, the volcanic speck in the sea which had been the scene of one of history's bitterest battles, and of which our forces did not yet have complete control.

As we approached the island, a squadron of P-51s came out to escort us in. Then, suddenly, there it was—the sharp cone of Suribachi volcano at one end, high cliffs and pounding surf below. But the tropical calm had been overcome by the evidence of men at war, wrecked ships and landing barges, and the dark surface of the little island looking like one huge airfield. That, in fact, is what it was—fighter strips, a longer strip for B-29s in distress on their way back from a bomb run over Japan, and the tents and Quonsets of the tens of thousands of men who flew and serviced the hundreds of aircraft, now lined up and ready to go.

For its size, Iwo Jima had cost the U.S. more lives than any battle ever fought by Americans. The Marines had stormed ashore barely three months before and had won the Suribachi heights four days later, February 23. On that day, photographer Joe Rosenthal took the picture that won him instant worldwide fame, four soldiers struggling to implant the American flag on the volcanic peak. The cost of raising the flag had been fearful: 4,000 killed and more than 15,000 wounded and missing. The Japanese had lost nearly 30,000, and when I was there early in June, they were still being flushed out of caves with flame-throwers and grenades.

Broadcasting from a mobile transmitter at the base of Suribachi, I told of the base commander's boast of Iwo having the only heated airfield in the world. Smoke and fumes from the volcanic fires underlying the island were actually seeping up through the runways. And I reported that General Arnold, who had come here to pin medals on the breasts of the men whose valor had wrested this eight-square-mile basaltic rock from the Japanese, had won all their hearts with one well-aimed wisecrack. "I traveled a long way to see what all the fighting was about over this place. Well, I've seen it." Pause. "Can anybody tell me why we bothered?"

But of course he knew, as did they all. Every B-29 that flew in with gas reserves gone, or after having been shot up in the skies over Japan, was eloquent testimony to the importance of this volcanic spit. Without it, those planes and their crews would have gone down in the trackless sea; with it, refueled and repaired, they could fly on to their bases in the Marianas and return again to carry the war to Japan.

Iwo was also the most extreme outpost from which our fighters could fly escort for the huge B-29 Superforts, and extreme was a well-chosen word, for it was a 1,600-mile round trip to Honshu, the main Japanese island. In my broadcast, I described the mission of one of those young fighter pilots:

You get into your P-51. You take off from the edge of a cliff and fly 800 miles or so over the Pacific to have a go at the Japs. Maybe you are shot up. But you still have to fly back for 800 miles and find this mountaintop jutting out of the sea.

One lad, bound for escort duty over Tokyo, is on his first mission. Dense fog covers the western Pacific and he is separated from his outfit. His directional instruments are out of commission. He flies around until he picks up another squadron on his radio. So he tags along with them, for he must stay within radio range, and instead of flying to Tokyo he flies to Osaka. Then, still without seeing the planes he is with, he follows them back. As they talk him in, he looks at his fuel indicator: it registers empty and he calculates that he may have a couple of quarts left. So though he doesn't know where he is and can see nothing but milky haze, he lets down. And lo and behold, there is old Suribachi and his own landing strip just below. He touches down, but right in the middle of his landing roll the engine goes dead—not a drop of gas left—and he has to walk the rest of the way home.

I left General Arnold for a time to fly on to Okinawa where, though the outcome of the battle was beyond question, the Japanese fought on fanatically. The U.S. ground commander, Lieutenant General Simon Bolivar Buckner, who once served in Alaska so that we had many mutual friends, had sent word that he would wait for me at his headquarters. But when I landed, a Marine Corps officer took me first to see his C.O., Colonel Melvin Joseph Maas, a former Congressman from Minnesota. As might be expected of any successful contender for the public's vote, Colonel Maas was a persuasive speaker and gave me a long and eloquent account of his outfit's activities on Okinawa. In doing so he may have saved my life. When I finally did reach

General Buckner's headquarters, he had gone on to the front, leaving word that I should have luncheon with his staff and he would see me later in the afternoon.

When he had not yet returned by 4:00 P.M., I decided to have a closer look at the Nanda airfield, another phenomenon of the Pacific war. The runways were completely obscured by a giant dust cloud, fed and fattened by the planes landing and taking off at two-minute intervals. The incoming planes simply disappeared in the brown haze, which also coated everyone in a mile-wide radius, like a silent rain of cinnamon. This prevailed the year around, I was told, except in the wet season. Then the airfield became a brimming bay of mud.

As I stood flapping my hands in front of my face so I could breathe, a specter in what was barely recognizable as a naval uniform appeared in the murk and said to me, "Lowell, you're the dirtiest s.o.b. I've ever seen. What the hell are you doing here?"

It was Admiral Cal Durgin, a friend from the time he had been on Navy Secretary James Forrestal's staff in Washington. Now he commanded a flotilla of carriers in the Japan Sea. After some backslapping, I told him how I had missed General Buckner and he said, "Come on out to my flagship and we'll give you a bath and a decent dinner."

Would he leave word for Buckner?

"Done!" With that, he walked me over to a Grumman Torpedo and instructed the pilot to fly me to his ship. Five minutes later we broke out through the dust cloud and were high over the ocean.

My first ride in an airplane had been in 1917, when one of Allenby's World War I aviators did a series of aerobatics with me above the pyramids and the Sphinx, an introduction to aviation I'll never forget. Since then, I suppose I've flown some six million miles—more than any other passenger in history, say those who make it their business to calculate such things. But few of the flights in between packed the punch of that short hop out to Cal Durgin's flagship.

After an hour over the empty blue sea, the pilot pointed to a black dot at the end of a long white wake. We were going to land on *that*? Apparently the pilot felt the same way. He swooped down until the speck became recognizable as a "baby"

Cartoonist Paul Webb's version of Paul Revere.

First TV newscast (below) ever made. Hugh James, far left,
Charles Warburton, NBC production man, beside me.

Count Felix von Luckner, "the Sea Devil," whom General Patton saved from the Russians.

T. E. Lawrence on the racing camel he accidentally shot in the head in the battle at the Wells of Abu el Lissal.

Soglow puts me in my place.

A portrait of Jimmy Doolittle (far right) by McClelland Barclay.

"The majority of radio commentators take a standing or sitting position."

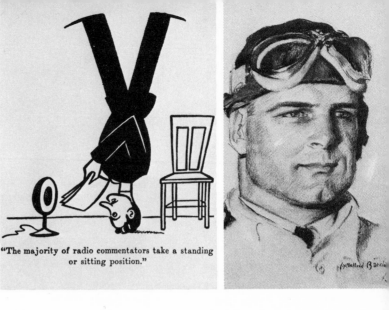

Many believed him to have been the greatest all-around athlete of all time; the legendary Jim Thorpe with Lowell, Jr., at Taft School.

L.T., Jr., and his mother.

L.T., Jr., while training Free French airmen during the war.

One of my favorite photographs of Fran.

Long after World War II, L.T., Jr., and his flying pal, Ed Seiler, found the first world flight Douglas amphibian on the mountain in Alaska where it crashed in 1924.

Hammersley Hill and Lake Hammersley. The water hazard (below) is in the center of the aerial photo.

The history of civilization fireplace at the Quaker Hill community center clubhouse.

Fran and Sun Oil tycoon Joe Pew.

President Hoover and my dad.

My favorite photograph of Herbert Hoover.

carrier, lined us up with the heaving flight deck—and at the last instant pulled up and sharply away.

As he banked around for another try, he turned to show me a feeble smile. Again he made a pass at the carrier, its deck full of tensely poised men who looked as though they were prepared to catch us in their arms if they had to. But again, with his wheels almost on the deck, the pilot aborted the landing. This time I didn't even get the smile.

Once more we swung around. I was beginning to wonder if I were doomed to spend the rest of my days in this limbo, like some Flying Dutchman of the sky. But this time we went straight in, bouncing once before the cables grabbed and brought us to a jolting halt. For a moment we both sat there. Then the pilot twisted around in his seat and said, "I guess I should have mentioned it to the admiral, sir, but I've never landed one of these things on a small carrier before."

After a much-appreciated bath, Admiral Durgin took me to his radar room, then the ship's nerve center, as it was on every ship in the western Pacific in those days. These were the final days when the entire Japanese air corps had become a *kamikaze* force, every pilot ready to dive his plane into an American ship in suicidal tribute to his land and his emperor. It was a hopeless, futile gesture, for the war was irrevocably lost and the explosives-packed Zeroes were shot down in droves. And yet the *kamikaze* were Japan's most terrible weapon in the last months of the war, sinking or severely damaging some three hundred of our ships and inflicting more than 15,000 casualties. So it was that radar became the fleet's lifeline, for its electronic sensors provided a moment's warning for the gunners and for initiating the evasive maneuvers that might take a ship out of the path of a plunging Zero's death dive.

Around 2:00 A.M. I was awakened by one of Admiral Durgin's officers, who said they had just received a message from Okinawa asking me to come ashore, at once. Half asleep, and positive there was a mistake—who in Okinawa would be wanting me there at this hour?—I turned over and went to sleep.

In the morning, I climbed into another Grumman Torpedo and was catapulted off the carrier deck for the return flight and my long-delayed meeting with General Buckner. But there was a pall over his headquarters that made me suspect the worst even before I heard the news. Buckner had gone off to the front without me. And there, standing in a trench observing the battle a mile or more away through binoculars, he had been hit by the burst of a lone mortar shell and killed instantly.

I sat down in the nearest chair. Buckner was the only top American commander to be killed in the Pacific. And as I sat there, I realized if it hadn't been for the long-winded former Congressman from Minnesota, I would have been standing alongside him at the time.

Have you ever had someone say: "Remember me?" And did you answer as I have made the mistake of doing a number of times when I didn't recall the person at all, "Oh yes, of course, and what are you doing now?" Years after the naval officer had aroused me in the middle of the night on that carrier in the Japan Sea, I was presiding at an aviation banquet at the May-flower Hotel in Washington, the day Colonel Bernt Balchen was, by Congressional decree, made a citizen of the United States and given the permanent rank of colonel in our Air Force. Balchen was a Norwegian who had been the first to pilot an airplane over both the North and South Poles, and who had been with both Amundsen and Byrd; he had made a great record in World War II rescuing downed airmen on the Greenland icecap, and had served also with the Norwegian underground in Scandinavia and later as the airman who commanded our Tenth Rescue Squadron in Alaska. The banquet hall was crowded with our leading air people. I had been assigned the role of toastmaster, and arrived rather late, after doing my evening broadcast. When I dropped into my chair I looked up and down the head table, and off to my extreme right a man waved to me. A few minutes later he came over and said: "Remember me? I was the one who woke you up in the middle of the night to tell you they wanted you to go ashore at Okinawa." Whereupon I made quite a faux pas. I said: "Yes, indeed, I remember. And what are you doing now?"

"Oh, I'm the Secretary of the Navy!" It was Tom Gates, who in civilian life later was chairman of Morgan Guaranty—and more recently the U.S. State Department representative in Peking.

A few days later I rejoined General Arnold on Guam and

spent some time visiting the B-29 bases on Saipan and Tinian. My pilot was General Barney Giles, twin brother of General Benny Giles, who had been my thoughtful host in Cairo at the long-ago beginning of this trip. Barney amused himself by handing the controls of his Superfort over to me—"Turn this, push that"—and calmly instructing me in the handling of that silvery, sixty-ton behemoth as we flew over the Pacific.

Back at Guam, I attended the early morning briefings given the top generals and admirals on the theater-wide actions of the previous twenty-four hours. Lieutenant General Curtis E. "Iron Pants" LeMay, commander of the B-29 attack force, conducted the briefings himself. He reported that all the Japanese industrial centers had been flattened, with Tokyo the hardest hit. The Japanese navy was neutralized and their vast fishing fleet destroyed, with the result that the civilian population was on the verge of starvation. The battle charts showed the home islands ringed with our submarines, making it increasingly difficult for the enemy to maintain communications with, let alone supply, his forces on the Asian mainland. Having devastated the major cities, our B-29s were turning to secondary targets.

One evening, I sat over coffee with the bomber pilots just back from raids over Shizuoka, Toyohashi and Fukuoka. More than four hundred planes had swept over the three cities and had virtually wiped them off the map. Returning, the pilots said they could still see flame and clouds of smoke at a distance of 120 miles. The score to date: fourteen cities reduced to ashes.

Broadcasting home on June 21st, I tried to summarize the hopeless state of the foe:

> As you no doubt have heard, all of the major cities of Japan have been knocked out by our B-29s. The pictures taken by our airmen show in grim detail how their industrial centers are flattened, docks smashed and rail centers destroyed. Brigadier General Tommy Powers, who commands one of our B-29 bombardment wings here in the Marianas, told me how the heat generated by bombs his airmen were dropping on Japan was so intense that over wide areas everything has been burned out, including underground wiring and pipes.

How long could Japan hold out? But somehow Washington was misreading the intelligence data, clinging to the notion that the Japanese people remained fanatically convinced that annihilation was the only alternative to victory. We were told we must be prepared to invade the home islands, a massive land operation sure to result in immense loss of life on both sides.

General Buckner, originally named to command the invasion of Japan, had now been replaced by Vinegar Joe Stilwell. One day I was sitting on a stone wall at Admiral Nimitz's headquarters, high above the sea, with the admiral and Generals Arnold, Giles and LeMay, when General Stilwell joined us. He had been flying back to America when word reached Washington of the death of General Buckner. Over the Pacific a radio order reached Vinegar Joe telling him to fly to Okinawa and take over the army command. "Joe," General Arnold said, "you might as well get back aboard your plane and head for home. This war is over."

From all I'd seen and heard, I believed him to be right. But only Arnold knew just how right he was, for he knew, as I did not and Stilwell was yet to learn, that an atomic bomb, successfully tested at Alamogordo, New Mexico, was already on its way to the Marianas. It would destroy Hiroshima and then Nagasaki, killing another 200,000 people and driving the Japanese to immediate surrender. But it also loosed a whirlwind of nuclear proliferation and international blackmail, and its menace still hangs over our head.

Did we need to drop those bombs? Without an invasion, and with only the continuing, steadily constricting pressure of the U.S. Navy and Air Force, the Japanese would have been forced to quit. If so, would the world today be a different place? Surely the collective American conscience would be less troubled; or have we already forgotten? At any rate, President Truman decreed otherwise and, for better or worse, the path of the nuclear age was set that momentous summer of 1945.

The day after our talk on the stone wall at Nimitz's headquarters, "Hap" Arnold and I took off in his *Argonaut IV*, for Guam, Hawaii and home. For me, the war was over.

Thirty years before, in the midst of another war from which he would never return, the English poet Rupert Brooke wrote:

If I should die, think only this of me:
That there's some corner of a foreign field
That is forever England. . . .
A body of England's . . .
Washed by the rivers, blest by the suns of home.

Returning, I felt as did those who had fought and survived—"blest by the suns of home,"—and I meant to stay put for a good long time. But within a few days there came an invitation I could not turn down. It was from the commander at Turner Field in Georgia, where Lowell, Jr., was serving as senior flight instructor. Would I deliver an Air Force commencement address there? If so, the C.O. would waive one of its rules and send young Lowell to fetch me and later fly me back.

How could I refuse? For one thing, the Air Force had been inordinately kind to me in Europe and in the Pacific, and for another I had not seen my son in many, many months. Even before the war, Lowell was well launched on a career of travel and high adventure, having gone along as assistant cameraman when, in 1939, President Roosevelt sent three battle cruisers on a goodwill tour around South America, the first such voyage since the opening of the Panama Canal. He was not yet sixteen. Then, soon after Pearl Harbor, he and a group of his classmates organized a Dartmouth Air Squadron and petitioned the Air Corps to enlist as a unit. My son had personally put this up to General Arnold, who was all for it, but for other reasons the group broke up and Lowell wound up a pilot instructor. Now, because of his experience and because he had some knowledge of French, he had been given the hazardous assignment of teaching night flying to De Gaulle's fledgling Free French pilots, none of whom spoke or understood English.

The flight down to Georgia and my address to the hundreds of young airmen about to get their wings were not notable. At least I remember little about them, whereas I am unlikely ever to forget even a single detail of the flight north. L. T., Jr., was flying a war-wracked Mitchell bomber, a twin-engine B-25 that had been mauled and patched and mauled again. In the cockpit, behind the seats for the pilot and co-pilot, there was a jump seat for me, the canvas backing torn away to reveal a maze of wires running through and disappearing into the starboard bulkhead. The co-pilot for this return flight was war-weary, nervous, a disturbed young man who had been shot down over Europe and was now going home to be mustered out. With shattered nerves and still ailing from his ordeal, he was actually unfit for flight duty, but as he lived in New York and our trip seemed perfectly routine, the C.O. at Turner had assigned him to us as the quickest means of getting him home.

I was busy with a thick manuscript. My old friend Chris Young, who had been our cameraman throughout the European tour of the Rover Boys, had written a 200-page narrative poem about our experiences, disguising me, I don't know why, with a pseudonym, Carlton Spears. Having seen an evocative but undecipherable surrealist film Chris once made, this seemed just the time to read his bulky verse version of World War II, and as soon as we were airborne I began Chris's story, which appropriately opened aboard a troop transport:

Whether it's day or night
Whether or not you want to sleep
Whether or not you think it's right,
When you arrive at your allotted cot,
You must, you *will* get into it at once
With your duffle, rifle, bedroll, pack
And everything else you've got.
This is an order, which, like many another,
Might seem ridiculous, but the purpose
Grows obvious—to leave room in the aisle
For all the other men to pass.
And it's amazing with how little fuss
In space as small as such
So many manage with so much.
You envy the officers, who
Can be up there above all this mess
With plenty of room to walk around
And fool around, with the girls, more or less.
And you ask yourself: "Why the hell didn't *you*
Go to O.C.S.?"

The weather forecast for our flight north was good—some scattered clouds and a shower or two, but smooth sailing otherwise. When we ran into rain over the Great Smokies in North

Carolina, Lowell turned east looking for clearer skies. I read on.

Having arrived in England, Chris is assigned to a photo-graphic darkroom:

> Meantime there's a war on.
> Across the Channel, an hour away,
> There's shooting, suffering and dying,
> Sleepless weariness,
> Mud and cold and blood.
> You see and handle every day
> The true images of all this.
> You hold a picture of a dead man
> In your hand and say:
> "This is underexposed."
> You mean the picture, not the man.
> He was overexposed when he was hit.
> At last, an assignment!
> You've been requested by name
> By Carlton Spears, top correspondent,
> As a photographer to accompany
> Him into Germany, perhaps to cover
> The entrance to Berlin.

The old B-25 seemed to be trying to dance out from under me. I looked up and saw that it was growing dark but, ominously, my watch showed that it was not yet 2:00 P.M. I tightened my seat belt and wondered if that Turner Field meteorologist had known what he was talking about.

> A day or so later
> The party boards its private plane
> And flies to a field at Eschwege
> Near Weimar. Then in jeep and command car
> They ride down roads that pass between
> Rows of blossoming trees,
> To a camp of death—on the way seeing
> The men with gray faces,
> Who wear gray striped pajama-like
> Uniforms, filthy and stinking
> Of their infamous prison.
> They are free now to go anywhere,
> But they don't know where to go or how.
> Next day the interview with General Patton.
> He picked for his HQ the most luxurious,

And, above all, the most conspicuous
Quarters in the region, a set of tremendous
Barrack-like buildings on top of a hill,
A former German officer school,
Visible from afar, that any fool
Could see and drop a bomb on.
The General is a man who is loath
To hide himself—even from the enemy.
You wait for him to come out,
He comes with the correspondents.
Today is the first day he has his four stars on.
He has them on his shoulder, his shirt collar,
On his helmet liner shiny with shellac,
On the license plates of his car,
On the sign, front and back,
At his parking space, saying: *Reserved for*
the Commanding General's Car.
(Star, star, star, star).
He says Congress has not approved
His promotion to full general yet. "Therefore,"
He says, "you better not release this picture
Until such time as they do."

I chuckled to myself, remembering that moment. Then I looked up and became suddenly aware that this milk run of a flight from Albany, Georgia, to Stewart Air Force Base near West Point had become a nightmare. Flying blind, Lowell, for obvious reasons, had turned away from the peaks of the Great Smokies and the Blue Ridge Mountains. Now, he told me, having come far to the east, we were somewhere over Cape Hatteras on the mid-Atlantic coast—in the mysterious Bermuda Triangle. But we still hadn't broken out of the murk. Instead, an apparently wide-ranging storm system had us firmly in its grip. The plane bucked and shuddered. Driving rain slashed against the windows and the co-pilot, white-faced, grew increasingly apprehensive. I tried to read on, but there was hardly enough light in the cockpit; my concentration flagged and I soon gave it up altogether.

I knew we were in real trouble. Twice Lowell tried to climb up over the storm, but could not. Then he began circling, cautiously letting down in hopes of spotting a Virginia landmark to fix our position and enable him to set a course for some airport.

This entailed the real danger of flying into something poking up into that shrouded sky—a hilltop, a building, a radio tower—but we seemed to have no choice. I kept squirming around in my seat, straining to catch a glimpse of the ground.

All at once, as though we hadn't enough to worry about, one of the engines began sputtering. A moment later, it ran smoothly again, then cut out altogether, as though a giant hand had closed over it. We began dropping swiftly. As Lowell worked furiously at the controls, the hand opened and the engine roared to life. But five minutes later it happened again.

Suddenly the co-pilot slipped out of his shoulder straps, pulled up on the parachute beneath him and cried out, "I'm jumping!"

"Stay where you are," Lowell commanded.

"*You* stay where you are! I'm jumping—it's our only chance!" He was on his feet, adjusting the parachute harness.

Swinging his fully-extended right arm sharply backward, Lowell caught the distraught man in the chest and knocked him back into the seat. "Listen, son"—Lowell was then all of twenty-two himself—"I'm going to land this airplane in one piece, and when I do you're going to be in it, understand? Because if you make another move to get up you'll get it with a monkey wrench!"

The co-pilot sagged back, eyes closed. Even so I felt sorry for him, as did Lowell. Still tormented by his visions of what he'd been through in Europe and only a few hours from home and respite, he was trapped in a storm-tossed airplane, with one engine gone and the pilot lost. The last shreds of his nerve may have snapped. For that matter I may have been just as scared as he was. At any rate Lowell coaxed the ailing engine back to life. When it began sputtering again, he turned in his seat and said, "We're losing the starboard engine, Dad, and I think it's your fault."

He was right. Having eliminated every other possibility, it had occurred to him that the wire controlling the carburetor mix might be shorting out. Checking its path, he figured maybe when I sat back I was pushing against the exposed wire, choking off the starboard engine. When I sat up there was a comforting roar from the right wing. And from then on I leaned well forward.

But his neatest bit of flying was yet to come. We were still spiraling down, peering through the downpour with the hope of picking up some landmark and not making violent contact with it. And we did—first the shiny green of a farmer's soaked field, then a village. Lowell swung around, searching, the weary old B-25 practically standing up on one wing. Then he pointed, grinning a mile wide. Below was a railroad station, its name printed in huge white letters on the depot roof. Lowell pulled up. A moment later he had found the place on his chart and set a course for Stewart Field; we were on our way.

"I told you we'd be all right," I said to the co-pilot.

He nodded. He asked Lowell if there was anything he could do. There was some color in his face again, and he gazed calmly through the rain-streaked windshield, toward home.

Satisfied that the male line of our family was no longer threatened with imminent extinction, I went back to the end of Chris Young's epic:

> Spears and the General are closeted.
> You meet Spears at the airport afterward.
> As previously said,
> He is one ever calm and collected,
> Even in times that are crucial.
> But now he seems even calmer than usual.
> Epstein and you rush up to him to say:
> "Hadn't we better get started?"
> For flying to the front that day
> Is what you had intended.
> But Spears just says, "Relax, boys! It appears
> There isn't any front to fly to.
> The war has ended."

Less than a week after our flight north from Georgia, another B-25 bound for Newark, New Jersey, dropped down through a dense fog over New York City looking for a landmark. Minutes before, the control tower at LaGuardia Field had warned the pilot, a combat veteran, Lieutenant Colonel William Franklin Smith, Jr., that the area visibility was extremely poor and advised him to land. "I can't even see the Empire State Building," said the tower operator.

Neither could Colonel Smith. But as he broke out of the overcast, Fifth Avenue just off his left wing, there it was, looming directly in front of him. Witnesses later reported that the Mitchell lurched up in a last desperate effort to climb clear, but it was far too late. Flashing across Thirty-fourth Street, it smashed into the north side of the twelve-hundred-fifty-foot skyscraper with a thunderclap heard two miles away. Sheets of flame swirled up from the huge gash it tore through the masonry and steel at the seventy-eighth floor. A piece of the wing landed a block away on Madison Avenue. Glass littered rooftops for hundreds of yards around, and a shower of blazing gasoline set others afire.

It was a nightmare disaster, the tallest building in the world struck by a lost airplane. And had it not been early on a Saturday morning, with only a fraction of the 50,000 people normally there on an average workday, the toll in human life could have been calamitous. As it was, the three men aboard the ill-fated B-25 were killed, as were ten others inside the building. It took twenty fire trucks and the greatest aggregation of fire-fighting equipment ever assembled in New York to quench the flames that raged out of control over six stories of the Empire State Building.

I recount this episode, not only because of the eerie co-incidence—two lost Mitchell bombers in the same week; two dramatically different endings—but to introduce another colorful character, Newsreel Wong. As the longtime voice of Movietone, I had known of Wong's fine camera work in China for the rival M-G-M Metrotone News—it was he who had given the world a classic face of war, the heartbreaking picture of a crying baby sitting alone on a track at the Shanghai railroad station during a Japanese air raid—a picture published over and over, everywhere. But we had never met. Then, when I heard he was in New York and had shot those spectacular films of the plane pinned near the top of our loftiest skyscraper, I invited him up to Quaker Hill for the weekend and we heard his fantastic story at first hand.

For years "Newsreel" had covered the Generalissimo and Madame Chiang, accompanying them on all their journeys. But he had never visited the United States, so when Madame Chiang and her escort set off for Washington in the summer of 1945 to cajole President Truman into sending still more arms and more dollars, Wong was a part of the delegation. Then since New York was so close to Washington, he decided to spend a few days there and to visit his home office which, through two decades of employment with Metrotone, he had never seen.

Arriving in the city on a foggy July morning, he found his way to the M-G-M offices on West Fifty-fourth Street. The hour was early and there was no one to greet him. But it was an office whose doors were never locked. Newsreel just walked in and, from force of habit, picked up a ringing telephone and said, "Wong here."

"Who? Who the hell is this?" The voice in his ear was piping with excitement.

"Wong. Newsreel Wong. I'm a cameraman from . . ."

"I don't give a damn where you're from! If you're a cameraman, grab your camera and get your tail down to the Empire State Building where an airplane has crashed into it, is still hanging there and the whole top of the building is on fire. Get going—fast!"

The line went dead and Wong, who didn't even know where the Empire State Building was and hadn't a camera with him, was suddenly on assignment. Hurriedly checking through the offices, he found where the cameras were kept, grabbed one and hailed a taxi. When he got to Fifth Avenue and Thirty-fourth it was just as though he'd been covering New York all his life.

His war correspondent's uniform was all he needed to persuade the first harried policeman on duty to let him pass. First he filmed the scene from outside. Then up he went, by elevator as far as he could, and trudging on up twenty flights to where the fire was raging and one of the bomber's engines had smashed through an elevator shaft serving the upper floors and had severed the cables. He ranged all through the disaster area, shooting away, pausing to lend the firemen a hand, then shooting some more. When all his film was gone, he made his way back downstairs—to find that he had been the only newsman to get inside the building after the crash. Across the street, more than thirty newsreel and still photographers were cordoned off behind the police lines—only rescue teams and firemen were now being allowed through. And so Newsreel Wong, by turning up at "Metro" before office hours and answering a ringing telephone, had the scoop of the year.

It was not his first triumph. Three pictures had seared themselves into the world's consciousness around that time, com-

ing to symbolize the war-torn 1930s and 1940s: a Frenchman
crying as the Nazis marched into Paris; those four Marines
raising the Stars and Stripes on the summit of Mount Suribachi;
and Newsreel Wong's crying baby, alone on the Shanghai railroad track, face and body blackened by a bomb blast, the debris
of the dead city all around. Newsreel told us how he came to
take that deathless photo.

The year was 1937. The Chinese army had just withdrawn
from Shanghai, leaving a blockade of sunken ships in the Whang-
poo River. "We heard the Japanese navy was going to blow up
the blockade and a bunch of photographers and correspondents
were on hand. But when nothing happened by late afternoon,
most of them left. I decided to hang around a while longer."

Just before 4:00 P.M. he heard planes overhead. Three Japanese bombers were coming in low from the direction of Nanking.
Seconds later he felt the concussion of exploding bombs, heard
the booming sound of the detonations following and then saw a
pall of black smoke rising from the railroad station. He thought
the Chinese arsenal near the river had been hit and, camera in
hand, raced for the waterfront. But when he reached the area
where the railroad tracks ran into the arsenal, he saw it was the
station itself that had been bombed. Whether the Japanese airmen had mistaken a crowd of nearly two thousand civilians waiting to be evacuated for Chinese troops, or whether they sought
to cow the populace with a show of terror, the result was mass
slaughter.

"It was a horrible sight. People covered with blood ran,
they didn't know where. Those who couldn't run lay moaning
where they'd fallen, many with arms and legs blown off. The
dead were everywhere."

Wong helped those he could, shooting film as he went
from casualty to casualty. When he stopped to reload his camera
he realized his shoes were soaked with blood. As he crossed the
platform, he saw a man put a baby down at the edge of the
track, then run off to carry a boy of about six to shelter. He saw
the mother of the two children lying dead on the track. All this
he recorded on film.

"I heard the planes returning and supposed they would
drop more bombs. As I was about to run, I heard the baby by the
side of the track crying. I had only a few feet of film left and

I used it on the baby. Then as I dashed toward him, intending to take him to some safer place, the father came back and I handed him over."

Wong's film was sent out of Shanghai on a U.S. Navy ship. It went to Manila and from there by Pan American clipper to New York. Two weeks later, the crying baby at Shanghai's South Railway Station was appearing on the cover of *Life* Magazine and on thousands of movie screens, and people around the world were jolted into new awareness of war in the mid-twentieth century.

But Newsreel's story wasn't over. The Japanese, outraged to be exposed in such a brutish light, insisted his picture had been faked. "One day as I was getting into my car in the British quarter, four Japanese plainclothesmen closed in and began pushing me toward their sedan. Luckily, I saw a British police inspector approaching and shouted for help. He told the Japanese to let me go, but they insisted I be kept in British custody until they brought written evidence against me."

Of course they didn't have any evidence, but they questioned him all that day and night at the British Municipal Council. He was accused of being a spy for the Chinese. When the British refused to turn him over to the Japanese, the Far East supervisor for "Metro" finally came to his rescue. Wong was released and two days later, with his family, left for the safety of Hong Kong. Later he heard the Japanese had put a price on his head and given him the dubious honor of naming him the fifth most wanted man on their blacklist.

I asked him how he had gotten the nickname "Newsreel." "Well," he said with a smile, "I was born Wong Hai-sheng, but Newsreel isn't a nickname any more." Then he told us how that had come about.

In 1927, he had gone off to cover a story in Tse-nan, a city controlled by the warlord Chang Tsu-chang. When the Japanese took Tse-nan and Chang fled, Wong followed to cover the fighting, leaving word at the hotel that he would be back in two weeks. But the fighting continued for a month and Wong had no chance to return. Meanwhile, his New York office was trying to locate him. Shanghai referred them to Tse-nan. They got in touch with the hotel there and asked the manager to telegraph collect any information on Wong's whereabouts.

Back came the answer, at length: there were many Wongs

in Tse-nan, too many. Which one did they want? And not knowing their man's given name, Metro in New York explained they
were after Wong the newsreel man. To which the hotel manager
promptly responded that, yes, now he knew who they meant—
Newsreel Wong—but he had no idea where he was, probably
dead.

"Fortunately, he was mistaken," said Wong, grinning, "but
it had a lasting effect on my life. From then on all messages from
New York were addressed to me as Newsreel Wong. This went
on for several years until I finally decided, what the hell, and took
Newsreel for my legal name."

And today of all the tens of thousands of Wongs inside and
outside China, "Newsreel" is the most famous.

Of all the long list of unusual personalities who were
Quaker Hill guests, and of the hundreds I have met whose lives
were full of swashbuckling adventure—perhaps the one who most
intrigued me was a lean, weather-beaten soldier of fortune named
Tex O'Reilly. By the time we met up, Tex had wandered the
wide world and been nearly everywhere a fellow might find employment in the game of death or where he could just raise a
little merry hell. I once calculated that he had been involved in
ten wars, from the Philippine Insurrection to the Riff War in
Morocco, and that he survived to die in bed at a ripe old age can
only be testimony that somebody up there liked him, too.

He had started out as a young reporter in San Antonio, but
found that dull and soon joined the Texas Rangers. The year was
1910 and, in retrospect, it seems inevitable that he would wander
south of the border to join Francisco Madero in his revolt against
dictator Porfirio Diaz. Three years later, when Madero was as-
sassinated, Tex joined the forces of Pancho Villa and one fine day
found himself leading a combined Villa-Zapata army on a trium-
phal entry into Mexico City. Suddenly the entire army was held
up—by a traffic cop with an Irish brogue as broad as the Liffey.
"You can't pass," the cop said.

"I admire your sense of duty," Tex said, "but you're holding up a war and sixty thousand men."

"I can't help that. Them's me orders."

Tex recognized a kindred spirit in both the brogue and the
courage. "What's your name?" he asked.

"Tim McGuire, what's yours?"

"O'Reilly."

Well, of course blood is thicker than water and Irish blood is thickest of all, and McGuire stood to one side, which is how the armies of Villa and Zapata got into Mexico City. And Tim McGuire and Tex O'Reilly became lifelong pals.

Tex missed World War I because they told him he was too old, thirty-seven, but for the likes of him there is always a next time. He happened to be in Morocco checking on some oil rights in 1926 when the fierce Berbers of Abdul Krim rose up in the Riff Mountains and threatened to annihilate the Spaniards. Working on his oil deal, Tex slipped through the lines and managed to rescue three prisoners, for which the French awarded him both the Croix de Guerre and the Legion of Honor.

Now the war turned really interesting for him. Along with his sidekick Tim McGuire as top sergeant, Tex joined the Spanish Foreign Legion and soon found himself senior officer of a skeleton battalion trapped between mountains and sea and with their retreat cut off by the Berbers. Inspired by a flag said to have been carried by the Mahdi at Khartoum in the days of "Chinese" Gordon, the Berbers charged again and again, slashing away at the thin Spanish line. Ordered to retreat, Tex replied that he would not come out without his dead. "That was only a way to shut the C.O. up: all I wanted to do was save the survivors, and I figured the only way to do it was to get that damn flag."

The distance was three hundred yards. Tex's flying wedge got deep into the Berber ranks before they knew what had hit them. Then came a yelling, shrieking melee, a whirlwind of *jalabas* and knives. Tex felt his arm slashed open, lost touch with the man behind him—and heard Tim McGuire's roaring brogue: "Begorra, I've got it, Tex! I've got the whiskers of God."

He was down under a tangle of Berbers, cut to pieces, but with the flag held fiercely in his arms. They picked him up and brought him out, nine of the original twenty-one, and by dawn the dispirited Berbers had melted away. But Tim McGuire had fought his last battle. "I gave him a bottle of cognac," Tex recalled, "and toward morning, drunk and happy, singing an Irish melody, he died."

The Sacred Flag of the Mahdi wound up in the Spanish War Office in Madrid, and Tex O'Reilly came to some highly perceptive conclusions about the ways of the world: "Pacifists tell us war is wrong," he once said to me. "That's not news to a soldier. But I've noticed that soldiers never start marching until civilians in high places fail at their jobs."

Between expeditions each winter I managed to get in a few weeks of Alpine skiing, often in Vermont and the Laurentians, and always for several weeks in the Rockies, the Wasatch and the High Sierra.

Frank Springer-Miller, a New York advertising man and ski enthusiast, had a daughter and son on our Olympic squad. So the father went out to Squaw Valley as a volunteer worker. Huge new road-building equipment had been brought up to the Valley to pack the snow over an area they planned to use for a parking lot. Frank had bought a sporty Karmann-Ghia. Two or three days before the opening Olympic ceremony the heavens opened and dropped six feet of snow on Squaw Valley, completely covering the Karmann-Ghia. When the packing monsters did their job they ran right over Springer-Miller's sporty new car and flattened it. The snow was so deep that when screen comedian Mickey Rooney came up from Reno where he was appearing and stepped out of the bus, he disappeared.

The Winter Olympics have always had a special fascination for me because over the years I have often skied with youngsters who later have been on our Olympic team. In 1968 Arthur K. "Dick" Watson flew a few of us from Paris to Geneva, from where we drove through the mountains of Savoy (Savoie) to Grenoble. Although the De Gaulle government had spent nearly a hundred million dollars on roads, high rise buildings to house the Olympic teams, a great new ice arena and other facilities unmatched anywhere in the world, they were overwhelmed by the spectators who came.

Unlike Squaw Valley, where nearly everything was in an easily accessible area, at Grenoble the Olympics were spread over a region that made it necessary for visitors to spend far too much time on the highways, often in stalled traffic. Fed up with this, Jack Simplot, sports editor Hack Miller and a few more of us decided to stage our own private Olympic games in the French Alps at the Haute Savoie, staying at an ancient but comfortable hotel in Aix-les-Bains. From there each morning we would head for a famous nearby ski area, Val-d'Isère, Courchevel or Megève.

In the latter we heard a story that surely ranks as one of the most unusual in the history of skiing.

At Megève our host was Ivor Petrak, who, as a young hotel man from Prague, for a few years had been the manager of our Mount Mansfield Lodge at Stowe, Vermont. Ivor hold us how Megève had become one of Europe's major ski resorts. Along in the twenties soon after World War I, when down-mountain skiing was a new sport in Switzerland, the wife of Baron Maurice Rothschild booked a room at what at the time was the number one hotel in St. Moritz. Wartime prejudices had not faded and the Baroness had made her booking and was assured there would be no Germans staying there. But when she arrived the first person she ran into was one of the Krupps.

Whereupon the Baroness left and a few days later made a deal with a Norwegian ski pro. She told him to find an area in the French Alps as spectacular as St. Moritz, and she put no time limit on his search. A year later he wired "Eureka!" and asked her to meet him at the little mountain village of Megève. She agreed it was just the place, and she and Baron Maurice Rothschild built on the mountain above the village one of the most luxurious hotels in the world, Mont d'Arbois. Eventually they even put in a landing pad for helicopters so they could fly direct from Paris and in moments be in their apartment.

When Hitler's Panzers overran France early in World War II, for several months the Nazis didn't bother about occupying the Alps. Finally paratroopers were dropped into the mountains. The German general in command must have known about the luxurious Rothschild hotel. One day when he strode into the manager's office at Mont d'Arbois and looked around the room, he saw a picture of a skier. Said the Nazi to Francesco Paradi:

"Are you the manager?"

"Oui, mon Général."

"Are you the one in the picture?"

"Oui," replied Paradi. "The day that picture was taken we were both competing. You won the gold medal, and I—came in third."

Whereupon the commander of the German paratroopers saluted Paradi and strode out.

It had been the intention of the Germans to take over Mont d'Arbois as a rest and recreation center for Hitler's officers.

When Baron Rothschild heard about all this he was so elated that he set up a trust fund to take care of Paradi for life, and also made generous arrangements for members of his family.

Today, a son, the Baron Edmund Rothschild, is the owner of Mont d'Arbois and each weekend flies there by helicopter.

III. Bottoming Out

It is my considered opinion that no man in
the annals of humankind, who had so little
interest in gambling, strong drink or fancy
women, has ever managed to unload as much
money as has Lowell Thomas.
        —Frank M. Smith, financial wizard

Quaker Hill is actually a twelve-mile-long ridge, two-thirds in New York and the other third in Connecticut. It has never been classed a village, nor has it had any legally recognized boundaries. In fact, it includes parts of three townships. Over the years such community affairs as required attention were often seen to by the Akin Hall Association, named for a patriarch who was descended from one of the early settlers. For decades its meetings were held in a somewhat run-down Victorian frame hall or next door in a stone edifice, a library, whose design the architect also used for a jail in a city 2,000 miles away. When we invaded the Hill these Akin Hall meetings always ended up in bickering between Akin heirs and their few neighbors. Not long after I became a member of the Association, back in the early 1930s, the old Mizzentop Hotel at the top of the Hill was dismantled, whereupon Fran and I thought it would be appropriate to move Akin Hall to the inn's spectacular site. Our suggestion only caused some eyebrow-lifting. Even if it could be done, which no one believed possible, who wanted to spend a lot of money moving the building?

Whereupon, one winter when most of our neighbors were away, we brought in a Bridgeport firm with impressive new-type equipment, and it was done. Then, all of us, with much enthusiasm, had the building redesigned in graceful Christopher Wren style, with portico and steeple, and since then, as before, it has been used as a nondenominational house of worship on Sundays, and as a meeting hall.

Evidently I like to move things, even hills. We had one which I was sure would look better if it were moved for a mere quarter of a mile. When I mentioned this to Fran, she said, "Now, Tommy, be reasonable. How can you move a *hill?*" I had heard of a steam shovel idled by the Depression, got it for a bargain and, a few thousand truckloads later—no hill. The flattened-out hill had enabled us to raise and level a rather extensive front lawn that had been a nightmare for our farmer, Pat Clark, to mow.

When the increasing popularity of our softball team, The Nine Old Men, began drawing crowds that interfered with the Sunday pleasures of our local golfers, Fran and I, using the same steam shovel, gouged out a new ball field. When the Quaker Hill population outgrew a short, obsolete course that was said to be the third oldest in America, Robert Trent Jones, world's pre-eminent golf architect, laid out a new one, and we remodeled a half fallen-down barn dating back to the early seventeen hundreds, making it into a clubhouse and neighborhood center.

It even seemed that our growing Hill crowd could use a ski tow and chalet, so Fran and I had them built. Then came bridle paths, which entailed clearing brush from a hundred miles or so of ancient, overgrown trails and long-abandoned roads. At the highest point on the Hill, there was an obsolete three-tier observation tower, successor to one built in colonial days, which afforded superb views—and was said to be the only place in America where one could look into five states. But its timbers had rotted; we replaced it with a steel tower.

And so it went over the years until a financial genius named Frank M. Smith took over my affairs in 1946, after I'd spent myself into insolvency. Said Frank to my attorney: "It is my considered opinion that no man in the annals of humankind, who had so little interest in gambling, strong drink or fancy women, has ever managed to unload as much money as has L.T."

The fact is, much of my cash went into a decade-long effort to save Quaker Hill from developers. This began with the death of Fred F. French in 1937. French had never been a social force in Dutchess County—far from it—although he was our wealthiest neighbor and had fulfilled his ambition to own enough land so "I can look from horizon to horizon and it's all mine." Fred F. French, a poor boy who had fought and dared his way to a fortune, seemed to be destiny's darling. Builder of skyscrapers and towering residential complexes like Tudor City and Knickerbocker Village in New York, and several more in London, he became one of the fabled headliners of the booming 1920s, a driving force in the political and economic life of New York City.

But for his private life, French preferred the tranquillity of the country. After acquiring some two thousand acres on Quaker Hill, including still-unspoiled Lake Hammersley and its entire watershed, he spent millions removing buildings and making it all a dream come true. For his family he built a baronial mansion not only lovely to look at but put together like a fortress, its concrete and steel innards fireproof and probably earthquake proof, as well. He also planted over 600,000 spruce and pine trees, with wide fire lanes. To keep out all intruders, French put up a high fence between the only road and the lake. Then, within the borders of his personal monarchy, taking little notice of any community activity, the family lived in splendid isolation. Fran and I visited them once or twice, and Fred French told us they had had only one other guest, an Englishman who once came to arrange for him to build a new London suburb at Golders Green.

Given time, he no doubt would have mellowed. Fran and I found them friendly and attractive. But time suddenly ran out for Fred French. Hit hard by the Great Depression, during the economic storm, he saw his vast holdings shrink, his real estate empire swept away. One day in 1936 he confided to me how up to that hour he had lost twenty million dollars, perhaps the equivalent of sixty or eighty million today. Then, in the bleakly familiar progression of those dark days, French, still in the prime of his years, died of heart failure.

For a while his widow hung on to the Quaker Hill property which, with some insurance, was all she had left. Soon, though, with her four children away at school, she found its memories too much to bear and its demanding costs too much for her dwindling resources. With the help of her husband's former associates, she tried to find someone who would buy the domain. But there were not many in those days with enough cash to take on a multi-million-dollar home, and one day we got the news none of us wanted to hear: Mrs. French was entering into an agreement to sell all her holdings to high-pressure developers, to whom Lake Hammersley and the unspoiled country around it represented a real bonanza. Their plan was to subdivide it all and sell off hundreds of small lots and cheap houses, forever ruining—for any newcomers, as well as for us—the peace and natural beauty that made Quaker Hill so appealing.

Impulsively, without any clear idea of what I might do, I went to Mrs. French and asked if she could give us a little time; maybe we could come up with something. She agreed, for she too had been unhappy about the pending deal.

What to do? I certainly hadn't the kind of capital required, but as I searched my mind for a way out I thought of someone who did—my broadcast sponsor. Soon after, I was in Philadelphia, in the office of J. Howard Pew, president of Sun Oil, explaining how while I didn't know if I could ever recover the investment, I was willing to take almost any gamble in order to preserve Quaker Hill.

"How much do you need?" he asked.

"Three hundred thousand dollars for a down payment."

"Go see Davidson at the Central Hanover Bank in New York. I'll phone and tell him to give you the money."

I went away pleasantly dazed. Had I mortgaged my soul to the Sun Oil Company in order to acquire an enormous domain entailing endless expense with no immediate prospect of any returns? Maybe, but somehow I felt it would work out all right for all of us.

One thing I knew was that I didn't need thousands of acres to satisfy some ego disorder. From this there followed an idea: divide the bulk of the property into fifteen- to one-hundred-acre parcels and sell them to city people or suburbanites longing for a place in the country. I was sure all we had to do was attract people of the type I had in mind—solid citizens—and they would fall under the Quaker Hill spell. Presto, I would solve the financial problem and assure the preservation of our unique life. But it turned out to be one more classic instance of the optimistic amateur innocently wandering into the complex maze of the real estate world.

The first firm with which I formed an alliance, Brown, Wheelock, Harris & Stevens, assured me the plan was viable, but urged me to build a few fine homes to start the ball rolling. I did so, and also remodeled some others. But by the end of a year we hadn't made much progress. The aftermath of the Great Depression was still with us. However, one of the company's top people, Byron Parks, was so taken with Quaker Hill that he and his talented wife—who had played a major role in creating Scarsdale —said they wanted to move to the Hill and run things for us.

But still I kept slipping deeper into the red. Even when we finally began to sell a few places, we were not able to meet the taxes and the costs of running the operation. I did have offers from developers eager to take the entire property off my hands, but despite what may have been sound advice to the contrary, I clung to my dream. I kept telling myself that what was at stake was the future of two superb lakes and many square miles of surrounding countryside, with Clover Brook, our own home, right in the middle of it all.

Incidentally, not until eight years later did Fran and I give a thought to leaving the farm into which we had put so much of ourselves. The big white house, the farm, roads, gardens, swimming pool, gymnasium, tennis court, fur ranch, and our five hundred acres of meadows and forest had all begun to seem part of us. We had hoped to sell the French house, plus appropriate acreage. That too turned out to be no easy task, for the house alone was valued at between two and three million. So as the months and years went by we arranged for various friends, including the Norman Vincent Peales and the Charles Murphys (he was then New York City's Corporation Counsel), to occupy it. Finally in 1945, with Fran eager to redo the much too somber-looking interior, we moved over to the thirty-four-room Georgian mansion on Hammersley Hill.

The first important turning point in our real estate fortunes was accidental and came about because I accepted the presidency of the Advertising Club of New York. I don't know exactly why I did it—I had only indirect connection with the advertising world and certainly didn't have any time to spare. But then my whole life has been a series of unanticipated involvements, few of which I have ever regretted. In any case, I was impressed with the stalwarts of the Ad Club—Bruce Barton, Thomas J. Watson, Stanley Resor, New York *Sun* publisher Gilbert Hodges, Roy Howard, Grover Whalen and the other men of eminence on its board of directors. And I did enjoy presiding over those standing-room-only luncheons and dinners for national heroes being honored by the City of New York—conquering airmen, returned explorers, all paraded up Broadway in a blizzard of ticker tape, with the climax a function at the Ad Club.

My immediate predecessors as president of that then-prestigious institution were Corporation Counsel Charley Murphy and G. Lynn Sumner, head of the International Correspondence Schools. They had been my special sponsors, and we invited them to spend several weekends with us at Quaker Hill. They later confessed it was love at first sight and asked if we would sell them each some property. Both built houses on the Hill and their families became major assets to the community.

Then we hit the jackpot. The *Herald Tribune* carried an item to the effect that the rackets-busting young district attorney, Thomas E. Dewey, was planning on taking his family to Connecticut for the summer. Although we had never met, I picked up the telephone and called him. After he thanked me for the favorable notice I'd given to his continuing battle against big-time gangsterism on my news broadcasts, I told him I'd heard he was about to spend the summer in Connecticut. I said, "Mr. Dewey, two questions: Is the State of Connecticut important to your political future? And, have you ever seen Quaker Hill?"

His instant reply was: "We'll be up to see you this weekend!"

When they came, they brought with them their close friends, Pat and Marge Hogan—which meant we had hit a double jackpot. Fran and I drove them from one end of our twelve-mile hill to the other, letting the serenity and the sweeping views do the selling. Then we took them to see the Haskins farm, which was not my property but was for sale, and maybe just right for the Deweys and their two young sons. All I wanted was to lure them to the Hill.

Tom and Frances Dewey were enthusiastic about the Haskins place, but there was a problem—money. The young D.A. said, alas, the price was far beyond his means as a public servant.

I thought this one over a while, then went to see Mrs. Haskins. I might have a buyer for her farm, I said, but additional persuasion was called for; how would she like to visit her son in Cincinnati and allow the Deweys to move in for the summer, at a modest rental?

She said my proposal seemed unusual, but she agreed to do it. And it all would have worked out perfectly—except that by autumn Dewey still didn't have the money. Nor did he have it by the following spring, though by then he and his family wanted the property more than ever. I knew Mrs. Haskins was not too happy with me, but I gathered up my courage and went back to see her. She grumbled. She complained. She said it was ridiculous. But I just kept talking and finally she agreed to spend the summer in Cincinnati again and the Deweys returned to Dapplemere.

However, this time it was for good. Dewey arranged to borrow enough cash for the down payment and worked out plans for a dairy operation he hoped would keep the farm self-supporting. He was to remain there happily for the rest of his life; he and his wife always found there on our Hill a haven from the political wars, and his sons grew to young manhood there. Furthermore, his move induced his friends, the Carl T. (Pat) Hogans, to buy a place nearby, and the Hill had two more fine new families.

The focal point of our community center clubhouse was a giant fireplace whose stones, many a foot square, were from the structures representing the high water marks of man's progress—the Cheops Pyramid, the Parthenon, the Great Wall of China, the Taj Mahal, St. Peter's and the Coliseum, Westminster Abbey, the Washington Monument, Mount Vernon and all the way down to the Empire State Building and Rockefeller Center, in our own era. Together, they capsulize the story of our civilization. And on the mantel, chiseled in Sanskrit, is this saying: "He who allows a day to pass without practicing generosity or enjoying life's pleasures is like a blacksmith's bellows—he breathes but does not live."

Therein, I suppose, lies the best explanation I can make for the softball field, the golf course and all the other amenities Fran and I promoted at Quaker Hill. They may have been considered acts of generosity by some, but the truth is we introduced them, all of them, in our own pursuit of life's pleasures. I would have been equally happy if someone else had done it, or if a committee had been organized to make them community projects. But I wanted to ride, play ball, swim and golf right then, not in some vague tomorrow, and at the time there was no one quite as hopped up as I may have been. And as everyone knows, committees were invented for conversation, not action.

Not long after acquiring the French domain, Fran and I invited all of our Quaker Hill neighbors to use Lake Hammersley just as if it belonged to them. Later, fifteen hundred acres of the adjacent woodland area were turned over to Nature Conservancy, a quasi-public institution devoted to taking over unspoiled lands and keeping them forever wild. They had been doing this from coast to coast, and we knew they would help protect Quaker Hill from future developers. And I felt access to the lake would give our neighbors a shared feeling of all being in this together. Of course, I hoped it might also stimulate the selling of real estate when word got around that Quaker Hill was a unique and wonderful place to live.

Alas, soon there were restless stirrings in our little paradise; perhaps it would have turned dull otherwise. Opening the lake to all didn't work out quite as we had hoped it would. Some neighbors were reluctant to impose themselves as constant guests, but others brought relatives and the relatives brought friends and on the occasions when we appeared sometimes we would find strangers and there was mutual embarrassment. Soon Fran and I quit using the lake altogether on the theory that what we didn't know wouldn't hurt us.

It was Byron Parks who came up with what seemed a solution. Suppose I invited each of the Hill residents to buy a small parcel of the former French estate at an exceedingly low price and, along with it, deeded them permanent lake rights. Wouldn't this make them feel like real partners, eliminating the awkwardness some felt at using someone else's beach, and also giving everyone good reason not to abuse it?

It sounded right, so we worked out an arrangement whereby I would sell any Hill neighbor approximately seven acres for $3,500 (today worth some $21,000). In addition to the land, the money was buying lasting rights to a multi-million-dollar lake and beachfront. Ah, but I had misjudged human nature. Many rushed to choose for themselves our best acreage, prize parcels that would have been most attractive to the outsiders I was trying to attract as purchasers and new residents.

I've always felt the fault was mine. I should have explained my plan to each neighbor in person instead of leaving it to By Parks who, with the best of intentions, perhaps went at it like any competent real estate salesman would have done, emphasizing how each family could increase the value of its own property and do L.T. a favor at the same time—for a mere thirty-five hundred. So it cost me dearly. But I was still learning and, after all, it was only money.

I had some other small problems. A neighbor ran into trouble with real estate commitments. I provided some cash—and lost both cash and friend. Which is the way it's supposed to be, isn't it?

Another neighbor dies and his heirs, failing to find a suitable buyer, come to you and, with a show of genuine regret and reluctance, say they will be forced to put the property on the open market. The implied threat is unmistakable; you wind up buying the property yourself. This happened now and then and, far from recovering my investment by selling off portions of the French holdings, I found myself the owner of an additional thousand acres—in self-defense against developers—when the Sheffield Milk company put their showplace dairy on the auction block.

Inevitably, I suppose, I heard how one of our neighbors had referred to me with some colorful profanity as the self-anointed King of Quaker Hill. I can see how it might have appeared. Perhaps I did precipitate the fundamental changes that made the Hill what it is today. But none of it was to gain or exercise power—something never of any interest to me. My reasons were much more basically selfish—to realize all the possibilities of the Hill so Fran, young Lowell and I could enjoy them now, with congenial neighbors, doing the things that add to the zest of life.

And despite occasional disappointments, I think we succeeded in fulfilling most of our dreams for Quaker Hill. All those years of young Lowell's growing up were a golden age as far as I was concerned, a halcyon time when my professional life was booming and, at home, there seemed to be an exciting challenge with every passing season. If I ever noticed that my financial well was running dry, I paid no heed.

Not long ago I was invited to serve as Grand Marshal of the celebration in St. Louis commemorating the fiftieth anniversary of Lindbergh's epic flight across the Atlantic. I accepted. I also agreed when the Explorers Club, which includes most of the active explorers of our time and those who support their work, asked if they could send out a letter over my signature asking famous men to lend their names to a committee to help organize the Lindbergh anniversary celebration. One of the most eminent explorers of our time replied that he never lent his name except when he really wanted to play an active role.

That's one extreme. I suppose I am at the other, joining clubs, boards, committees and the like at the drop of an invitation. Many years ago, when my secretary, Electra, quit framing my membership cards, there were well over two hundred. Why am I such a joiner? I don't know, unless it is that in my work—except for technical help—I have always been a loner. And of course joining up has given me the opportunity to meet a truly remarkable roster of achievers. Which brings me to George Pierrot.

A journalist who had worked his way through the University of Washington and the first lean years after by canning salmon in Alaska, working at a Billy Sunday tabernacle, mining coal and roaming the world as a deckhand, Pierrot became an editor for two famous magazines, *The Youth's Companion* and *The American Boy*. In 1933, he was asked to help the Detroit Institute of Arts out of serious financial difficulty and launched a travel film series in their auditorium that soon became the best known in the world. And that's how we met. Along with Roy Chapman Andrews, head of New York's American Museum of Natural History; Fred Black, a vice president of the Ford Motor Company; and a handful of others, Pierrot thought I had the prestige to help get his series off the ground. So, I became a member of his board—now the last survivor.

Pierrot could have duplicated his series all over the world —it was certainly copied often enough—but he and his wife devoted part of each year to long journeys. He was a remarkable man: no one has done more to promote travel than my dynamic, eloquent and humorous friend, George Pierrot. Whatever help I gave him was more than rewarded by seeing how he rescued the Detroit Institute of Arts and what he did for others in the fields of travel, exploration and entertainment. And all I had done was to lend him the use of my name.

Golf, which has been described, not unfairly, as less a sport than a disease, has afflicted me for more than half a century. Most men, similarly plagued, play a round once or twice a week and are momentarily appeased. As for me, I build golf courses, am a member of eight golf clubs on three continents, and am one of the founders of the National Golf Hall of Fame. The irony of it all is that I have seldom played often enough to establish a handicap, and when I break ninety—anywhere! (one hundred at Pine Valley)—it is an occasion for celebration.

It all began on an otherwise pleasant autumn afternoon in 1920. Having presented a show featuring films and a narration about the exploits of General Allenby in Palestine and Lawrence of Arabia for more than a year in New York and London, I had been invited by Prime Minister Billy Hughes to bring it to Australia. There, at a luncheon given in our honor by Sir John Monash, commander-in-chief of all Australian forces in World War I, I met amateur golf champion Ivo Whitten, who invited me to play a round with him at the Melbourne Metropolitan Club. That I did represented a certain foolishness on both our parts, for golf is not a game to plunge into without preparation and much practice. For most of the eighteen holes, I was all over the landscape, appearing on the fairway only to cross from one rough to another. But on one of the short holes, by accident of course, my tee shot plunked right down on the green and rolled to within a few inches of the cup. When I sank it for a birdie two, Whitten was so unnerved that he sliced his next drive into the deep bush. Whereupon he broke the shaft of his club over his knee and threw it after the ball.

That was my first lesson in the complexities of golf. It is, at bottom, an exasperating game, and you are your own most relentless opponent. Anyway, I was hooked, and later took some lessons from young Joe Kirkwood, who had recently won the Australian championship. He must have forgiven my vagaries as a student, for in later years he often came to visit us at Quaker Hill. I named a golf hole for him, and we remained friends until he died.

In New Zealand, I bought my first set of clubs. They were the wooden antiques you now see in museums. I carried them inside the big padded trunks built for our projection equipment, always hoping to play wherever we stopped to do the Allenby-Lawrence show. But that happened only twice, and twenty years were to pass before I swung a club again. It was as though I had never previously held one in my hands.

By then, in the perverse way of the world, the game had caught on everywhere. At Quaker Hill, the short nine-hole course —said to be one of the first in America—which had served the Hill people for decades, became inadequate for the increasing number of our golfers and their sharpened skills. So one day I invited Gene Sarazen, a Hudson Valley neighbor, to stop by. He took one look at a large field on the brow of North Quaker Hill with its magnificent views and proclaimed it ideal for a golf course. It was also Gene who suggested Robert Trent Jones, the world's number one golf architect, to lay it out, and in that post-Depression period, we were lucky to get him to do it at far less than what it would cost today.

Soon after the course was completed in June, 1940, Governor Dewey and my other Quaker Hill neighbors presented me with a set of clubs and a handsome bag with a silver plaque. But I rarely got a chance to use them until, a couple of years later, in Tucson, I took a few lessons from Leo Diegel. I was still such a neophyte that I didn't know what a legend Diegel was in the golf world, two-time winner of the P.G.A. and at the top in countless other tournaments. He was a chain smoker and so nervous he had to putt bent over with his head at waist level, his arms locked at rigid angles so only his shoulders moved and his club swung with a sort of mechanical pendulum motion. When he offered to play me on one leg and give me a stroke a hole, I didn't see how I could lose. Of course I did, but his performance left an indelible mark on me. If jittery Leo Diegel could beat me on one leg then surely, even at age fifty, I could master this maddening game.

And perhaps I would have had I devoted even a couple of afternoons a week to it. But I never seemed to have the time.

And though I have since played with and taken lessons from the likes of Horton Smith, Tommy Armour, Sam Snead, Willie Turnesa, and even Arnold Palmer and many more masters of the game, all with highly diverse styles—I only succeeded in becoming the most confused golfer in America.

Yet somehow, through the years, golf and the splendid men associated with it have given me much pleasure. One October day, a man named Ralph A. Kennedy, whom I'd never met, telephoned and asked if he could play at Quaker Hill. It would, he said, be his two-thousandth golf course. Although we had officially closed for the season, I didn't see how I could deny such enterprise, so I arranged for a member, Paul Reinhold, to play a round with him and attest his scorecard. Then, years later, when I had all but forgotten the incident, an article in the *National Geographic* caught my eye and I read in detail about Ralph Kennedy's remarkable achievement. By that time he had been searching out new golf courses for forty years and had played more than 3,000 of them, by far a world's record, walking 27,000 miles of fairways in fourteen countries on six continents and in every one of our then forty-eight states. He had played a course in Uganda where crocodiles were a hazard; in India, where the caddies ran ahead to keep ravens from flying off with the ball; and on fairways in Panama made of earth dredged up from the Panama Canal. There was the highest course in the world—12,000 feet up in the Andes, near La Paz, of which I now am a member; and the lowest—the Devil's Golf Course in Death Valley, California. Kennedy had played them all. Golf was not a diversion with him—it was a mania.

The high point of his obsessive quest had been his round at the Royal and Ancient Golf Club at St. Andrews, Scotland, where golfers first began crying, "Oh, no!" after their shots in 1754, and which has since become the Mecca of golfdom. Kennedy was in thrall to St. Andrews, where the streets had names like Golf Place and The Fairway, where the bus stops were called stances and where only infants and the infirm among the 10,000 townfolk do not play "the royal and ancient game."

The day Kennedy approached the starting tee there, quite a crowd was assembled, including a goodly number of photographers, and he asked his partner what it was all about. "Pay no attention," was the reply. "They've come to see some famous golfer tee off."

"Well, look," said Kennedy, as thoroughly in awe of the great golfers as a small boy might have been of Babe Ruth, "let's stand aside and watch, too."

But his partner shook his head and smiled. "No, they've come to watch a guy named Ralph Kennedy play his three-thousandth golf course."

Kennedy reported that at these words his knees buckled. But then came the age-old St. Andrews starting signal—"Play away, please!"—and he did a waggle or two and sent the ball booming down the fairway for two hundred yards, beginning a round that was to cap half a lifetime of golf, 27,000 miles following a little white ball—and every one on foot, for he was a man who scorned golf carts!

In time I came to realize that, as the old saw goes, you drive for show and putt for dough, a vivid way of saying that a golfer's score is more apt to reflect his skill on the green than his strength on the fairway. A canny old gentleman I sometimes played with, Glenn McHugh, one of the heads of the Equitable Life Assurance empire, although ten years my senior, never failed to come within a few strokes of the best amateurs or professionals in our foursome by the simple expedient of dropping his approach shot close to the pin and often holing out in one putt, never more than two. How did he manage this wizardry? He had a practice green at his home and spent an hour or two putting almost every day.

This started me thinking; a self-generating chain of events with awesome consequences was about to begin. First I laid out a practice green. After all, who wants to be "low man on the totem pole" with the highest score in every foursome? But when I was away, Fran kept Felice and Rocco busy in her flower gardens and nature worked her ravages on my green. Then I heard of a golf course builder named Billy Mitchell who would bring you a golf course—tees, fairways, greens and all—and have it ready for play in three weeks or so. He had done this at our Stowe, Vermont, ski area. I phoned him.

"Look," I said, "I don't want a golf course. I just want a

putting green. If you ever get down this way, drop in."

And of course he did, whereupon I compounded the felony by bringing out a rough sketch once done by a Boca Raton, Florida, golf architect of how four holes could be laid out around a body of water on our place. Mitchell took one look at it and said, "Why bother with a putting green? Let me put these four holes in for you—you have a perfect set-up for them."

That was my last chance to back away from the toboggan slide down which I plunged. "Why not?" I said blithely, and soon had four golf holes around our small lake.

Then Gene Sarazen came around to have a look. As he stood gazing out over the water, he pointed to a pine forest about four hundred yards away and said, "You ought to put another green down there, for an over-the-water shot and a second to the woods."

So I did, and named the hole for him. Other pros came and suggested others, and before I quite caught hold of what was happening, I had a twenty-one-hole course on Hammersley Hill, so any guest who had played the regulation eighteen and still had another half hour of energy left could play three more as a bonus. In my customary way, I paid little attention to the cost.

After it was all done, the money long spent, and Frank Smith had become my financial manager, he lost no opportunity to needle me about the course, about the folly of all this expenditure when we already had the Robert Trent Jones course two miles away which I had built for our neighbors. "A pitch and putt course," he called my new one. It was true I had put in what may be the shortest hole of any regulation golf course anywhere, an eighty-yard over-the-water par 3, but the others were standard length. Still, I thought I ought to show Frank how two could play at the needling game. I tracked down Trent Jones in whatever part of the world he happened to be then and asked him if he knew the length of the longest hole anywhere. He did. It was at Johannesburg, South Africa, a 650-yard par 6. So I put one in, 780 yards, double dog-leg, over a grove of tall pines. All this when Frank was laid up with a bad knee and unable to play. By the time he was fit again, the hole was all set and named for him. When Joe Kirkwood saw it, he said it had to be a par 7. Another golfing friend, the British diplomat Sir Berkeley Ormerod, who had played with Bobby Jones the historic year of the "Grand Slam," threw down his club midway up the fairway and asked, "What's the suicide rate on this hole?" And when Frank finally saw it, he closed his eyes as in silent supplication, then said, "Lowell, before I cross swords with you I am going to lock up your checkbook." But I think he was secretly pleased. Several years later I put in an 830-yard, par 7.5 hole, which to my surprise all pros enjoy playing.

Having my own golf course did not restrict me to playing at home. Along with Lowell, Jr., and Trent Jones and others, I even became involved in building a course in Hawaii, the Royal Kanapali at Lahaina on the island of Maui. We lost our shirts on it, but it was a magnificent course; eventually American Factors, one of the pioneer Hawaiian firms, took it over, and now it is thriving.

In time, like the peripatetic Ralph Kennedy, I chalked up some rounds in some of the world's unlikely places. One was the Low Tide Golf Course on Wake Island. It had been organized in the early days of trans-Pacific flying by Pan American air crews who sometimes had to kill a couple of days on that lonely atoll in the middle of the Pacific while kinks were ironed out of their Clipper planes. To while away the time, they played golf on the beach—*when the tide was out*—hence the intriguing name.

The Royal Hong Kong Golf Course is so near the Chinese border that if you sliced your tee shot on the sixth hole, forget it, it belonged to Chairman Mao. In New Delhi during World War II, on a course built around some Mogul tombs, my host handed me a single golf ball, explaining how difficult they were to come by in wartime India. Whereupon I hooked it into the jungle on my first shot.

But if golf can burden you with monumental embarrassments, it can also favor you with an occasional moment of transcending bliss. Already properly awed to be playing the challenging "Old Course" at Scotland's St. Andrews, I was assigned a caddy named Andrew Carnegie, a grizzled old Highlander who had seen the best and probably expected the worst from me. I imagined him to be gloating in anticipation of my flubs and hackings. Instead, he gave me what he called "the tiger line," the most direct route to the green, and with his encouragement I was shooting a fairly tolerable game.

Then came the memorable eleventh, a 160-yard par 3. With the guidance of Andrew Carnegie and the blessings of Lady Luck, I put my tee shot right up against the cup and holed out. Retrieving the ball, Carnegie cleared his throat and said, "I suggest you put a note on your scorecard to telephone Mr. Gene Sarazen when you get back to America, sir, and let him know your score on the eleventh. It was here that he took a triple bogie that cost him the British Open!" Maybe some day I'll write more about unusual golf experiences in Africa, South America, Japan— in many lands—mebbe.

In 1957, George Carroll wrote an article about me for *Ski* Magazine in which he said that perhaps five million Americans called themselves skiers—the number has more than doubled since then—and he added that I was their best friend. Well, writers do exaggerate, but the truth is for the past five decades I've been a ski addict and have urged others to take up the sport. During this period I may have devoted more time to it than to any other single endeavor. Maybe it is all a result of having grown up at ten thousand feet in the Rocky Mountains. I feel at home on a mountain. But nothing I could say by way of explanation would adequately describe my feeling about skiing. If you have ever come down a long mountain run over fresh powder snow on a clear winter day, you know. If you haven't, just take my word for it: no other sensation approximates it. And there was also the pleasure of the unusual people I came to know as a skier.

It began in the Italian Alps during World War I. That was when I had visited the mountain lair of the *Arditi,* one of the first military ski outfits ever organized. Commanded by the Marquis Nicolas degli Albizzi, a dashing cavalry officer whom I later came to know well, these crack Italian troops, clad in white, did their thing high up on Monte Rosa, on nine-foot skis. Through the convoluted logic that sometimes prevails in wartime they didn't spend much time in battle, since it was a holding operation on a static front; nonetheless, I was impressed with what I saw.

One winter a decade later, Prince William of Sweden was our first guest at Clover Brook while I helped him prepare for a national speaking tour. The Prince was a towering six-foot-six Scandinavian who rarely left the house. His aide, a captain in

King Gustav's army, gave me a few lessons in ski touring and each day we went out across our Quaker Hill fields. Then came the historic Winter Olympics of 1932 at Lake Placid, New York, where young Lowell and I had the good fortune to get acquainted with Erling Strom, a young Norwegian who was a pioneer in the development of skiing in America.

Erling had been an officer in the King's Guard. But he was also a stutterer and, one day, more nervous than usual while putting the Guard through its close-order marching routine in the presence of King Haakon and his guests, poor Erling was unable to give voice to any saving command and the rigidly disciplined troops marched straight into the palace wall. Whereupon Erling took his honorable discharge and became a cowboy in America.

Norway's loss was our gain. After a stint on an Arizona ranch there followed some spectacular skiing exploits in the Rockies. In 1926, Erling and another top skier, Lars Haugen, made a spectacular 110-mile cross-country trip over the three highest ranges in the Rocky Mountains. When they reached Steamboat Springs, their destination, and some doubting Thomases scoffed at their story, they turned right around and did the same route in the other direction!

I think Erling would agree that his most sensational exploit was climbing both the north and south peaks of Alaska's mighty Mount McKinley, a feat never before achieved—and Erling and his party did it on skis! It wasn't, as he later put it, "that I really thought a trip to McKinley would offer snappy downhill skiing—I knew too well what one can and cannot do with sixty pounds on one's back." But on the other hand, how many people would ever be able to claim to have stood on skis and looked out on 20,000 feet of downhill in all directions. And so in the spring of 1932, he and Al Lindley, with two Alaskans, Grand Pearson and Harry Liek, did it—and had the added thrill of finding a thermometer left behind by an earlier McKinley adventurer. It was frozen at a hundred degrees below zero and had a poignant little accompanying note: "Please read carefully and return to Archdeacon Hudson Stuck, 281 Fourth Avenue, New York City." The note was dated June 7, 1913.

In the late 1920s, Erling was invited to become ski instructor at the Lake Placid Club in the Adirondacks; it was there that young Lowell and I fell under his spell. We took some lessons, and Lowell, Jr., age nine, and Lowell, Sr., age forty, became ski addicts for life.

In 1940, Erling moved on, first to Mont Tremblant in the Laurentians, and then to invest in his own lodge at Stowe, Vermont, near Mount Mansfield, which was to become the eastern ski center of the United States. Eventually he and the Marquis established another ski camp at Mount Assiniboine, near Banff in Canada, and that's where he can be found these days, still standing tall on his skis.

I have been skiing with Erling Strom for forty years now, and with another skiing pioneer, Alf Engen, almost as long. Today, well into his sixties and still going strong at Alta, in Utah, Alf has taught uncounted thousands of youngsters the fine art of Alpine downhill skiing and in the process he himself has become one of the best-known—and best—skiers in the world. Alf, too, is a Norwegian, one of three famous skiing brothers, who came to America to seek their fortune. Alf found it particularly hard going at first, walking the streets of Chicago without money to buy even food, unable to speak English. Then one day he found himself wandering in Grant Park along the lakefront where some stalwarts were playing soccer. This was like a whiff of home and Alf sidled up to the coach and somehow made known his interest in getting into the match. Well, he was so weak with hunger that the first time he made bodily contact he was knocked out cold.

But fortune comes in strange guises. Soon the other players managed to glean the truth of his circumstances, pooled some money to get him started—and Alf became a professional soccer player. Then he became a professional ski jumper, the best in the country. He had started skiing, as had most of his countrymen, in what are still called the Nordic events: jumping and cross-country. Skiing in Scandinavia has historically been a mode of transportation, on long skis, but like every mode of transportation, it eventually became a sporting event featuring high-speed races. And so developed the big boom in downhill skiing all over the world. Alf Engen was to help lead the way.

I was skiing with Alf at Alta a couple of years ago when we were witnesses to one of the most freakish survival stories in the history of the sport. We had just rounded a turn high up on

Mount Baldy when the avalanche alarm sounded. Joining the ski patrol, we went poking in the deep snow with long rods because it was impossible to account for how many people had been on the mountain. And so we came on Ron Perla, a ranger who, with two other men, had climbed up on a huge snow cornice to plant an explosive charge so the overladen snow could be triggered when there was no danger to skiers. Somehow, though, the avalanche took off on its own, just as Ron perched himself at the top, and off he went in a great swirl of snow traveling at terrific speed. He kept his head, though, and was in superb shape which, together with the under-the-snow swimming motion recommended for such exigencies, saved his life. Out of sight, he had ridden the avalanche for half a mile at 100 miles an hour. Ron Perla has moved over to the Colorado Rockies, where today he is that state's avalanche expert.

From my first lesson, until now, I have continued to ski my way not only around this country, but all over the world. When young Lowell was off at school, I would take Fran, a secretary, a radio engineer, a Western Union telegraph operator and a few friends and be off following the snow from one ski area to another, having a glorious time. I usually did my broadcast with a local background, which brought joy to the hearts of those brave souls who were putting in the first tows, chair lifts and ski lodges in those tentative beginnings of the ski boom.

All this meant considerable extra expense for me—line charges and travel costs which I had to assume—for my contract specified that I was to do my broadcasting from New York City. So when I took off for the White or Green Mountains of New England, the Adirondacks or Canadian Laurentians, or west to the Rockies and High Sierra, both American Tel and Tel and my network added the heavy radio line charges required to my travel bill. Each year, this additional expense came to between twenty-five and forty thousand dollars; it takes only a bit of figuring to see that it all totaled out to something more than a million dollars over the decades since I was first bitten by the ski bug. And this, I suspect, less than my skill, is why I have been so generously honored by ski organizations and have been elected to both the U.S. and Canadian Ski Halls of Fame, and why ski trails were named for me in the Adirondacks, the Rockies and Canada, and also why I was made an honorary member of our U.S. Olympic team, and likewise of the 700-member Professional National Ski Association members.

Honors apart—and they are undeserved—skiing has introduced my family and me to an endless list of exciting people and to an array of fabulous places. One of the first was a famous old inn, Peckett's-on-Sugar-Hill, near Franconia in New Hampshire. It had an inspiring view of the Presidential Range and a glittering roster of summer guests including President Calvin Coolidge, Chief Justice Charles Evans Hughes, John D. Rockefeller, Jr., and his son Nelson, authors Kenneth Roberts and Alexander Woollcott. Then one year in the early 1930s, Katherine Peckett came home from a holiday at St. Anton in the Austrian Alps and talked her father into opening their inn for the winter season. She also engaged four Austrian skiers, and Peckett's became the first place in North America where instruction in Alpine (downhill) skiing was offered to the general public.

Sig Buchmayr, the most colorful of these Austrians, was the head of this, the first formal ski school in the United States. With the inn's long-established reputation and the charismatic presence of Buchmayr—who, said *Vogue* Magazine, was "a veritable Nijinsky on skis, always looking elegantly Tyrolean and dazzling onlookers with his relaxed grace"—Peckett's became the winter resort *du monde*, entertaining four thousand guests during the twelve-week season, with as many as two hundred fifty in the ski classes. Recalled one of those neophytes: "We would take toboggans out for those who cracked up; somebody was always waiting around for the ambulance from Franconia or Littleton." And L.T., Jr., was one of those early casualties—but a broken leg hardly even slowed him down.

Young Lowell and I were among the first to take up Alpine skiing at Peckett's, with Sig Buchmayr, Kurt Thalhammer and others who later joined them. Heading west, we skied with most of the other Austrians who soon were lured to America. Among them was Otto Lang, who organized ski schools in the Pacific Northwest and later at Sun Valley in Idaho, where the Hollywood set found a glamorous new winter home. Otto gave instructions to Norma Shearer, Claudette Colbert, Gary Cooper and the supercharged Darryl F. Zanuck, who even skied with that long cigar in his mouth. Zanuck, recognizing latent talents in his ski instructor, talked him into going to Hollywood, where Lang first became a cameraman and then moved on up as a top director. Years afterward, when I became involved in Cinerama, Otto went with us to the Himalayas, to Nepal, Kashmir and Hunza, to direct our *Search for Paradise.*

Otto Lang was not the first head of the ski school at Sun Valley, that glamorous resort in the Sawtooth Mountains which Averell Harriman had the foresight to establish along the route of his Union Pacific Railroad. That distinction first went to a rangy, good-looking Austrian ski champion named Hans Hauser— but not for long. Hans was a romantic, not the everyday kind, but one who was so dazzled by visions of what he *wanted* to see that he was blinded to simple reality. No one was more fun to ski with, but skiing seemed to be where Hans Hauser's ability to cope began and ended. Every time I saw him I sensed a man coming ever closer to a tragic end.

When it became clear that he wasn't cut out to be director of the Sun Valley ski school, Harriman replaced him with Friedl Pfeifer—and later with Otto Lang, Johnny Litchfield and Sigi Engl. With the coming of World War II all the Austrian instructors at Sun Valley (now technically enemy aliens), with one exception, chose to serve in the American army. Some of them made brilliant records in the newly-formed ski troops. Only Hauser chose to go to a detention camp instead.

But his troubles didn't really start until a November day in 1949 when, back at Sun Valley, he was assigned as a ski student a full-bosomed, flamboyant sex bomb called Virginia Hill. Now it may well be that Hans had no idea who the ever-undulating Miss Hill was at first—he was an innocent sort. But there was simply no way to avoid finding out. To begin with, she went down to the Piccard ski shop and unloaded $5,000 to equip herself for her new pastime, paying cash from a wad tucked into her stocking top. That started tongues wagging, and soon it was all over Sun Valley that Virginia Hill—yes, my dear, *Virginia Hill!*— was in residence: the woman in whose living room the notorious gangster, Bugsy Siegel, met an untimely end when someone stuck a rifle through the window and pumped him full of bullets. Nor was Bugsy the only hoodlum with whom Virginia had consorted since cutting a swath from Liscomb, Alabama, to the big time. She seemed to have a predilection for mob types, and the list of those who had enjoyed her favors before and after the ill-fated Mr. Siegel included Frank Costello, Lucky Luciano and Joe Adonis.

Virginia spent six memorable weeks at Sun Valley, during which time, as Hans once told me, she received a shoe box full of money, delivered by a messenger, each and every week. The smallest denomination was a fifty. And this was a practice that was to continue almost to the end of her life. But money was not on Miss Hill's mind during that winter idyll: Hans Hauser was. She was on the slopes with him all day and threw gala parties for him at night; and one day when it snowed a blizzard and no one was out, she called from her room and wanted to know where her instructor was. "But, Miss Hill," they told her, "it's snowing too hard for a lesson."

"Yeah, well send the s.o.b. up here and I'll teach *him* a couple of things," she said.

Apparently she did. Soon it was painfully clear that Hans was seriously hooked, in love. His friend Otto Lang sensed this, and stayed up half that night, pleading with Hans not to get involved. Otto told him there could be no happiness in an alliance with the so-called Queen of the Underworld. Finally Hans said he saw the light, blessed Otto for his patience and understanding and said he had decided to break off the romance. At 2:00 A.M., Otto went to sleep convinced reason had prevailed. And sometime between then and breakfast, Hans and Virginia Hill eloped. Now they were both on an icy downhill track.

Hans' life was never the same after that, while unhappily Virginia's didn't change much. There were still the mysterious ties to the underworld, still shoe boxes full of money arriving, every week or two, wherever they were. Hans and I did some skiing on Mount Spokane in the State of Washington not long before the roof fell in, and he seemed to me a man with a heavy burden.

No wonder. That spring, Senator Estes Kefauver convened the public hearings of the Senate Crime Investigating Committee and of all the underworld characters who enthralled millions of American television viewers with their testimony, none had a greater impact than witness Virginia Hill. Not that she made any startling revelations. Her memory lapses were breathtaking. She didn't remember the sources of her considerable income, or much about her relationships with the likes of Bugsy Siegel, Frank Costello and Joe Adonis. "I just seem to be drawn to underworld big shots like a magnet," she said coyly. She certainly had nothing to say about underworld activities. But the fact that she looked like precisely what she was and the obvious scorn in which she held her interrogators and the press made her a ten-day American sensation.

It is, perhaps, all for the best that the TV cameras were excluded when, in private session, Senator Charles Tobey, staid and elderly, asked her in all candor why men should have given her such large sums of money. She tried to convey the message by lowering her eyelids and saying she'd rather not be specific. But Tobey went blundering on, insisting, in a gentlemanly way, that she be frank with the committee. What was it, he asked, that impelled so many different and notorious characters to be so generous to her? So Virginia put it on the line: "It's because I'm the best goddamn lay in the country," she replied. Senator Tobey had no further questions.

What poor Hans thought of all this is not a matter of record. But he stood loyally by her when, soon after the hearings, the Internal Revenue Service calculated that she owed $161,000 in back taxes. Some say it was this loyalty that caused Hans to run into visa trouble. In the summer of 1951, he flew to Chile, one step ahead of deportation. Virginia joined him there soon after, one step ahead of an indictment for income tax evasion. And, flying in during my rovings on behalf of the first Cinerama film, I ran into Hans in a Santiago hotel lobby. We promptly organized a skiing trip to the high Andes and had a fine time. It was, he said, almost like the old days. But of course I had to move on eventually and, for Hans Hauser, the old days were over for good. I never saw him again.

He took Virginia and their infant son to his native Austria, to a family-owned inn near Salzburg. But none of it could have been Virginia's style. In 1954, the United States government issued a warrant for her arrest, but as long as she was abroad she was safe from Uncle Sam. However, she couldn't hide from the demons inside. She and Hans separated and one spring day in 1966 they found her dead in the snow outside the little village where she lived. An autopsy revealed that she had taken an overdose of sleeping pills. Then, in 1974, there came word that Hans was dead, too. He had hanged himself.

The early ski masters were inspired people. Mathias Zdarsky, who developed the Lilienfeld method, an adaptation of bindings and technique for Alpine terrain, had the astonishing foresight to write—in 1916!—that

> Alcohol and nicotine are two unequal enemies of the nerves. Alcohol is the milder, for it has the virtue that it betrays itself easily. Nicotine is a sneaking fellow and a hypocrite. This enemy of our nerves, of our hearts, leads us gradually into debt. In the amiable form of cigarettes, it offers us an insignificant loan which we accept from the pleasant fellow year after year. We don't know how much we owe him. Suddenly he lets his mask fall and stands before us grinning, scornfully, with his total bill presented.

Some of my early ski memories are linked with Lake Placid. After the 1932 Winter Olympics—which nearly bankrupted the place—the Chamber of Commerce tried to recoup by staging annual ice carnivals and pageants. For reasons never wholly clear to me, I was selected to be the first sovereign of this extravaganza, the King of Winter, and thereafter usually participated in a role requiring me to wear the elaborate costume of a pseudo-Archbishop of Canterbury. But even more vivid in my recollection is the bobsled run down Mount von Hovenberg, two miles of twists and curves between walls of ice, with not much margin for error. At some places if you hit the wall too high, bob, riders and all would go catapulting out into space. One day, after watching Olympic team captain Hubert Stevens and his team come flying out of the chute at the bottom of the mountain, I said to him, "That must be a tremendous thrill. I wish I could drive one of those bobs."

He looked down his six foot three and replied, "You're driving the next run."

Of course I survived, thanks to assistance from a world champion. But it was only the beginning. One morning Ron Wagner, head of publicity for General Electric, phoned and asked me if I would be willing to strap shortwave equipment on my back and do a broadcast describing the thrills of careening down

Mount von Hovenberg. He reassured me by saying his G.E. engineers would make a test run to be sure it was feasible, and WGY in Schenectady would send my broadcast live all the way around the world. In my usual leap-first-look-later style, I said sure, and went off to nearby Mount Whitney to do some skiing with Hubert Stevens.

I should have stuck around. The General Electric engineers took one look at that icy chute from the top and declared that neither Lowell Thomas' well-being nor anybody else's would induce them to ride it to the bottom. Did the General Electric P.R. man tell me this? He did not. They just strapped fifty pounds of batteries and radio gear to my shoulders with a three-foot antenna above my head. I was assigned the number three position on the bob, and since I needed both hands to hang on, they rigged a microphone in a baseball catcher's mask which they clamped over my face just before Paul Stevens, Hubert's brother, ran us forward and jumped aboard.

As we picked up speed and went into the first curve, centrifugal force, working on all that weight on my back, just about ripped me right off the bob. Clutching the hang-on straps for dear life, I somehow managed to stay aboard. Next surprise: there was no time to say anything more than sing out the name of the curves we were taking: "Entering Shady! Leaving Shady! We're in Zig Zag! Leaving Zig Zag!" Hardly the sort of commentary to make one feel like a particularly perceptive broadcaster.

But I needn't have worried. It seems that when Paul Stevens had shoved us off and jumped on the sled he somehow fouled the radio equipment. Result: nothing I said was being transmitted to WGY, or anywhere. I was broadcasting to myself and to the whistling wind.

But even if I'd known it at the time, it would not have been a matter of paramount concern. Mainly I was intent on surviving the run. Had I been thrown off with all that gear, I'd probably still be in flight. Somehow, though, we made it—and then the G.E. men admitted they had made no test run! Irrepressible Ron Wagner next turned his charm on Torger Tokle, national ski jump champion.

Torger, who was later killed while serving with our 10th Mountain Division in Italy during the war, was one of the most famous and spectacular skiers of the pre-war era. Would he, Wagner asked, be willing to wear the same shortwave outfit, mask, microphone and all, and describe the sensation of jumping on the big Olympic hill? Tokle, casual as I was, said yes. Fifty pounds heavier rigged out in all that radio gear, he climbed to the top of the Intervale hill. There, high above a crowd of spectators, he put on his jumping skis, went into a crouch and sped down the run. But he didn't do much broadcasting either. Leaving the take-off and soaring into the air, he let loose with an enlightening, "Jee-sus Kee-rist!", which actually did go out on the air.

Then there is the saga of Toni Matt and the Tuckerman Headwall. Toni was a nineteen-year-old racing star who had already won everything there was to win in his native Austria when he came to the United States and began doing the same. Then he was told about The Inferno, an aptly named race down New Hampshire's Mount Washington. Though he had never even seen the mountain before, he was talked into entering.

Now Mount Washington, at 6,200 feet, in some ways is a more formidable peak than many more than twice as high in the West. Among other things, it was the home of what at the time were the highest winds ever recorded. If you stand on its summit in winter, as I have done, you can easily imagine yourself deep in the Antarctic.

The upper part of the mountain, in good weather, is a skier's dream, an almost perfect cone where in the spring you can have a ball. But at the base of the cone you are suddenly staring out into empty space. Below you is the famous Tuckerman Headwall, a thousand-foot precipice, beneath which lies Tucker-man Bowl where the snow may reach a depth of a hundred feet by the end of April, snow that has cascaded down the sides of the mountain. When it is this deep in the bowl it clings to the Headwall at an angle of about what you'd get if you placed a board on your toes and leaned the top against your chest. Top flight skiers can get down—maybe—by making zigzag jump turns. But most of them fall for at least a few hundred feet, tumbling head over heels.

The day Toni arrived for The Inferno, the mountain was typically stormy, with an eighty-mile-an-hour wind shrieking across the summit. Having never skied there, he planned to make a late start and follow the path set by Dick Durrance, our Olympic star who held the Inferno record, or some of the others who knew the mountain. But with the chaos created by the gale winds, something went wrong and the officials sent him off in the lead. His English imperfect, understanding only the starting signal, Toni turned downhill and away he went. By the time he had run the first mile to the bottom of the cone, he had picked up such speed that he shot right over the lip of the precipice. Once on the Headwall he was moving so fast it was impossible for him even to attempt to check and make a turn. As Toni tells it there wasn't even time to think.

For what happened next, he belongs on everyone's list of history's rivals to Paul Bunyan. Hanging on somehow, he shot straight down the almost perpendicular wall, keeping his feet in some miraculous way. Then, slamming down into the bowl, where the best of them, traveling at lesser speeds, have crashed in a windmill of arms and legs, he sped across, then over the Little Headwall and on down the Sherbourne Trail. Not only did he break the record set the previous year, he actually cut it in half—perhaps the only instance in the history of sport for an existing record to be actually halved. Nor has anyone, before or since, run the Mount Washington Headwall—straight. Since then The Inferno has been scratched as too dangerous.

Race or no race, that Headwall kept taunting me. I chose April 6, 1942, my fiftieth birthday, with a few diehards who, forsaking worldly considerations and common sense, joined me at giving it a try—doing it cautiously. At the summit, we paused long enough to catch our breath—there was no point in *thinking* about it any more—and took off. Speeding down the smooth cone filled me with a heady sense of euphoria. Even as I went over the lip of the Headwall and started down the almost vertical precipice, I knew I'd never make it. Actually I held it for 200 feet or so, but just before a wide crevasse, in a flash of sky and snow, over I went. And once you fall there's no way to stop, nothing to do but go end over end which I did for some 800 feet, winding up bruised and somewhat battered. But at the time it seemed an appropriate way of entering the next half century. One of our group, Sigurd Vinsness, who had escaped the Nazi invasion of Norway on skis, bounced over the same crevasse and ended his fall with a broken arm.

It was Joseph Bondurant Ryan, grandson of the legendary Wall Street buccaneer, Thomas Fortune Ryan, who developed magnificent Mont Tremblant in the Laurentians north of Montreal for skiing. We climbed the mountain together the first time he saw it. In fact, Ryan was a hitchhiker in our party, having talked his way into a seat aboard the small plane that flew Lowell, Jr., and me to Lac Tremblant at the foot of the highest peak in Eastern Canada. We made it in deep powder on a sunny day when the pine trees were glistening with rime ice. Said Joe: "I've never seen anything more inspiring anywhere in the world."

It was one of those rare days of crystal clear skies, in the wake of a three-day storm. Spread out before us was the panorama of the Laurentians with many frozen lakes glittering in the sun. Gazing into the distance, he said, "It's perfect except for one thing—it's too damn difficult to get up here."

Half-joking, I said, "Why don't you do something about it?"

"I believe I will," he replied.

He was a spectacular-looking young man, broad-shouldered and powerful, with a million-dollar smile and, when he wanted to turn it on, enough charm to win over a firing squad. But there was another, darker side to Thomas Fortune Ryan's grandson. For all the millions he had inherited from the old man, he'd had a confused, sometimes bitter youth—divorced parents, trouble in school and an early acquaintanceship and subsequent attachment to John Barleycorn. At his doctor's urging he had been off to the Canadian bush with an Indian guide as his sole companion and, after isolating himself from temptation for several months, had just returned to civilization, fit and clear-eyed, when we ran into each other in the bar at the Wheeler Gray Rocks Inn.

A spurt of determination took hold of him after he had seen Tremblant. A year later, he telephoned to invite me back. Having badgered the Canadian government into giving him a ninety-nine-year lease on the mountain, he wanted me to see what he had been doing. Roads were in, and a chair lift up the south side was under construction; also a ski village at the base. I was amazed to find that he had built a handsome base lodge and a restaurant for the public, which I named Chalet les Voyageurs, the name it still bears; there were also shops and some forty cottages.

I suggested he give all the buildings French names in keeping with the *habitant* surroundings, which he didn't do. Soon he
was also cutting trails on the north side of the mountain, one of
which he named for me.

But not even his success at Mont Tremblant could swerve
Joe Ryan from what seemed an inevitable track toward disaster.
Often he disappeared for weeks at a time, drinking heavily and
occasionally phoning back from a thousand miles away demanding that everybody be fired. As the years went by, he became
over-extended financially. Then the tragic ending. Did he take
his own life? He had enemies, and there were those who believed
he was murdered. The only thing we know for certain is that one
day flamboyant Joe Ryan came to the end of the line on the
pavement beneath a lofty hotel window in New York.

Meanwhile, I had become a regular in the Laurentians.
For more than thirty years after the first visit, I did a week or
so of evening news broadcasts from the north country nearly
every winter. During the first five or six years, when I skied at
Tremblant, I broadcast from the Canadian Pacific Railroad depot
at St. Jovite, a dozen miles away. The station agent, Oscar Landry,
had his home on the upper floor and down below the only available place for my staff and me and all our electronic gear was the
ladies' room. So here, each evening, some twenty or thirty skiers
from the Wheeler Gray Rocks Inn and Mont Tremblant Lodge
would sit around on the floor as I did my show.

For each of these remotes, I did a fifteen-minute warm-up,
talking about the problems of putting on a broadcast so far from
New York, telling anecdotes of earlier radio experiences and skiing adventures. Soon, sports reporters were coming around to
listen, with the result that we got unexpected publicity on both
sides of the border, all of which spread the word about skiing in
the Laurentians.

It also imbued my St. Jovite C.P.R. ladies' room "studio"
with a certain international chic. One member of the audience
was a celebrity from Washington, D.C., a young lawyer often
referred to as President Roosevelt's court jester—Tommy Cor-
coran, "Tommy the Cork," a gifted amateur entertainer who
would return to Gray Rocks after listening to my broadcast, get
out his guitar and do a musical imitation of my show.

Mont Tremblant was also the place where my inspiration

for a book on skiing began and ended. It had long seemed to me that the sudden burgeoning of skiing in America, together with the dramatic tales of the men and women who developed our major resorts, would make a great story. And what better way to tell it than through the eyes and typewriter of a talented writer, one who had never been on skis, as he took lessons at the great ski areas of the United States and Canada. This led me to my old friend and former shortstop on our Nine Old Men baseball team, sportswriter Ted Shane. Would he, I asked, be interested in such a project, one that might yield him quite a fat reward from book and magazine serial rights?

He wasn't too keen about the idea of putting on skis, but finally agreed, and away we went. Unable to begin at either Lake Placid or New Hampshire as planned because of a weather problem, we hied off to Tremblant, where the weather was some of the same but promising to clear. Ted started off by taking yodeling lessons at the lodge from Hans Faulkner, the ski pro from Obergurgl.

But next morning, the skies were blue and six inches of fresh snow lay sparkling in brilliant sunshine. This was my chance! I would inspire Ted by taking him up the mountain to see the whole winter wonderworld from the summit. And since, as I thought, I could bring my grandmother down in this light, fluffy new snow, Ted would have his first ski lesson painlessly.

The trip up was quite a thrill, he admitted. I let him absorb the view, then took him over to the Ryan Run, an intermediate trail, and got him into his bindings. For a hundred yards or so, he really did all right. Then, as we rounded the second turn, he crossed his skis in the deep powder and a split second later our literary dream was shattered—there lay my author with a busted leg.

I asked a third member of our party to go down and round up the ski patrol and a toboggan. But an hour went by, then another, and still no sign of help. It was getting late in the afternoon and as no other skiers came by, I began having visions of Ted out on that mountain all night—both of us, in fact. Finally I told him I'd have to ski down myself and get help. I said under no circumstances was he to move from where he was; we were on a mountain and if we had to go looking for him he might be preserved in ice by the time we found him.

Maybe he wasn't listening. Maybe a sudden sense of panic overrode common sense. All I know is that when we returned an hour later, with the ski patrol and a toboggan, Ted had vanished. He had crawled off the trail into the forest. Of course we found him, but by the time we did it was dark and he was half-frozen and hysterical. Bundling him in robes, we rode him down the trail. A local doctor put a temporary splint on his leg and we boarded the evening C.P.R. train for Montreal. The coaches were jammed with returning weekend skiers and old Ted gave them quite a time. Still a bit delirious, he stopped everyone tramping up the aisle and said, "Wanna hear how I broke my leg?" It was a long trip.

I assumed that all would go well once he was back home in New Canaan, Connecticut, but a week later a mutual friend, cartoonist Paul Webb, phoned and told me Ted was in trouble. It seems his family were all Christian Scientists and he hadn't consulted a doctor. The leg wasn't mending properly, and Paul concluded ominously, "Unless someone does something Ted's going to wind up a cripple."

Not wanting to become involved with the Shane family, I simply phoned Ted and told him I knew of an article opportunity for him; for a rather big fee, could he meet me in Grand Central on Friday? As soon as he arrived, Lowell, Jr., and I hustled him aboard the train to Littleton, New Hampshire, where we had an orthopedic surgeon waiting. We were met with a station wagon and before Ted knew quite what it was all about, he was at the local hospital. Ten minutes later he was on the operating table. And six weeks after that he shucked his cast and walked off as fit as ever.

So ended the ski book, but not the story. A year later, Ted told me *Collier's* had commissioned him to do a ski article and asked for my help. I was delighted. He came up one morning accompanied by a cameraman and spent the entire day with us on our Quaker Hill slope. Lowell, Jr., and I demonstrated ski techniques; filled him in on ski lore; did everything we could think of. Then he went home and wrote a scathing piece denouncing skiing and all skiers—and received a handsome check for it! I didn't mind at all.

Many years later, in 1976, some 700 ski professionals, when they met at Snoqualmie Pass in the Cascades, made me a member of their organization. A few weeks later the American Olympic team did likewise—honors richly undeserved.

Not long after Pearl Harbor, Lowell, Jr., an Air Corps pilot-in-training stationed near Nashville in a leaky barracks, was laid low by a malady that stubbornly resisted all treatment—rheumatic fever. Finally he was detached from his outfit and shipped out to a hospital at the Davis-Monthan air base in Tucson, the doctors hoping the warm, dry Arizona clime would help him regain his health. So it was that in the winter of 1942, Fran and I flew west to see our son.

As our plane came in over the Santa Catalina Mountains, I saw a fair-sized snow field on the north side. I hadn't heard of snow in the Tucson area and, as it turned out, neither had most Arizonans. But it occurred to me I might be able to contribute a lot more than fatherly encouragement to the restoration of young Lowell's health. Skiing always was an exhilarating and gratifying part of his life. I felt sure a hike to the top of these mountains—Mount Lemmon and Mount Bigelow, the highest peaks in the Catalinas—could help. Convincing the doctors of this, I rounded up some ski gear and a small party of ski-minded fellows from Dartmouth and Harvard. One fine morning we set off by jeep to the north side of the range, via an old mine road.

After following an abandoned road for a few miles, we were in snow so deep we had to leave the car and continue on foot. Nearing the summit, we entered a surprising new world—bracing winter temperatures, plenty of fresh powder snow and ponderosa pine forests reminiscent of the Pacific Northwest. I took one look at the expression of eagerness on Lowell's face as he tightened his bindings and decided I'd prescribed the right medicine.

After a couple of hours of almost ideal skiing, we returned to Tucson—and to a storm of controversy. The local newspapers, hearing of our adventure, gave it front page coverage. But the Chamber of Commerce, which called itself The Sunshine Club, was not pleased. The officers grumbled that for years they had been advertising Tucson as one place where people could get away from snow and winter; now along come some outlanders blabbing it to the world that there was snow and skiing right at their door. They denounced us in no uncertain terms.

We paid no heed. All this Santa Catalina snow was our son's road to recovery and we went back again and again. Others joined us, including some state forest rangers who admitted they'd never been to the top of the range in winter—no reason to go there. Officers from the air base, intrigued, asked if they could send some of their men with us to evaluate Mount Lemmon as a possible place for rehabilitation. Fine, we told them, but be sure they were adequately dressed. What did that mean? they asked. As though they were going with Byrd to the Antarctic, I replied.

Of course it's hard to heed such advice when you're in balmy Tucson, and the airmen showed up wearing regular summer issue. By the time we got them back to the base, they were swathed in every spare scrap of clothing we could muster, their feet wrapped in burlap. They looked like the survivors of Napoleon's retreat from Moscow.

In March, we staged an end-of-the-season party at the Arizona Inn. Just for a joke, we organized the Sahuaro Ski Club, named for the giant cactus through which you must go at the foot of the Catalinas. It was all done in the spirit of fun—and my personal gratitude for young Lowell's recovery. We sent handsome elaborate membership certificates in this southernmost ski club in North America to a hundred or so top skiers, then thought no more about it. But the seed we had planted took root. Ten years later, upon returning to Tucson, we were met by a band and a dozen or so members of the Sahuaro Ski Club, some of them people I had never met. They now had a lodge on the mountain, tows—even lights for night skiing! And we were told more than 100,000 happy skiers had run the slopes we had pioneered as an experiment in physical therapy.

I have had some rather special moments while skiing, and Lowell, Jr., has shared some of them—which is not surprising, since we have skied together from Quaker Hill's slopes and trails to the rugged glaciers of southeast Alaska. One of our early thrills came soon after we "discovered" Mount Lemmon. When Lowell returned home for a month of recuperative leave, we went up to Vermont and signed up for the annual national father-and-son race. There were always some top skiers entered in this event, but Lowell, back in his old racing form, gave us a good lead. In fact as I sped—not too rapidly—toward the finish I heard him yell: "Stand up, Pop, and we've got it!" I managed to hold on and when I made it to the tape we took the trophy as Father-Son National Champions for 1942.

Once, after the war, we were skiing in Idaho's Sawtooth Mountains when I noticed a snow cornice hanging out from the top of Lookout Bowl. Wouldn't it make a dramatic snapshot, I said to Lowell, if he dropped down a few yards and took my picture looking over the cornice with my ski tips out over the edge and outlined against the sky? But as he was adjusting the camera, I heard a groan behind me and looked around to see a crack in the snow only four or five feet from where I stood. When I turned back, L.T., Jr., was gone, already heading down the slope. My weight on the overhang had been enough to trigger an avalance. Although the cornice itself held, tons of snow just below had broken loose and were roaring down the bowl. Luckily it wasn't a major slide, and slowed after a couple of hundred yards with Lowell still on top. But two days later, another slide swept down the adjacent Christmas Bowl wiping out an inspector, two pupils and a steel lift tower.

To go back to World War II for a moment, when I was with General Mark Clark in Italy, he told me our Tenth Mountain Division in some ways outranked every other American military outfit. It was made up of young men from our colleges and universities, and had by far the highest I.Q. The Father of the Tenth Mountain was C. Minot "Minnie" Dole, a Yale man who had done more for the American ski world than any one individual, having created the National Ski Patrol, an organization made up of volunteers. As a result of our long friendship "Minnie" had prevailed upon me to help recruit college athletes, experienced skiers. Much of the Tenth Mountain training was done on the western slope, in Colorado, at Camp Hale. I spent several weeks there and each evening did my radio broadcast with many old friends and ski companions around me.

The three generals at Camp Hale, non-skiers, insisted upon my staying with them. Although they were cordial and gracious, I suspected they wanted to keep an eye on me. Maybe they thought I might give America a distorted picture of Camp Hale. If I was their house guest maybe I might be less critical. I did hear of some incidents which would have bothered them.

For instance, one of the many with whom I skied there in the High Rockies near Leadville was a veteran Swiss mountaineer with whom I had spent many happy days at Franconia in the White Mountains. Not only was Peter Gabriel an expert at rock climbing, and a veteran ski pro, he also knew as much about avalanches as anyone in America.

One day, with a major in command, he went into the nearby mountains. When the major ordered his platoon to take a certain route Peter demurred—said it wasn't safe. This angered the major. Peter Gabriel insisted the safety of the platoon was his responsibility. Said the major, who had no experience as a mountaineer: "You'll carry out my order, or you'll be court martialed."

Gabriel had only one trump card left. He said: "Before these men go any farther, sir, let me fire a round with this gun." The major, who may have sensed he might be wrong, told him to go ahead. When Peter lobbed a shell up the slope down came the whole side of the mountain. Had the platoon gone where the major had ordered they all would have been wiped out.

Eventually the Tenth Mountain gained far more experience in the Apennines, and at the end of the war was acclaimed one of our crack divisions. Perhaps "Minnie" Dole should have been in command of the Tenth.

Lowell, Jr., and I, both before and after the war, had many unforgettable experiences in the mountains in New England, eastern Canada, our western Rockies and Alaska. Of course, none equaled the journey we later made across the Himalayas to Inner Tibet, to visit the Dalai Lama at Lhasa. But among our experiences one had to do with a mine which provided the gold that paid for one of the most famous of all jewels, the Hope Diamond.

When heading for the Rockies I often would call up a friend and urge him to join me. In Colorado I would phone a former high school or college pal, usually a mining engineer. Harold Worcester, my most studious high school classmate, scaled the heights in the mining world and was made president of the Western Mining Congress. At Telluride on the Western Slope, he was in charge of several mines which in the boom days had been major gold producers. Telluride, long a semi-ghost town, with its background of precipitous mountains, is one of the most picturesque places in the Rockies. At the time nothing had been done about skiing at Telluride.

Not far from Telluride another even more picturesque semi-ghost mining camp is named for a famous Indian of an earlier era. Ouray was a tall, eloquent chief of the Utes, who made quite an impression on our first explorers and prospectors. Up the canyon from the town named for him was one of the richest gold mines in America, the Camp Bird. During and after World War II it was a mining property operated by another of my schoolmates, Blair Burwell, a mining engineer from the University of Denver. Although he was not a skier, his mine superintendent was. Blair invited Lowell, Jr., and me to do something he said no one had ever tried, take the mine lifts to the top of the range, crawl through an abandoned tunnel, and then ski down through an area known as the Chicago Basin.

In most mines your cage takes you down to the lower levels. At the Camp Bird it was the reverse. Aboard the usual small electric mine train, off we went for a half mile or so deep into the mountain. There we transferred to a cage which whisked us up a couple of thousand feet. Again we transferred to another train, and then a smaller cage shot us past a few more levels to the top of the range. The "Super," who had recently come from a mining operation in Alaska, led us into a tunnel abandoned for years. Since it was near the top of the range, surface water seeping through had added a thick layer of ice to the roof. This forced us to crawl, dragging our skis for several hundred yards until we emerged into the sunlight. As we sat there contemplating the spectacular views of other 13,000- and 14,000-foot peaks around us, the superintendent told us about the mine.

Prior to World War I, when prospectors were combing the Rockies for gold and silver, there was an ore buyer by the name of Tom Walsh, whose job was to roam the mountains, buying "pay dirt" from small operators and then hauling it to the nearest smelter. One day Walsh climbed the mountain up to this same tunnel through which we had just crawled. It was before the larger mine had been developed, and when the tunnel here was a mere "prospect drift" where the old boy who had been digging hadn't yet struck it rich—that is, he didn't know he had! When Walsh arrived the miner was still in the tunnel. As the ore buyer sat on the dump waiting, he did what you often do. You casually handle the rocks on which you are sitting, maybe throwing one or two at a chipmunk. Tom Walsh, who knew more geology than the prospector, noticed that a rock he had in his hand was rich in calaverite, a combination of gold and silver.

When the miner emerged he told Walsh he was having no luck, no pot of gold at the end of his rainbow, and was about to give up. Whereupon the ore buyer bought him out for a song. And that was how Tom Walsh came into possession of what became the great Camp Bird Mine, from which he took one of the largest fortunes in the history of mining, a part of which he spent on the fabulous Hope Diamond for his daughter Evelyn, who as Washington's famed hostess, spent some of those Camp Bird millions. Through several administrations she gave parties which made her a legend—Evelyn Walsh McLean.

Putting on our skis, the three of us started off on a rather thrilling long, down-mountain run. It's an awesome thing to be at the top of the Rockies, in an area where few if any skiers have preceded you. It was a glorious spring day, and by mid-morning the sun was loosening the snow on the more exposed slopes, touching off many avalanches. On all sides we could hear them, and we lost little time in making our run.

Near the bottom we sped through a narrow canyon where our Camp Bird "Super" told us years before there had been a bunkhouse for a hundred or more men. He said a spring avalanche had roared down this same valley and the air pressure built up by this phenomenon—the pressure alone—had crushed the building and killed many of the miners.

While the avalanche is a familiar hazard in the Alps, the Andes and the Himalayas, seldom does anyone lose his life as a result of one in North America. This is mainly because in our Western mountains there are so few people living where there is an avalanche problem. In the period between the Civil War and World War I, when many gold seekers roamed our Western mountains, many a prospector disappeared. But when F.D.R. took us off the gold standard most of our gold camps became ghost towns, and today only a cross-country skier is likely to hear or see an avalanche, let alone get caught by one.

There have been other similar incidents, and I have had a skier's usual assortment of broken bones, sometimes in the most unexpected places. Once, at Quaker Hill, giving a beginner some pointers, on an intermediate slope, a ski tip went through a crust and there I was again. But for every splint and cast I've worn, I've been rewarded a hundred times over. Recently the National Ski Patrol gave me a plaque, the National Professional Ski Association inducted me into their organization, our Olympic team did likewise, and at age eighty-five I'll have to brush up on my technique to keep from disgracing them. However, for me, skiing is its own reward. People occasionally ask me to tell them my number one skiing thrill. Simple. It happens every time I start down a mountain.

By the beginning of 1946, I was just about at the bottom of my financial barrel. Anyone who has read this far will know I had a rather good time getting there, but this doesn't alter the basic circumstance. I had earned a lot of money, and still did, but wartime taxes were now taking a large bite, and I'm afraid my predilection for doing all the things I wanted to do took care of the rest, and then some. Those were the days when Fran and I had up to two hundred people for supper nearly every Sunday night. "Lowell," Governor Dewey once said, "you keep this up and you'll soon be broke." He was right.

Finally I went to Philadelphia to see my sponsors, Joe and J. Howard Pew, heads of the Sun Oil Company. And they said they would be willing to help me, but in exchange they wanted me to sign up with Sun for life. It was a super compliment, but for reasons I'd probably never be able to make clear to anyone, I just couldn't do it. Life was such a long time.

The Pews seemed unhappy with my reaction; of course, I was already deeply indebted to them for helping me on the French estate matter. I went home to think things through. Apart from my pressing financial problems, I hated to see the warm relationship I'd always had with the Pew family end in this way. They had been my sponsors for more than fifteen years, taking over so smoothly when my original sponsor, the *Literary Digest*, dropped out of radio that I hardly noticed any transition.

Radio had come a long way since those pioneer days. Almost as soon as it passed the crystal set stage, the *Literary Digest*, quick to take advantage of the new medium, had put the spectacular Floyd Gibbons on the air with the first regular news broadcast. He had begun early in 1930, and by summer it seemed everyone was talking about the colorful former war correspondent and his machine-gun delivery of the nightly news. But Floyd was a two-fisted drinking man and this did not accord with the sober, not to say solemn, mien of the top people at the *Literary Digest*. He was let go, and on September 29th I took his place and began my forty-six continuous years in radio.

The *Literary Digest* had been losing money for some years, and when it bowed out of radio and Sun Oil became my sponsor, it didn't seem to mean anything to me, for I just kept right on broadcasting. From time to time I went to Philadelphia to chat with the Pews, heads of one of the world's major oil companies —J. Howard, the older brother and president, a tall, austere-looking man with magnificent presence and bearing; and Joe, tall, good-humored, on the surface more outgoing. They made an impressive team, Joe better suited to the public aspects of the business—communications, advertising and politics—while J. Howard handled financial policy matters, the building of pipelines and refineries and the operation of the huge Sun tanker fleet. Both were remarkable men.

There was no secret about the Pews' politics—they were a power in the Republican party, in fact its major contributors. I always thought they were a little to the right of Ramses II, but never did they question or interfere with me when it came to our greatest national pastime. My broadcasts remained, as in the past, straight down the middle, without favor to either Democrats or Republicans, so the Pews, like the general public, may not have known what my political preferences were. They never asked me. Once, at a luncheon at one of Philadelphia's principal clubs, I overheard someone ask Joe Pew if he knew what his broadcaster's politics were. "I think he's an anarchist," said Joe.

Over the years, the Pews visited us at Quaker Hill and Fran and I were happy because they seemed to consider me part of the Sun Family. Since they did not operate coast to coast they actually helped me pick up other sponsors in the West, including giant Standard Oil of California, so that my broadcast covered almost the entire United States. There were a few gaps, and I couldn't help envying people like Amos and Andy and Jack Benny who had nationwide coverage with coast-to-coast sponsors. Still, I would never have contemplated leaving Sun on that account. And yet, we had now come to an impasse, and it troubled me as much as did my money problems. At that bleak moment in my career, I had an inspiration. I thought of Frank Smith.

I had come to know Frank when, as executive vice president of Trans-American Broadcasting, he produced an elaborate radio show for General Motors, *Victory Is Our Business*, in which I had a part. *Victory* ran for a year or more, during which time Smitty even lined me up to participate in other programs, some sponsored by *The Reader's Digest*. I was much impressed by this dapper, self-assured dynamo of a man who always seemed in absolute control of all the stray odds and ends of business connected with major radio production. For a refugee from the hills of Tennessee, Frank M. Smith had come a long way.

But of course in no sense could Frank be called a refugee from anywhere, as I later learned. He was the son of a prospering banker and had acquired considerable polish while earning degrees at Washington and Lee University and at Harvard Business School. But like a good many bright young men from the hinterlands who flocked to New York seeking their fortune during the Depression, Frank was a long time finding work. Finally he won an interview with Milton Biow, who headed his own advertising agency, and though the only thing the two had in common was that neither was more than an inch over five feet tall, Biow was taken with Smitty's courtly manner and hired him.

Biow: "Report to work at nine A.M. Monday."

Frank: "Sir, that's a very early hour. I could never start work at nine A.M."

Biow (stunned): "Why not? I start work at nine A.M."

Frank (courtly as ever): "Yes, sir, Mr. Biow, but that's because you're the boss."

To his everlasting credit, Biow gave Smitty the job anyhow, and he was an instant success. Soon he went on to become advertising manager of the Bulova Watch Company, then general manager of radio station WLW in Cincinnati, flag station for Powell Crosley, and finally an independent partner of Trans-American, which packaged soap operas and other entertainment programs and probably had more shows on radio through the 1940s than any other independent producer. At just about the time I had dug myself deep into a financial hole, Smitty had sold out his Trans-American interests and, though still a partner, was at loose ends.

But he seemed to have disappeared from the face of the earth. Smitty was one of those people who presented a serene face to one and all while churning within, and periodically he disappeared to calm his nerves and recharge his batteries. Desperate, I tracked him to Daytona, Florida, and took the first plane south. There, sitting on the beach, Smitty listened to my story, asked a few questions, then, in his best Southern gentleman manner, said, "Lowell, I believe I might be of some help to you."

He made it sound so easy. Maybe that's how it is with miracles. Anyway, before I fairly knew what was happening, he had gone to Philadelphia to see Joe Pew, worked out the details of a long-term contract for me with Procter & Gamble, then headed by Neil McElroy and probably the second most important radio sponsor in the country. The arrangement included coast-to-coast coverage for my nightly news broadcast, and required me to shift over to CBS, Procter & Gamble's network of choice. My indebtedness to Sun Oil was taken care of by a complicated but effective mortgaging arrangement whereby eventually I sold off a portion of my Quaker Hill property to satisfy the note.

Smitty, the hero of this story, thereupon undertook to manage my personal affairs. He took over my books and my bank account, paid my bills and, though I managed to sneak a few extravagances behind his back, not only rehabilitated me financially, but guided my investments with such devotion and skill that for the first time in my life I was saving more money than I was spending.

Though the stakes had been high and tensions had built between us, the Pews ended our professional relationship with a civilized and unprecedented gesture. They staged quite a farewell party for me at the Waldorf-Astoria, inviting hundreds of our radio friends and presenting Fran with dozens of red roses and me with a handsome set of diamond cufflinks. Joe Pew even laughed when H. V. Kaltenborn, one of the most gifted extemporaneous speakers, pulled his leg by saying that Sun Oil was now hiring *three* high-powered broadcasters to take the place of the one they'd let get away. But there were tears in Joe's eyes when he made his own farewell talk, and mine weren't too dry either.

There still remained a few legal knots to untie, but H. V.

Kaltenborn, in his infinite wisdom, had introduced me to a young lawyer as gifted in his field as Frank was at finance. It was through him that I met Gerald Dickler, and when I tell you how he handled a balky CBS, you will understand why he is still my lawyer. First of all, CBS, in its corporate pride, ruled that Procter & Gamble could not supply the broadcaster for its program, but that the network had to do it. Fine, said Gerry: How about Lowell Thomas? So, in an intricate three-way deal, that was ironed out. Then we sat down with Bill Paley, and with Ed Murrow, who was miserably uncomfortable as CBS vice president in charge of news—to go through the contract. Came a clause which, in essence, said that Lowell Thomas would conform to all the policies of CBS News. Innocently Gerry asked, "Where are these policies written down? We'd like to see them."

Paley looked at Murrow, Murrow looked at an aide. There followed the most intense scurrying and paper shuffling, but the only thing produced was acute embarrassment. Finally, agonized, Murrow said, "We don't seem to have anything on paper."

"Okay," Gerry replied briskly, "when you get something we'll be glad to have a look. Meanwhile, I think you'll agree that this clause better be stricken."

Thirty years passed and we never heard another word about CBS News "policies." Probably neither did Daniel Schorr.

"Smitty," in some ways one of the boldest men I ever knew, was also a victim of claustrophobia. It was almost impossible to get him into an elevator, or lure him into boarding a train or an airplane. Once, when he knew he had to go out to Hollywood on a project in which we were both involved, he had his doctor give him a drug that knocked him out for the duration of the flight. Even geniuses have their weaknesses.

IV. The Journey to Shangri-La

If the valley is reached by a high pass,
Only the best friends or worst enemies are visitors.
                              —*Tibetan Proverb*

Has anyone ever had to respond to the question, "How was your trip?" more often than I? Maybe, but I don't know who. Starting with a journey to Alaska in 1914 and down to last week, I have been endlessly prowling the earth's surface, seas and airways, seeking the magic that, for me, lies beyond every horizon. I have always presumed that growing up on a mountaintop had something to do with this insatiable craving to go places. As a boy, from our vantage point high in the Colorado Rockies, I could see in the distance the beckoning snow-capped peaks of the Sangre de Cristo range and sense the world's breadth. Ever since then I have been irresistibly drawn toward the farthest horizons. A pair of crutches, propped against an attic wall and unused for nearly three decades, stirs the memory of the most thrilling trip of all, and the most unusual—across the Himalayas.

It all began early in 1949 when I learned that for the first time in my life I was to have a real vacation. Radio had grown up to an awareness that even the most popular programs lost much of their audience during July and August, and many regular sponsors—except the automobile and oil companies of course—had begun taking a summer hiatus. This they were allowed to do without losing their prime time period on the air. Informed by

Neil McElroy that I was to have ten weeks off beginning July 2, I began at once to think of all the things I had wanted to do. The world's so-called "forbidden lands" had always intrigued me —especially "Holy Arabia," and Afghanistan and Tibet, all three "closed" countries. During World War I, while in the Middle East, I had ridden the Arabian desert with the legendary T. E. Lawrence. A few years later, to the surprise of officialdom in India, I was invited to take the Khyber Pass route into Afghanistan as the guest of the Amir himself. But Tibet, remotest and most mysterious of all, had remained beyond the pale. Only a bare handful of Western travelers had ever made the journey across the Himalayas to Lhasa, little-known capital of Inner Tibet—that isolated fortress land guarded by the loftiest peaks in the world and ruled by a reclusive young man known as the Dalai Lama, the Living Buddha, who was worshipped as a god. To that time, only six Americans had ever laid eyes on him.

No matter. Without ado, I sent a long radio message to Loy W. Henderson, our ambassador to India. I congratulated him on his appointment, then added:

> NOW THAT YOU ARE IN HINDUSTAN, A LAND OF
> MIRACLES, HOW ABOUT PERFORMING A MIRACLE
> FOR ME? CAN YOU ARRANGE FOR ME TO TAKE
> A PARTY OF FIVE TO TIBET? IS THERE ANY CHANCE?

Well aware that there wasn't much hope on this, I set about lining up a backup project, a restaging of the historic first flight around the world by four Douglas special biplanes in 1924. This time, if we could swing it, for a 25th-anniversary commemoration flight, the trip would be made by an Air Force Globemaster, then the largest aircraft in the world—a goodwill global flight which Air Secretary Stuart Symington and head of the Air Force Hoyt Vandenberg quickly okayed. My plan was to take with us all the surviving participants in the first world flight: Les Arnold, Erik Nelson, Leigh Wade, Hank Ogden and Al Harvey; also General MacArthur, if he would join us. A return wire from Ambassador Henderson only caused me to redouble my efforts on the world flight. He said the doors to Tibet remained as closed as ever, and the United States hadn't any diplomatic contact with Lhasa.

Having thus dashed any delusive notions I might be harboring, Loy Henderson—who later told me he was indeed intrigued with my idea—talked it over with Sir Girja Bajpai, Nehru's secretary for foreign affairs, who, luckily, I had known when he was India's first ambassador to our country. They decided to somehow get my request to the Dalai Lama, along with their own expression of hope that it would be given favorable consideration. I knew nothing of this. As far as I was concerned, the journey to Shangri-La already was filed under Impossible Dreams and I was busy planning for a 25th-anniversary world flight. Then, one midnight in July, I was awakened by a telephone call from Washington, the State Department relaying a radio message to me from New Delhi, from Ambassador Henderson: "You are invited to Lhasa. Come at once."

You can imagine that I did not get much more sleep that night. There seemed a thousand things to do in a desperately short time, first among them a cable to Lowell, Jr., in Iran.

A MIRACLE HAS HAPPENED. MEET ME IN CALCUTTA.
WE ARE ON OUR WAY TO LHASA.

DAD

Young Lowell hadn't exactly been standing by. I suppose it is true that the fruit does not fall far from the tree; from the time he was fifteen and voyaged around Cape Horn with a United States Navy squadron, L.T., Jr., had been on the move, too. Now, at age twenty-six, he had already climbed mountains in Alaska with a scientific expedition, served as an Air Force pilot in World War II, been at Bikini for the atom bomb tests and continued on around the world with Stuart Symington, then Secretary of the Air Force. Now he was in Persia with Supreme Court Justice William O. Douglas, studying the native tribes and making a film. My cable, as he subsequently reported, was delivered by camel to where he was with the Bakhtiari tribesmen in a remote region, and the prospect of leaving Iran for a trek to the roof of the world filled him with such joy that, to the amazement of his colleagues, he turned a couple of cartwheels on the spot.

But having thus expressed his exuberance, he promptly packed, made his way to the Iraqi port of Basra, legendary home of Sindbad the Sailor on the Persian Gulf, and from there flew to Calcutta where, in the days before my arrival, he busied himself rounding up equipment and supplies we would need for a journey across the Himalayas. Meanwhile, I had my own problems to solve, foremost among them the bleak fact that two weeks of my vacation had already gone down the drain and I could no longer hope to make a caravan trip to Tibet and get back in time to resume broadcasting in September. All this I put up to Neil McElroy, the genial and dynamic chairman of Procter & Gamble, and his able colleague Howard Morgens, together with a suggested solution: how about trying to do my program from Tibet? It's true there were no radio facilities there, so far as we knew, but why not take along a portable recorder and keep a day by day record of our wanderings and transmit them by caravan to India and thence to the United States? This was something never done before. Between my own broadcasts from the world's farthest reaches, which surely would stir the imagination of an American audience, prominent guests could take my place at the CBS microphone. McElroy didn't think twice. "Done!" he said, shaking my hand enthusiastically. Naturally, I was pleased when President Eisenhower named him Secretary of Defense in 1957, which put Howard Morgens at the head of the P & G empire.

Next problem on my long list: only young Lowell and I had been cleared by Lhasa for the trip, not the party of five I'd requested. No motorized transport—not even yak-drawn carts— were permitted in Tibet. I had asked permission to include a surgeon, an expert on Oriental affairs, and a top-flight cameraman from Hollywood. But only Lowell, Jr., and I were invited. We were to enter from the Himalayan state of Sikkim, via the caravan route over Nathu La, a 15,000-foot mountain pass. Who would guide us? What did we need to know? What to take? For this would be no summer jaunt into the countryside; if we overlooked some essential piece of equipment there could be no turning back, nor any stopping to stock up at some friendly general store en route.

Then, I thought of Suydam Cutting, a naturalist and expedition leader who in 1935 had been the first of those few Americans to be allowed into Tibet. We made contact, and I was to be grateful for Suydam's guidance every day in the months that followed, and particularly when we were on the trail. He told us to organize our caravan in Gangtok, capital of Sikkim, there to round up guide, bearers, cook, interpreter, and animals. He said that if we packed each of our supply cases as a complete unit—

food, clothing and medical supplies—we would avoid endless shuffling through the boxes at each of our stops. We were to take gifts for the Dalai Lama, officials along the way and the dignitaries we would meet in Lhasa. Visiting cards and white silk scarves, the *kata*, were de rigueur; they were elaborately exchanged during visits and we had best be well-supplied. The list of his invaluable suggestions went on and on, and without them we would have been lost.

On July 13 I was in Philadelphia, where the Democrats nominated Harry Truman for President, despite the revolt of the Dixiecrats and the disaffection of Henry Wallace's Progressives. A few days later, I was winging my way westward, my heart already in Tibet, but my broadcasts still concerned with politics. For when I landed at Honolulu, I found all Hawaii in the grip of a major longshoremen's strike decreed by labor boss Harry Bridges, a strike that all but isolated the islands for weeks. In protest, the women of Oahu—rich, poor, Hawaiian, Caucasian, Chinese, Japanese and Filipino—were picketing the waterfront, marching in front of Aloha Tower and wielding brooms as a none-too-subtle symbol of their urge to sweep Bridges and his longshoremen into the Pacific. Knowing this would make a colorful broadcast, I joined the protesters, recording their angry complaints and interviewing their leader, a famous Hawaiian beauty, Winona Love, best known of Hawaii's hula dancers.

Winona was a charmer. Some time before, she had fallen in love with a young millionaire, Francis Brown, who, much as he wanted to, was unable to marry her. It seems that in his oat-sowing days, Brown had already married several times, so aggravating his grandfather, fount of the family fortune, that after the third or fourth divorce, the old gentleman decreed permanent bachelorhood for his heir. If Francis ever married again, the grandfather stipulated in his will, he was to be disinherited. Brown lived up to the letter of the old man's expressed wish. He and Winona simply set up housekeeping in a lovely home in Honolulu and another in Monterey, California, a secret to absolutely nobody, living happily ever after.

When I had completed my interview, Winona turned the tables on me: would I address the picketing ladies at a local auditorium where they met briefly each day at noon? I protested that I was on the first leg of a long journey and had many things on my mind and so on. But she was most persuasive. She even promised to do her famous hula for me if I agreed. How could any man refuse? And so I spoke, but then had to head for my plane and was unable to collect on my side of the bargain. Neither of us forgot it, though. Years later, when I premiered the *Danger Island* show of our "High Adventure" television series in Honolulu, Fran and I threw a gala party—dinner for a hundred under the giant banyan at the Moana, after that to a theater for our South Seas film, and then on to the Barefoot Bar for further festivities. And it was there—before an audience that included the Governor of Hawaii; Duke Kahanamoku, one of the great swimmers of all time; an Olympic star, his fellow movie Tarzan, Johnny Weismuller; Earl Thacker, known around the world as "Mr. Hawaii"; press tycoon Roy Howard and the others—that Winona Love kept her promise and did her exotic dance. It was worth waiting for.

Flying on to Tokyo, I had an interview with General MacArthur, then the American pro-consul in Japan. In his office and at his home with his sparkling wife Jean, we talked mostly about my forthcoming expedition to Tibet. MacArthur told me how he already had envied me for having had a chance to cross the forbidden border into Afghanistan—he had once gotten as far as the Khyber Pass—and now, he said, he had cause to envy me again.

By the time I reached Calcutta, young Lowell had managed to round up most of the gear we would require. It had not been an easy task, for it was the height of the monsoon season and the heavens poured rain; the city's streets, already packed with millions of India's ever-wandering poor, were now ankle-deep in riptides of rushing water as well. Still, between what Lowell had purchased on the spot and the equipment flown out with me, we had put together what appeared to us to be the sort of kit needed—saddles, army cots, sleeping bags, special clothes and rubberized rain suits for the rain forest, plus medical supplies (which were to prove inadequate in the time of our trouble), pots, pans, a primus stove and eight cases of food, each weighing sixty-five pounds and, together, holding enough to sustain us for nearly two months. As we expected to live mainly off what we could buy and hunt on the trail, that seemed a comfortable reserve.

We converted about a thousand dollars into rolls of Indian rupees—this at Suydam Cutting's suggestion that the Tibetans preferred hard coin to any paper currency. The rupees went into bags and the bags into three specially-made wooden cases, each of which, filled, weighed sixty pounds. Thereafter we bowed many a mule and yak under their weight, slept with them between our beds, worried lest they wind up strewn across a canyon floor or lost on some river bottom as we wound along the narrow trail. And for our pains, we were rewarded to learn on arrival in Lhasa that since Cutting's last visit the Tibetan economy had become attuned to paper money and tradesmen either shunned our rupees or discounted them to their own generous advantage.

In the last hectic days before our departure, Lowell and I had a chance to wonder aloud at our great good fortune. Why had we been invited to Tibet when, over the years, the requests of so many others had been denied?—even those of the indomitable and persistent Sven Hedin, foremost of all Central Asian explorers. And as we talked it through, we came to realize that the only logical answer—to be chillingly confirmed in Lhasa—was that the Dalai Lama and his ministers had come to fear the intentions of their elephantine neighbor, China. For by that summer of 1949, it had become clear to them, as it would be soon to the rest of the world, that the Communist forces of Mao Tse-tung were winning their bloody civil war against Chiang Kai-shek and would soon complete their mastery over the vast land that pressed down on the northern and eastern borders of Tibet. Better, then, to yield their cherished isolation, reasoned the government in Lhasa, in hope that foreign visitors would make Tibet's peril known and so help engage the world's sympathy. Our request had reached Lhasa at just that crucially decisive moment.

Why would a lofty, rugged, mountain-locked, stubbornly independent country be prized by the Red Chinese? Apart from the inherently aggressive urge of revolutionary Communism, Mao saw in the conquest of Tibet two golden opportunities: a chance to extend the Chinese influence over Buddhist Asia, and an eighteen-hundred-mile-long staging area from which his troops could menace India, and if he chose, strike southward into parts of India only an hour by air from New Delhi! Now, as recorded on a dark page of history, we know the Tibetan fears proved all too real. Only months after our visit, the Chinese overran Tibet and soon drove the monks from the lamaseries. In 1959, the Dalai Lama himself had to flee for his life, a grim story recounted by Lowell, Jr., in his later books, *The Silent War in Tibet* and *The Dalai Lama.*

Nor, it turned out, was the Soviet Union entirely disinterested in Tibet at the time of our expedition. After our return, the Kremlin weekly, *New Times,* attacked us on the grounds that we had been sent to Tibet to alienate it from China and turn it into an American colony. Our trip, said the *New Times,* was actually "a dirty adventure" sponsored by the U.S. government, and "Lowell Thomas, who modestly calls himself a radio commentator, is actually an agent of the O.S.S."

I must confess to being flattered. For what a secret agent I was! Not only did I neglect to consult with anyone in Washington about the trip—not even my old classmate Allen Dulles— I even forgot to take a letter or a gift to the Dalai Lama from President Truman, the most common courtesy. And of course, considering my regular broadcasts and the news coverage we got, the entire affair was conducted with all the secrecy of a World Series.

We left Calcutta on the evening of July 31, feeling not unlike the proprietors of some Oriental circus as a battalion of coolies loaded our thirty-seven cases of gear aboard the night train for Siliguri, a railroad center in the Himalayan foothills 300 miles away. Having heard many a gory tale about train passengers being murdered and robbed in their sleep, we bolted our compartment windows and piled cases against the door—and slept fitfully during that long night. As soon as it was light, we could see the stark wall of the Himalayas rising from the Bengal plain, knowing that just beyond was six-mile-high Kanchenjunga, the world's third tallest mountain, dominating the snow-covered peaks around.

At Siliguri a truck, long superannuated by the British military, awaited us, along with a volatile driver known only as Lulu, who tongue-lashed a swarm of G-string-clad Bengali bearers as they hauled our cases and cameras and recording machines off the train. Then we set off for Gangtok, a seventy-mile drive up a steep and winding mountain road, rank jungle on one side and the monsoon-fat Tista River on the other. At a native village, we stopped and bought some delicious pineapples and bananas. A little farther along, we crossed into Sikkim, rumbling over a bridge festooned with white prayer flags, each one, as it flapped in the rain-swept breeze, ostensibly sending its supplication off to the Buddhist spirit world.

Apparently there was even a prayer for such as we. Within twenty miles of our destination, Lulu suddenly shouted, slammed on the brake and, pointing, cried out, "It's a slip, a slip, an excremental slip!"

A rising cloud of dust filled the sky ahead of us. Driving closer, we saw a still-growing mountain of earth and boulders and up-ended trees. A whole section of the mountain had been torn loose by the monsoon and had thundered down to the river, burying a quarter mile of the road under a couple of hundred feet of debris and even creating a temporary dam across the Tista. It was painfully clear that we were going no farther that day. But had we not stopped for the pineapples and bananas, we might never have gone anywhere again.

Lulu sent someone off to find help. Then, we huddled in a crude wayfarer's shelter fortuitously located on our side of the slide. By morning, the rain had stopped and, stripped to our khaki shorts, Lowell and I clambered up over nature's newest mountain, sweating under a relentless sun and ducking boulders that still came bounding down from the heights. On the far side, we met some coolies sent to carry our gear over the avalanche. We arranged for another truck and, entrusting it to Lulu, found a jeep that would take us on over the last leg of our journey to Gangtok. Bare-chested and shivering in our shorts, we were blue with cold by the time we arrived at Sikkim's 6,000-foot-high capital, but still considered ourselves lucky. Not only were we alive and the first to get through, but two months later, when we returned, we learned that despite the efforts of an army of coolies with heavy equipment, the road was still blocked.

The Indian chargé d'affaires, Harishwar Dayal, proved to be our savior in Gangtok. He and his talented wife provided Lowell and me with warm clothing until our own things caught up with us, and his home was our headquarters during the three days we spent in that mountaintop town surrounded by terraced rice fields. One of the world's smallest capitals, Gangtok was a vital Himalayan trading center, a crossroads of caravan routes whose teeming marketplace was full of Sikkimese, Tibetans, Indians and Sherpas for hire.

From the polyglot crew, we made up our caravan. Our agent was a plump, ever-grinning Sikkimese named Rinzing Dorje, the pigtail coiling on his head rounding out the classic image of the cunning Oriental with a heart of gold. Dorje's fee was fat enough—and to it he added 10 percent of the salary of every man he hired for us—but anything we questioned about his accounts only elicited an even broader grin and the inevitable pronouncement, "Subtract. Just subtract it." The fact is that we questioned very little: stories of pack trains beset with troubles caused by unhappy bearers were all too common; we wanted to be spared that and, thanks to Dorje's expertise, we were.

Our interpreter, Tsewong Namgyal, was a Tibetan who had come to Sikkim as a child, then studied at an American missionary college in India. This was to be his first return visit to his homeland. As neither Lajor, our *sirdar*, as the head bearer is known, nor Norbu, the cook, nor any of the six coolies in our party could speak a word of English, it can be seen that Tsewong became the motive force by which our caravan operated.

During most of the three days we spent in Gangtok, our equipment lay strewn about the courtyard of Harishwar Dayal's residence; we had discovered that the cases were too big for the pack animals and so had to rebuild and repack each of the wooden boxes. We also made the first of our recordings for my radio program and sent them back to the U.S. via Pan American Clipper. Finally, early on August 5, we set off for Lhasa, the Holy City, three hundred jungle-covered, mountainous and wind-swept, gorge-cut highland miles away—just your typical, everyday caravan: nine pack mules; interpreter, *sirdar* and cook shouting final instructions at each other and the six bearers, all colorfully garbed in G.I. shoes, tattered field jackets and other U.S. Army castoffs; and the two *sahibs*, wearing rubberized navy storm suits to round out the unlikely expedition.

Soon we had left Gangtok behind and were deep in a rain-drenched bamboo forest. Leeches pounced on us from the wet foliage and quickly fattened on our blood, finding every bit of exposed skin, fastening themselves inside the mules' nostrils and sending them into paroxysms of sneezing. On one side, the jungle shut out the world, but on the other the world fell suddenly away, to be lost in the mists thousands of feet below. We had had a wild hope of trimming a week or so off the normal twenty-one-day trip to Lhasa, but there was no persuading the mules of any urgency. Besides, it took only one day on the narrow, ever-climbing trail before we realized that we would be lucky to make fifteen miles a day. Caravans such as ours had been plodding this trade route for hundreds of years in just this same careful way, at just this maddeningly slow pace.

We spent our first night in a bungalow maintained for travelers by the Sikkimese, where we were joined for dinner and the night by the genial and well educated Crown Prince, who had followed us, curious to know what our plans were. A few years later he married an American girl, Hope Cooke, and after he became the Chogyal—the ruler—we met again at the coronation in Nepal, and several times in America. Next day we were high in the Himalayas, trying hard not to look down from the winding, dizzying heights to the bottomless gorges and chasms that swept away from the trail's edge. My mule had a predilection for getting right to the brink of the abyss, and then bending farther forward to nibble at a stray plant, so a few times I felt myself all but propelled out into that endless space. Soon we dismounted and entrusted our fate to our own two feet.

At 12,000 feet, it was still raining and bitterly cold. We pushed on toward Nathu La, the high mountain pass at the Indian frontier, fighting our way uphill against the treachery of the mud and wet stones underfoot. No customs official greeted us at the border—only three wild yaks, who glared down at us from a ledge; and at an altitude of 14,800 feet, we crossed into Tibet. As was the custom, we bowed low, then threw rocks to chase the evil spirits believed to live in the mountain passes and lie in wait for unwary travelers.

We stopped for lunch, then continued on foot down the slope of Nathu La, in keeping with an ancient Tibetan saying: "If he doesn't carry you uphill, he is no horse; if you don't walk down, you are no man." Wet and cold as we were, an overriding excitement, a sense of achievement and well-being had hold of us. We had crossed the main barrier wall of the Himalayas; we were inside forbidden Tibet!

A few miles over the border we said "so long" to cameraman John Roberts, who had been allowed to go this far with us, and who at least could say he had been in Tibet.

Early the next morning, bound for the town of Yatung, we descended to an enchanted forest, the trees wound with a delicate golden moss; the sun flickered brightly through, for the rain had stopped at last. Here we encountered a huge monkey, all white except for his wise black face, examining us carefully as we filed beneath the tall branch where he perched. He had no fear, for most Tibetans are devout believers in reincarnation and would no more harm an animal or fish than they would a family member for, obviously, the two could be one and the same.

Not far from Nathu La, we came upon our first monastery, a turreted stone building on the mountainside called Kargyu Gompa. Here lived a sect of the Red Hat monks, who, long ago, ruled all Tibet. An old priest, sitting Buddha-like at the entrance, regarded us serenely, and soon an abbot came to offer us food and shelter for the night. Unfortunately we had to decline, for we were determined to hold to our schedule. But the sight of this remote monastery, seemingly lost in time, served to remind us of the preeminent place held by religion and ritual in Tibet.

The fourteenth Dalai Lama ruled the world's only theocracy by reason of his consecration as the Living Buddha; he was to be reincarnated after death, a perpetual self-succession. There were nearly 250,000 monks in the land, a quarter of the entire male population, and they were supported, as were countless monasteries like Kargyu Gompa, by all the rest of the people. Outside, the world had moved into the atomic age; continents could be spanned in a matter of hours by high-flying jets, and oceans in the time it took to say "shortwave radio." But locked inside its mountain fortress, infinitely more concerned with a spiritual rather than a temporal life, the Tibet we had come to see would have been absolutely familiar to the first Dalai Lama —whose rule ended more than five hundred and fifty years before!

In Yatung, the Tromo Trochi, a government agent, provided us with Tibetan passports, the *lamyik*, without which further travel was impossible. He wore a royal blue robe tied with a ceremonial red sash, a four-inch earring of turquoise, pearl and gold dangling from his left ear and, on his head, an ordinary gray fedora. We exchanged the traditional silk scarves, whereupon

General Patton wearing his fifth star before it was confirmed by the Senate.

Radio newsmen with General Ike the day the Germans capitulated. Others around him include Quincy Howe, John W. Vandercook, Burnet Hershey, Howard Barnes, Joe Karsh, Johannes Steel and George Hamilton Combs.

With the Generalissimo and General Albert C. Wedemeyer.

Captain Eddie and General Jimmy help me celebrate an anniversary.

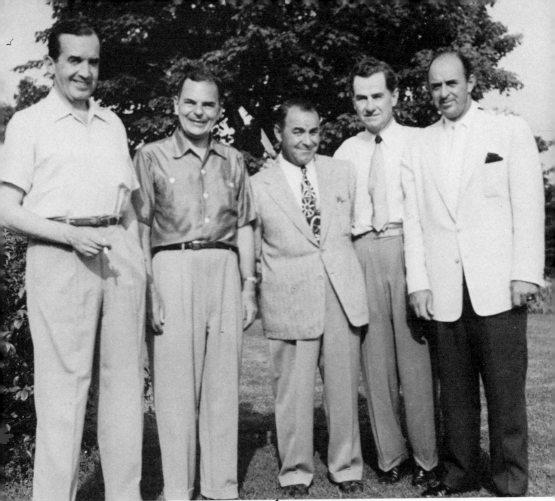

Edward R. Murrow, Thomas E. Dewey, Gene Sarazen, L.T., Sam Snead.

Walter Hagen, perhaps the greatest golfer of all time.

With the famous Tommy Armour.

The Marquis degli Albizzi, super athlete.

Erling Strom, conqueror of Mt. McKinley.

I tried in vain to make skiers of two ex-heavyweight champions: Eddie Eagan (amateur) and Gene Tunney.

Sig Buchmayer executes an acrobatic jump on the Tuckerman Headwall.

Toni Matt, the only skier ever to schuss the Tuckerman Headwall on Mt. Washington.

Each evening Lowell Thomas, Jr., paid the Tibetans who had provided the caravan for that day.

L.T. recording the first broadcast ever made from Tibet—the first ever made anywhere with battery equipment.

The Potala—one of the wonders of the world—built without elevators and no steel.

With L.T., Jr., Rimshi Kypup, Luishahr Djoza Lama, and Dorje Changwaba.

The Dalai Lama, age sixteen, on his throne at Norbu Linga. The Lord Chamberlain is with him.

On an outdoor throne with Tokra, a high lama selected to rule until the Dalai Lama came of age.

he bestowed on us the *lamyik*, a long scroll with the Dalai Lama's seal, whose provisions were as impressive as the Tromo Trochi himself:

> From Yatung right up to Lhasa, let it be known to all officials and to all others that a message has been received from the Tibetan government that two Americans, with an interpreter and servants, have permission to proceed to Lhasa. And that sixteen pack mules and six riding animals be given to them, and coolies if required. . . . On the route, preparations for lodging, servants for the kitchen, skin boats to cross rivers and any other requirements such as milk, eggs and vegetables are to be given to them at the current rate. The wishes of the two Americans are to be fulfilled at a moment's notice. For this journey let them be given everything without fail, as Americans are very good friends of Tibet. If they wish to proceed forthwith after arrival at each stage of the journey, let their wishes be gratified.

We left Yatung with an official guide, Nima Gyabu of the Tibetan army, a young man who presented a dignified demeanor although his pigtail and a long earring bounced gaily under his campaign hat as we rode along. Perhaps it was the silver portable altar and prayer box he carried on his hip. We followed the Amo Chu River, climbing out of the valley up to the shoulders of the Himalayas. This time, though, we were afforded some spectacular views, for the mists that had dogged our way this far melted away under brilliant sunshine. By midday we had reached the immense Central Asian plateau, an elevation of 14,000 feet and more, as high as the highest of our Rockies. And as we rode along, the tinkling of the mules' bells providing lively accompaniment, great snow-covered peaks rose yet another 5,000 feet and more all around us.

That afternoon we saw a herd of yaks, that most remarkable animal distantly related to the American buffalo and, for untold ages, the backbone of the Tibetan economy. The yak is an ideal beast of burden, strong and sure-footed and able to forage for himself in those sparsely-grown heights. But more, he willingly pulls a plow; his wool makes clothes and tents, his hide leather, the hair of his tail strong rope and, exported to America, superior Santa Claus beards. In a land without coal and almost no trees from which to cut wood, dried yak dung provides nearly all the fuel, and yak butter and milk are staples of the Tibetan diet—as is the meat among herdsmen who worry less about the afterlife than being well-fed here on earth.

We stopped next in the town of Phari Dzong, a place with little to commend it to the traveler except for a chance to replenish supplies and rest for the night within the shelter of four walls. A motley assemblage of sod and stone houses, Phari was once described as "the highest, windiest, dirtiest town in the world," and no one who subsequently passed through had reason to quarrel with that succinct characterization, not even the founding fathers. It seems the name Phari Dzong, where the streets are piled high with the accumulated garbage of the ages, translates into Hog Hill.

We pushed on to Gyangtse, crossing 15,000-foot passes and, in double-time marches of twenty-five miles or more, covered the distance in four days. Here, in the third city of Tibet, a trade and commercial center dominated by fortress walls and the inevitable monastery, we were visited by the Rimshi Lobsang Tsewong, a monk who was also one of Gyangtse's highest officials. After the ritual exchange of white scarves and presents, he told us, through Tsewong, our interpreter, that all of Tibet's four million people were wholly devoted to the thoughts of Buddha, Nirvana and their next incarnation. "Therefore, any of your Western ideas, science or inventions are superficial and trivial and have no importance to us."

That was a conversation-stopper if I ever heard one, and we were glad to go off for a visit to the monastery. There we saw a man praying before a stone Buddha. Suddenly he flung himself forward, face to the ground, in an attitude of prostrate submission, then rose and repeated the performance. We were told the man, a religious pilgrim, had been going through this arduous ritual all week, from daybreak to dusk, and meant to keep it up for three weeks more. Maybe the Rimshi hadn't exaggerated.

We were now halfway to Lhasa, and at the farthest limit of Western influence. Neither the Indian mail service nor any but a handful of travelers or traders went any farther; the austere *dak* bungalows which, at the end of a hard day on the trail, had come to seem luxurious, now vanished, to be replaced by the hospitality of ordinary Tibetan villagers, whose hearts were certainly in the right place, but whose homes were, in a word, primitive. Typically, the ground floor was occupied by yaks, goats and chickens, the living quarters reached by ladder and, except for Buddhist images lighted by yak-butter lamps, virtually devoid of furniture. I think my journal, written in the intensity of the moment, conveys some of the domestic aspects of our life and times on the trail in far Tibet:

> We are sitting in a Tibetan kitchen with ten other people. In one corner two women are trying to start a yak-dung fire in a stove made of stone and mud. One of the women is vigorously pushing up and down on a goatskin, a Tibetan bellows. Six others are watching Tsewong Norbu as he putters with Lowell, Jr.'s primus stove.
>
> The spectators squat around me, drinking the omnipresent Tibetan tea, which is mixed with barley and rancid yak butter. One old crone and a patriarch are goggle-eyed as Lowell gets our pressure cooker going. They can't understand where that intense flame comes from. No doubt they think the Buddha works miracles through strange people.
>
> Three more persons have come in. I can hardly make them out through the smoke. Having no chimneys, only holes in the roof, Tibetan kitchens are black and suffocating. Out on the great plateau, they are always on the second floor because the animals, the chickens and the mud are in full possession of the first floor.
>
> Seated on Tibetan rugs around a charcoal brazier, by the light of a primitive oil lamp, we usually have quite a feast for dinner, our caravan food supply brought together from practically everywhere. A spot of Canadian Club from MacArthur's second-in-command in Tokyo, then pea soup from Switzerland, concentrated in a block an inch square. Next, ragout de veau with gravy from Switzerland, or yak steak or mutton—the gift of a *dzong-pön* (a district governor)—stewed together with fresh turnips, cauliflower, beets and carrots, all local products. Usually we have a plate of rice from the sack presented to us by a noble Tibetan official, seven-foot Rimshi Dorje, at Phari. We top off our banquet with pancakes made with Australian flour and strawberry jam from Tasmania, and Klim, our powdered milk from America. It all tastes wonderful, due to the wizardry of cook Tsewong Norbu.

Our hosts invariably offered us the largest of the sleeping rooms around the patio-kitchen, but Lowell was afraid they would join us and I was afraid they would not, for I could not imagine where else they might find shelter against that piercing, ever-present wind. So we pitched the tent outside and slept on army cots. That is, *sometimes* we slept. Once, the wind mounted to such velocity that we almost blew away in the darkness, tent, cots and all. As I recall it, we spent half the night hanging on to the guy ropes while the canvas flapped wildly and threatened to launch us into flight. Another time a congregation of monks, apparently feeling the locality threatened by a demon, beat on their drums and blew into bone horns all night, so that sleep was impossible and sanity menaced. I can only assume the demon was as terrified as we were. I know he was luckier—he, after all, could leave.

After more than two weeks on the trail, midway on our longest day's march—some thirty-two miles that would take us fourteen hours—we reached the pass at Karo La, a craggy, narrow path pressed tight by a massive glacier wall. And at this point, with nothing to do but advance or retreat, we encountered a long caravan of yaks. Something obviously had to give, and our bearers decided on the yaks. Beating at the great beasts with whips, they drove them off the precipitous edge of the trail to what looked to Lowell and me like a 16,500-foot drop and certain death. But the remarkable yaks, with their cloven hooves clinging to almost perpendicular slopes, hung on, waited patiently until we had passed, then clambered back up and continued on their way.

Wearing as the demands of the trail were, we now set out on each day's march with high spirits and the heady feeling that we were actually going to make it. The Holy City, the dream we had journeyed half a world to realize, was finally within reach!

At Nyapso La, we crossed the final pass between Lhasa and a now remote outside civilization. When we reached the Brahmaputra River at Singlakenjung, we climbed into skin boats and for sixteen luxurious miles rode downstream to Chusul Dzong, start of the last lap. But there we found the highest flood waters in four years. Often the trail simply disappeared under the muddy waters, and sometimes the bearers had to carry the loads so the donkeys could swim. But late one evening, as we walked ankle deep in the Lhasa valley, we caught sight of our destination, the roofs of the Tibetan capital agleam in the last sunlight and standing like a toy city of gold under the dark mountains in the distance. We camped five miles away and prepared to make our entry the following morning.

✻ ✻ ✻

Just outside Lhasa stands Drepung, the largest monastery in the world, at the time still the home and spiritual haven for ten thousand monks. As we went slowly by on that brilliant September morning in 1949, impressed by the endless tiers of stone buildings that crept up the mountainside, two Tibetan nobles rode out from the city to meet us and announced in labored English that His Holiness, the Dalai Lama, had given them the honor of acting as our hosts during our stay in Lhasa. Their names were Rimshi Kypup and Dorje Changwaba, both in the red and purple robes of high office. Thanking them, Lowell and I were outwardly solemn, as befitted the occasion, but our hearts were leaping with excitement. Then we all turned and rode on, across the bridge over the Kyi Chu River, and through the Western Gate.

We were inside Lhasa, the Forbidden City!

The Dalai Lama's winter palace, the golden-domed Potala, stood before us on the left, an architectural miracle towering story upon story up into the sunlight. It is 900 feet high, taller than all but our very highest skyscrapers, yet so skillfully designed that it is hard to tell where the hillside ends and the building begins. It was built with no steel, and, of course, no elevators. Beyond were a maze of streets full of sharply-angled shops, their open windows alive with banners and prayer flags. It was summer festival time, and the lords and ladies of Lhasa, ornately clad in rich robes and elaborate hats, mingled with peasants and muleteers in serviceable yak-skin clothing and rough boots. Benignly overlooking this storybook spectacle were the snow-covered mountains, like a guard of honor protecting and preserving the magical quality of this real life Shangri-La.

Dorje Changwaba led us through the city to the government villa that was to be our home in Lhasa. It was light and airy, and before we had finished unpacking, Dorje's servants appeared with gifts of mutton, eggs and fresh vegetables. Then came the most magnificent gift of all, a tin bathtub in which we could luxuriate while washing the tangible evidence of the long trail from our bodies. No guest at the most modern hotel was ever more pleased with his accommodations.

It would be some days before we were to be received by the Dalai Lama. Meanwhile we set about seeing the city, where no census had ever been taken, but whose population was estimated at 25,000. At the bazaar, thrown together with splendid Oriental rugs and jewelry, one could buy Western cigarettes, sunglasses, flashlights and soap—at prices that took full account of the long caravan journey required to bring them to Lhasa. But these expensive bazaar items were virtually the only traces of Western culture. Modern plumbing was unknown. Garbage was piled up in all the city's far reaches and collected infrequently—to be used as crop fertilizer. But the odors were not as noticeable as you would imagine. Luckily, the bracing mountain air, the almost constant wind, and the complete absence of flies and mosquitoes staved off a public health problem.

People who could afford horses or mules rode; everyone else walked. It was as though the wheel had never been invented, so that, travel apart, everything used in heavy construction—and there was a great deal going on—stones, wood beams and earth, had to be borne by men or mules or yaks. Why was this so? We asked Rimshi Kypup.

His answer was wonderfully Tibetan: his people had gotten along without wheeled transport throughout the ages; where was it written that they should change now? Furthermore, he said, to introduce even the crude oxcart would require widening the country's narrow trails, and this would violate the land and anger the holy spirits. He did not say, and did not need to, that proper roads would also be an invitation to foreign penetration.

On the last day of the summer festival, we were invited to attend the feasting and performances at Norbulingka, the Dalai Lama's summer palace. There, two Americans amid thousands of Tibetans, we attracted a fair share of attention with our pale complexions, skinny, sunburned noses and bizarre Western garb. But we were equally intrigued: the Dalai Lama and his party of high lamas sat in the adjoining pavilion, only forty feet away, and though protocol held that since we had not yet been received we were not officially present, it was hard to keep from staring.

The festivities consisted of the enactment of an ancient Buddhist drama by actors in the most spectacular costumes, with a narrative so complicated that not even our interpreters could keep us abreast. Since it lasted a numbing ten hours, I have a feeling we would have lost track even if we were in perfect command of the Tibetan language. Lowell, Jr., with his tape recorder, was permitted to wander in and out of the proceedings, and attracted as much attention as the drama. At midday we were fed stupefyingly opulent courses of yak cheese, rice, raisins and barley bread, washed down with the ubiquitous yak-butter tea. At the many-colored marquee of Tsepon Shakabpa, the Dalai Lama's finance minister, we noticed a man who obviously was a European. He turned out to be an Austrian mountaineer who had escaped from a British prison camp in India, and who later became famous as an author and as a climber with perhaps more firsts than anyone in the world!

Two days later we were received by the Dalai Lama. Then only fifteen years old, he was the Fourteenth Incarnation, found by the high lamas at Kumbum on the shore of Lake Koko Nor when he was only a child. He had immediately selected the articles belonging to his departed predecessor, Chenrezi, Buddha of Mercy, thus passing the test as the Living God of Lamaist Buddhism. Although Tibet was to be governed by a regent until the Dalai Lama's eighteenth birthday, his power, religious and temporal, was absolute, and rooted entirely in the love and reverence of his people.

On the morning of our reception, we were escorted to Norbulingka by our two nobles. In the courtyard, we dismounted as the wail of Tibetan conch shell and six-foot brass horns reverberated against the stone walls. A gong signaled the beginning of the morning reception and we took our places in the long line of the faithful, come to be blessed by the True Incarnation. Almost too soon we were in his presence, a smiling, bareheaded youth in red robes seated on a high, cushioned throne. I had wanted to savor these incredible surroundings, like an Oriental scene from an illuminated manuscript of the Middle Ages, but suddenly we were part of the scene and had to play our roles.

I held out the traditional white scarf. The Dalai Lama took it, together with symbolic objects representing the world, the body and the power of speech. As I bowed, he touched my head in blessing and presented me with a red scarf. Young Lowell followed, and when he had gone through the ancient ritual, we were directed to cushions in the audience chamber and served ceremonial bowls of rice and tea. Soon the ceremony was over, but it would live on in our memories forever.

Nor was our visit with the Dalai Lama finished. After an

interview with the seventy-three-year-old regent, His Highness
Tokra, we were told that the Dalai Lama had agreed to permit
us to photograph him, another shattering of precedent, so they
told us, for never before had anyone ever taken either color
photos or motion picture films of a reigning Dalai Lama. We
hurried off to a pagoda on the palace grounds, where the young
ruler awaited us, and for thirty minutes we shot away with four
cameras. It was a coup such as we had hardly dared hope for,
and the Dalai Lama's gracious willingness to smile and change
position at our request made the outcome a once-in-a-lifetime
triumph.

The next days swept by in a hectic round of receptions and
interviews. We spoke with the Foreign Ministers and other dignitaries, and without exception their main concern was a Chinese
incursion on Tibet's independence. In one way or another, each
asked the same question: what would America do if the Communists invaded Tibet? As private citizens, we were in no position
to offer more than the hope that public opinion would induce
Congress and the President to render all possible aid; certainly
American sympathies would be with the threatened, mountain-
locked land. But it was clear such answers were less than satisfying to our hosts. They did not grasp the sometimes cumbersome
workings of a democratic society. Sympathy was not arms; sympathy would not turn back the Red armies. Their fears, of course,
proved tragically real, but by the time they raised the question
of Tibet's defense, the grim answers were already written on the
winds blowing south and west from China.

"Inner Tibet," the vast realm then ruled by the youthful
Dalai Lama and his advisers, while regarded as the ultimate goal
for travelers, had been seen by few Westerners. Many had made
the attempt to reach Lhasa; even Sweden's famed Sven Hedin,
foremost of modern Central Asian explorers, was one of the many
who failed. Several did manage to reach Lhasa in disguise. One,
Theos Bernard, a young Arizona lawyer, spent years studying the
language and Tibetan customs in monasteries on the Indian side
of the Himalayas. Much later, when he returned to America, he
wrote a book and billed himself as "the white lama" on a lecture
tour. Whether the Tibetans heard of this and disapproved we
don't know, but when Theos attempted to return to Tibet he had

his throat cut at the border and nothing more was heard of him.

To our surprise when we got to Lhasa we found three West-erners, one a scholarly, rather young Scotsman, a product of Eton, St. Andrew's University and Oxford. At the time of Partition, when Nehru and his cohorts could hardly wait to get their former rulers out of India, they had asked the British Raj to allow just one of their people to remain. Hugh Richardson had been the British expert on Tibet; Nehru had no one to take his place, and so asked London to loan him to them.

Of the many impressive diplomats I have known, and they have been legion, Hugh Richardson ranks high on my list. I've often wondered why Whitehall failed to reward him. Surely few have been more deserving of knighthood or a baronetcy, or even elevation to the lofty status of a marquis. I suppose it's one of those miscues of history. After all, the British had been frustrated and saddened over the way they finally bowed out of India, "the number one jewel in Queen Victoria's crown." So, in their haste to forget, they overlooked the opportunity to honor a pro-consul who richly deserved it.

But, greatest surprise of all, we found not one but two Austrian mountaineers in Tibet, both escaped prisoners of war. At the outbreak of World War II they had been attempting to scale Nanga Parbat, in the Western Himalayas, the "killer moun-tain." Peter Aufschnaiter and Heinrich Harrer, two crack Alpin-ists, had been picked up in the Western Himalayas and put in a prison camp at Dehra Dun. After a number of unsuccessful at-tempts to escape, they had eluded the frontier guards. In an in-credible journey, finally dressed in skins of animals, and after months of near starvation, they crossed a pass never used in winter by anyone. When they turned up in Lhasa the Tibetans were so impressed they allowed them to stay and eventually gave them work to do, Aufschnaiter as an engineer, of which there were none in Tibet; and Harrer as a part-time instructor to the teenage Dalai Lama. We were the first to tell the outside world about these two mountaineers, who had been given up for dead.

Oh yes, and we found one other European, a chap whom some of our British friends in India referred to as a renegade. Reggie Fox, born in the slums of East London, had been a motor-cycle courier in World War I. Later, in India, he became a radio technician, accompanied a government mission over the border, liked the way he was accepted and treated by the Dalai Lama's people, married a Tibetan woman and was allowed to become a Tibetan citizen. In Lhasa he and his attractive wife raised a family and Reggie lived the life of a Tibetan noble—quite a contrast to his unhappy youth in London's Limehouse district. It might have been a real Shangri-La for Reggie, except for one thing: He suffered acutely from arthritic gout.

At the end of the Second World War, when we pulled all our forces out of Asia, Uncle Sam left millions of dollars' worth of equipment strewn all the way from the Pamirs to the South Seas. Even a decade later, on an expedition in New Guinea, we chartered a yacht captained by an Australian who had made a fortune scrounging for copper and other metals left behind by our people. At any rate, some unknown American officer even sent a caravan of yaks laden with electronic equipment over the towering Himalayas as a gift to Tibet, where Reggie Fox was the only one who knew what to do with it. We found him spending his nights monitoring shortwave stations around the world—Radio Moscow, Radio London, Radio Tokyo, Radio America and so on. He made notes of the news he picked up in this way, and the following morning turned it over to Surkang Dzaza, who presided over a new office in Lhasa. Surkang was the Dalai Lama's Foreign Minister.

At night, while I slept, Lowell, Jr., would spend memorable and rather exciting hours with Reg Fox, who one night said to him: "Is there anyone in America you would like to talk to?" Lowell's reply was: "Yes, I'd like to talk to a girl in Greenwich, Connecticut." Many American ham operators were constantly trying to get through to Reg, eager to reach the most remote city in the world. He now quickly got through to one in a Boston suburb, a bartender who patched up a phone call from Lhasa to Greenwich, Connecticut, which enabled L. T., Jr., to talk to the daughter of Sam Pryor, one of the heads of Pan Am. That night, from the roof of the world, Lowell proposed to Tay. Nine months later, twenty-seven years ago, they were married; they now live in our forty-ninth state, where they have been active in Alaskan public life. There is an odd sidelight on this episode. Lowell and Tay assumed they were having a shortwave private conversation. But, within minutes, the bartender had phoned Walter Winchell in New York, and the next day Winchell broadcast the story both in his column and on his own radio program!

While Lowell was spending those midnight hours with Reggie Fox in Lhasa, Reg picked up a report of a drug said to be a miraculous cure for rheumatism, gout and so on—a new drug they were calling cortisone. Reg, badly crippled by arthritic gout, begged us to investigate this upon our return. So one of the first things we did when we got home was to get in touch with George Merck; he called his scientists together at a luncheon, and they told us of the research they had done on this drug.

Although they said it hadn't been fully tested, they agreed to let us have several thousand dollars' worth of it, which we had flown to Calcutta via the State Department. By shortwave we got this word to Reggie, who made the long caravan journey over the Himalayas to India to get what he hoped would be a cure for his ailment. The Merck people had told us Fox must strap it next to his body on his return journey to keep it at an even temperature. They also gave him instructions as to how to use it—in limited doses. Alas, he suffered such intense pain that he failed to heed their advice.

A few months after we were there, when the Chinese Reds overran Tibet, Reggie and his family fled to India. When Lowell, Jr., and Tay were flying through southern Asia on their honeymoon, Lowell visited Reg at his Kalimpong home in West Bengal. Finding him in desperate shape, Lowell made arrangements for him to be taken to one of India's major hospitals. Reggie Fox died on the way.

As for one of our hosts in Lhasa, Tsarong Shape, a former Prime Minister who had saved the previous Dalai Lama's life, a year later Tibetans in exile told us how the Chinese Reds put him in chains, dragged him through the streets and killed him. He was the one who had loaned us the horse that spun me off the trail on Karo La, a high pass. We had promised Tsarong that some day, if his son ever came to America, we would loan him caravan animals for a journey from New York to Washington. His oldest son did eventually come to America and we put a grandson, Jigme Tsarong, through a university in Indiana where he made a fine record both as a student and as an athlete.

We had passed more than a week in the enchanted city, and the time had come to begin organizing our caravan for the return journey. It was already well into September and the winter snows come early in the high Himalayas. And so, on the twelfth morning, we set forth, sailing down the flooding Kyi Chu in skin boats to reach Chusul Dzong in six hours; it had taken us two and a half days to cover those forty miles traveling overland.

The yak-skin boat called a coracle is a remarkable craft. Ten feet long and six feet across at the blunt end, it easily carried the loads of twenty pack animals, along with eight passengers and two oarsmen—and was itself light enough to be portaged great distances. A broadcast we made as we went coursing downriver and including the haunting boat songs of the oarsmen proved to be one of the most popular of the entire trip.

We left Chusul Dzong for the high mountain country, trailing a file of donkeys and yaks, and accompanied this time by one of Tsarong Shape's traders, a man from Kham, leading two high-spirited, half-broken horses Tsarong hoped would fetch a good price just over the Himalayas, at Kalimpong in India. For five days all went well. We had reached the summit of Karo La and begun the steep descent to the plateau. Lowell and I began talking of being home in the first week of October, and perhaps that taunted some of the demons of evil who are forever lurking along the trail across the world's loftiest mountains. Or perhaps it was simply my hubris in mounting one of those half-wild Tibetan horses.

The fact is that they looked handsome and appealing after the endless hours astride an uninteresting, plodding mule. And for a day and a half, my riding experience, gained in my younger days in the Colorado Rockies, stood me in good stead. But late that afternoon, having dismounted to pick up some unusual colored rocks, I foolishly neglected to have anyone hold my unbroken horse's head when I started to mount him. That was the chance my steed—or the demon—was waiting for. Catching me with one foot in the stirrup and the other raised over the saddle, the horse spun and sent me flying out over the edge of the trail.

I felt the agonizing sensation of bones breaking in my hip as I came crashing down on the sharp rocks below. Almost at once I was struggling for breath in the thin air at 17,000 feet, struggling for consciousness. And even through the pain, I knew that in such a desolate place there might be little I, or anyone, could do to stave off an abrupt ending to all my years of travel. The first aid kit was miles behind in the slow-moving caravan, and even that had no morphine or anything else to ease pain and the effects of shock. It was only an hour before dark, and the next village still lay more than four miles across the plateau. And heaven alone knew how far we would have to go to find medical help.

Lowell was holding me in his arms, which helped to keep my other bones from breaking apart as I shook with the chills and fever that at high altitude come swiftly with shock and exposure. When the caravan came up, he wrapped me in blankets and eased me onto a folding cot. The bearers hoisted it up and we were off through the darkness to the village of Ralung, a trip that took four hours, during which time I alternated between fainting and delirium.

Neither of us slept that night. In the morning Lowell found a one-wire, usually-not-working telephone and managed to make contact with an Indian military medic in Gyangtse, thirty-three miles away. This Bengali medic, Brajendra Chandra Pal, made a forced march to Ralung in one day, but on arrival confessed that medicine, not surgery, was his field. Besides, he had been drafted into the Indian army even before he'd had a chance to complete his training. Years later he became a surgeon-commander in Nehru's navy.

"What can we do?" Lowell asked him. "Can we go on?"

"You have no choice," he said bleakly, then added encouragingly that my injury might be only a matter of torn ligaments. Once we reached Gyangtse, he hoped that could be seen to.

His medical assessment was off by quite a bit, as I suspected from the pain; and a month later, in New York, we learned that my hip was broken in eight places. But he was right about our options: we had to push on.

Young Lowell, without whose resourcefulness and determination to get me out alive I could never have made it, describes that harrowing journey to Gyangtse in his book about our Tibetan adventure, *Out of This World: To Forbidden Tibet.*

It sometimes took ten Tibetans to carry Dad's stretcher over the steep, rocky trails, which skirted chasms and swift streams,

moving at a snail's pace to keep him from plunging into the river far below. Strapped to the stretcher with his leg not even in a splint, Dad roasted when the sun was out and nearly froze when it ducked behind the clouds and the cold winds blew up. . . .
We reached Gyangtse on the third day, and the quarters seemed like paradise after those grim days on the trail.

For ten days I rested, eventually even managing to get to my feet and, leaning heavily on a cane, to hobble about twenty yards. But both Lowell and I knew the worst was still ahead of us. Although word of our plight had gotten to the outside, there was no possibility of rescue. No plane, no helicopter, no modern transport of any kind would be allowed into Tibet. If I was ever to walk properly again, we would have to march out the way we came in—and soon, before the deep snows blocked the Himalayan passes.

Just about the time we had counted on arriving home, we started out from Gyangtse, bound for Gangtok, more than two hundred miles away. We averaged no more than twelve or thirteen miles a day. In teams of four, the Tibetan bearers carried me in an improvised sedan chair, chanting, along with their prayers to Buddha, a refrain that translated to, "Oh Lord Buddha, lighten our load!" I obliged them, losing some twenty pounds en route.

We reached Yatung on October 5, to be met by a rescue team sent out by Ambassador Loy Henderson and Prime Minister Nehru. There was nothing they could do, so they simply joined us and we crossed the final high pass, Nathu La, together. Neither Nehru's surgeon nor Emily Bateman, the nurse from our New Delhi Embassy who, with Royal Bisbee, one of our younger diplomats, had come with the rescue caravan, could tell the extent of my injury. Emily, by the way, was a blonde, and the ultraviolet rays at those heights in the Himalayas caused her arms, legs and face to swell, so she too was a casualty. A year or so later she wrote and told me her principal claim to fame was that she had "shot John Gunther and Lowell Thomas in the ass!" Three days later, at an airfield just south of Gangtok, an Air Force plane picked us up and flew us to Calcutta, and then we were really on our way home. I calculated that the entire air trip, just about exactly halfway around the globe, even with a three-day rest at

London, took less than a third of the time we spent on that bitter thirty-three-mile route from Ralung to Gyangtse.

At the Harkness Pavilion (Columbia Presbyterian Medical Center), Dr. Frank Stinchfield found my hip had been broken in eight places and did some fancy surgery, and Dr. Hans Kraus performed a rehabilitation miracle. With it all, some doubted I'd ever walk without assistance. And it is certainly true that all through that winter and spring I was on crutches. But in May, when Lowell and Tay were married, I threw them away. And less than a year after that horse took it into his head to do me in, I flew north to the Alaska Juneau Icecap and went glacier skiing with the eminent glaciologist and mountaineer Dr. Mal Miller—and I haven't felt more than a twinge since.

In return for our being honored as few Westerners had ever been—invited to Lhasa as guests of the Dalai Lama—had there been anything they wanted us to do for them? The Kremlin had gotten word of our visit, and Moscow newspapers had labeled us American spies. Yes, the Tibetans did ask us to do them a favor. But spies we were not.

On the return to India we carried a parchment scroll on which was a message for President Truman and Secretary of State Dean Acheson. Two days before our departure from Lhasa, Surkang Dzaza had us as luncheon guests in his office. Others present were his associates, whose contacts with other nations had been limited to their neighbors, China, India, Nepal, Pakistan and Iran. Luncheon was served to us as we sat cross-legged on hassocks. The room was pure Central Asia, with no modern equipment of any kind. For a filing system they had strips of yak thong dangling from the ceiling; at the ends of each strip were tied official papers, all made of wood pounded out by hand.

The Foreign Minister had the usual long turquoise pendant hanging from his left ear. All were dressed in silk gowns, with their unique headgear indicating their rank in the hierarchy of Tibet, whether they were nobles of the first, second or third rank.

After the luncheon we were handed a scroll which we were asked to deliver to the President of the United States.

When we finally arrived in New York, and while I was in the hospital, Lowell, Jr., went to Washington, where he was warmly welcomed by President Truman, who told him one of his lifelong dreams had been to visit Lhasa, adding that he probably would never have the opportunity. He said he thought Lowell, Jr., had been a most fortunate young man.

In his book *Out of This World* my son described his visit to the White House as follows:

> The message I turned over to President Truman had been handwritten in Tibetan characters with a bamboo pen on parchment made from the bark of a Tibetan tree. It was dated—"the sixteenth day of the seventh month of the Earth Bull year (September 7, 1949)" and read, in Tibetan and in English:
>
> "Now that Lowell Thomas, Sr., and Lowell Thomas, Jr., have been able to visit Tibet, they are well acquainted with all facts about this country. Therefore, the government of Tibet hopes that from them the President of the United States, the people of America, and those who live in other countries as well, will soon come to know more about Tibet. That it is a holy, independent country, a religious country, ruled over by His Holiness the Dalai Lama, who is the true Incarnation of Chenrezi, the Buddha of Mercy. Furthermore, that all Tibetans, including the civilian population as well as the monks, are entirely devoted to religion.
>
> "We have learned that unfortunately, throughout this world at the present time, there is an absence of peace and happiness—this because of troubles between peoples, and disturbances and conflicts of many kinds. We, the government and people of Tibet, are much worried, deeply concerned over the present state of the world in which we all live. And we are eager to have it known that here in Tibet, a land that is especially dedicated to religion, all of our peoples, both lay and monk, are earnestly praying that God will grant happiness and everlasting peace to all humanity."

Some months later, still on crutches, I also went to Washington to pay my respects to the President and the Secretary of State. The visit to Dean Acheson reminded me a little of our Lhasa luncheon with Surkang. Dean Acheson, with a leg in a cast, was sitting on cushions on the floor, where I joined him. He listened to me tell about our trip across the Himalayas, but gave no indication it might be possible for America to help the Tibetans. When I went in to see the President I had an unexpected welcome from his press secretary, a Missouri schoolmate of President Truman—the thin, lean, western sheriff type. Charlie Ross greeted me warmly and said he had been hoping I would come to the White House. He told me how years before he had been editor of the daily paper in the Cripple Creek district, where I had been one of his successors.

President Truman not only gave me an hour or more— several times when I started to pick up my crutches he urged me to sit down and not be in a hurry. He also took me over to a globe and showed me where he said we were going to contain the Communists in Asia. He also had no promise of any help for the Dalai Lama and his people.

Early in 1951, only a year or so before he died, Sven Hedin, the titan of twentieth-century exploration in Central Asia, wrote to me about our Tibetan journey:

> My dear Lowell Thomas: A few days ago, Professor Sten Frieberg sent me the charming book "Out of This World" which had been presented to me by you and your son and for which I bring you my most hearty thanks. I had a really very good laugh at the distinguished title you gave me as Grand Lama of all Tibetan travelers. . . . At any rate, the journey you and your son undertook to the forbidden land of the Lamas was a clever and audacious achievement which I admire and the description of which has given me so much pleasure.
>
> Already a few months ago I was perfectly fascinated in reading about your adventures and experiences, published in the Collier's Magazine and I loved the brilliant illustrations.
>
> Now I am happy indeed to be the possessor of the noble book of your noble son and I will read it again without the interruptions of a periodical. . . . I hope our beloved Tibet will be saved from the Red Chinese.
>
> With hearty greetings and thanks to you both. Yours very sincerely, Sven Hedin (the wandering Tibetan Lama).

A year later, after putting aside my crutches, I made a pilgrimage to Stockholm just to pay my respects to the Swedish scientist who was generally acknowledged to be the foremost living Central Asian explorer. There was one thing about Sven Hedin that had caused him to lose many of his former friends and admirers. He and Kaiser Wilhelm had been good friends. The Kaiser, whose hobby was archeology, had often welcomed Hedin to his Berlin palace on the Spree. In fact Sven Hedin proudly showed me his array of German decorations and plaques. All of which didn't disturb me too much since World War I now seemed like ancient history. To me Sven Hedin was one of the greats of our time. I never did feel it was necessary to dislike a man because you disagreed with him.

V. The Wonderful Life and Premature Death of Cinerama

> Surely an historic occasion. . . .
> Audiences squeal, reel and sometimes
> faint. . . . Unprecedented crowds are
> lining up for a look. . . . Not since
> the birth of the talkies has a premiere
> agitated Broadway so. The New York
> *Times* plunked the story on Page One.
> —*Time, Life* and *Fortune* Magazines

Former President Herbert Hoover called it a revolution in motion pictures. In his breezier way, Ed Sullivan said it was the most exciting thing to hit town since penicillin. And the New York *Herald Tribune*, in an editorial entitled "Cinerama Takes Over," wrote:

> [It] is the sort of spectacle which is impossible to describe in
> words. . . . But it certainly will be difficult for anyone who has
> witnessed Cinerama ever to be satisfied with old-fashioned
> (that is the word) flat images of sky, water and countryside.
> Cinerama isn't a movie; it's an experience—and an experience,
> we believe, which millions of people are going to become familiar
> with in a very short time.

The *Trib* turned out to be dead right. But shortsightedness, folly and plain old-fashioned greed did Cinerama in, and though there are now wide-screen processes, the marvelous peripheral vision miracle of sight and multiple sound that took the world by storm on September 30, 1952, is now once again waiting for someone with the courage and cash to give it a new life. For some of us it was the equivalent of an oil gusher and surely will be again.

What happened?

It's a bizarre story, full of big names, big money and the most unexpected twists and turnings—and I was in it up to the top of my moustache. It began, as these fascinating adventures so often have begun for me, by the sheerest accident. On a September day in 1950, I happened to drop into the office of Hazard E. Reeves, an old acquaintance. I had last seen him twenty years before, when he was a sound engineer just out of Georgia Tech and we had worked together. I had heard of his rapid climb to the top in his field and I asked, "What's new, Buzz?" And Buzz, as he was known to his friends, came up with quite an answer. He said: "I've just bought out the Rockefellers."

Naturally I sat down.

It seemed that somewhere along the way, Reeves, who now had the most successful sound studios in New York, and had been active in real estate and even in the restaurant business, also constantly kept an entrepreneurial ear to the ground, and he had heard something about an extraordinary new film process backed by the Rockefellers, as well as the top brass of Time-Life. The trouble was that the thing, which was called Cinerama and involved three curving, interlocking screens, was a long time developing—more than a decade—and, as nobody knew quite what to do with it, a certain lethargy had taken over.

Enter Buzz Reeves to buy up the patents, add his own nine-track, stereophonic sound process to complement the wraparound effect of the picture and, now, to sit dolefully in his office unable to raise enough money to go into production. One by one, he had ushered the heads of the major movie studios out to the Cinerama laboratory on Long Island to sit through an experimental film, and, without exception, they had been stunned by what they saw. Sight and sound seemed to leap out at them from every direction. But the story was the same—what to do with it?

How could the tens of thousands of movie exhibitors on whom producers depend to show their films be persuaded to buy expensive new equipment and revamp their theaters to accommodate this revolutionary but still untested process? Joseph Schenck, a film tycoon and top money man, had summed it all up when he said, "Who am I to finance the Rockefellers?" Then, because he was far from a stupid man, he ruefully added, "I'll be buying this process someday, and it will cost me ten times as much."

I was intrigued by the whole story. Having long worked in the field of nonfiction film, I saw boundless possibilities for spectacular presentation of the world's wonders in a motion picture process that finally broke through the stringent limits of a small, two-dimensional screen.

Buzz, suddenly remembering I had had an unusual success with my Allenby-Lawrence production years before, became wide-eyed and pronounced me the Almighty's answer to his cash and production deadlock. I countered with a litany of all the projects I was currently involved with. And that part was true enough. But it was also true that since I'd put my affairs in Frank Smith's capable hands, I was trying hard not to undo his good work by plunging deep into cold financial waters on my own.

But Buzz, a true zealot, somehow decided the Fates had sent me to his rescue. A few days later he telephoned to say he was coming around in a car—I simply had to go out to Long Island with him and at least have a look at the experimental film. As soon as I hung up, I called Smitty in self-defense. When I had filled him in on the background, I said, "How about it, will you come out to Oyster Bay with me?"

He was agreeable, but added he'd like to bring a chap along whom he was trying to help and who at the moment had a musical show on Broadway—but was flat broke. This producer turned out to be a man I had never met, an exuberant, all-flags-flying showman named Mike Todd. When we arrived at the Oyster Bay studio I got another shock. I found the inventor of what we were to see was Fred Waller, a movie engineer I'd worked with back in the twenties, when I did a travel-adventure series for Paramount. He was, not to mince words, a wizard. Nominally, he had been in charge of Paramount's special effects department, but in truth he was their all-around troubleshooter, a genius at solving the most intricate technical problems. Little did any of us realize we were about to launch a new era in motion pictures comparable to the advent of sound or color film.

Todd in those days—long, long before *Around the World in Eighty Days,* long before he married Elizabeth Taylor—had by chance met my manager Frank Smith, to Mike's great good fortune. John Chapman, the critic, once described Todd as having "the soul of a carnival pitchman and the ambition of a Napoleon." He was living proof that such extravagant spirits are born, not made. At fourteen he was already promoting "Lost Our Lease" and "Must Vacate" sales for small shopkeepers. By the time he was twenty he had gone through two fortunes, a pattern he was unable to break out of for all his subsequent flamboyant show business successes. In a flurry of legerdemain, the profits would vanish and rare indeed was the backer who ever came away from a Mike Todd show with anything but memories.

This did nothing for Mike's reputation. Everyone credited him with originality, enormous drive and enough gall to intimidate a firing squad—the arch-promoter—but he must have been poor on follow-through, so that what came out on the far end, more often than not, was trouble. And trouble was what Mike had plenty of by the early 1950s. He had filed a petition for bankruptcy, but was unable to get a discharge of his debts because he could produce no records. All but hamstrung, he was trying to transact business using his son as a dummy.

Then Mike ran into the incredible Frank Smith, and his fortunes took a turn for the better. Smitty, who liked nothing so much as the challenge of a sow's ear and the promise of a silk purse, got Todd back on his financial feet, then sold him to Long Island State Park Commissioner Robert Moses as producer of a $400,000 extravaganza called *A Night in Venice* for the new Marine Stadium at Jones Beach.

Only a few months before, when he had a musical extravaganza playing at the Ziegfeld Theatre, he invited the Smiths and my wife and me to his show, and also for dinner. As always he did things with a flourish. Wanting Fran and Helen to have orchids, he had to borrow a few bucks from Smitty to cover the flowers and the dinner at the St. Regis. Mike was an incurable optimist, and an almost irresistible one.

He told me his real name was Avram Hirsch Goldbogen, and at an early age he changed it because he thought such a long one might be a handicap. Mike was one of the most fascinating and attractive men I ever knew.

He would do almost anything to get publicity. Recently, when vandals took his remains out of the vault, some who knew him said: "I wonder if Mike himself arranged it?" Of course he didn't, but some of the things he did, for publicity, were unbelievable.

Meanwhile, Fred Waller was closing in on his longtime dream, his wide-screen peripheral vision invention. He was no basement tinkerer, but an authentic mechanical and photographic genius with an impressive list of practical and timely inventions to his credit, from water skis to the Photo-Metric camera that measured a man for a suit of clothes in a fiftieth of a second.

"Fred," said a friend once, "is the sort of fellow who goes out to the barn to build a kitchen shelf and winds up inventing a better nail, a special hammer and a new kind of screwdriver."

Once, when Paramount needed a scene of a young couple clutching each other on the bow of a sinking liner, Waller built a model ship, put two tiny objects in the bow and shot the sequence. The producers were enthralled: How had he gotten those miniatures to move, wave their arms and gesture with such desperation? By trusting in the human imagination, Waller replied. The figures hadn't moved at all. They were two shapeless lumps of clay that didn't even resemble people. But Waller knew that the brains, not the eyes of the audience would give them shape and motion.

"I had learned," he later told us, "that sight is largely an experiential phenomenon. The eye lens actually paints a crude picture on the retina. The brain then fills in the details it knows from experience should be there."

In 1939, Waller was asked by the Eastman Kodak company to create a motion picture display for the inside of the Perisphere, a gigantic globe 180 feet in diameter which, with the sleek Trylon, became the symbol of the New York World's Fair. What he did was nothing less than revolutionary, designing a theater with eleven projectors which enabled the audience to stand on a turning platform and gave the illusion that the picture was revolving three hundred and sixty degrees around them.

Now Waller had the essential clue to his revolutionary movies. "I had been using flat screen because that's what I was used to," he said. "But of course a person sees a curved view in real life."

His Perisphere concept gave him the opportunity to project images on a curved screen, virtually enveloping the audience. But before he could perfect and present this epochal idea as a wholly new entertainment form, World War II was upon us and Waller was called upon to adapt it to a more pressing need, the aerial gunnery trainer. It proved to be indispensable, so Washington later said, and materially quickened the training process. Seated in a gun pit, airmen in training were surrounded by a huge spherical screen on which synchronized projectors threw movies of enemy planes, zooming, diving, attacking. In a realistic situation, the trainee was called on to think quickly, aim and fire away. By the time he had climbed into a real plane, he had had not only target practice that was just next to the real thing, but the emotional experience of attacking and being attacked. What Fred did was credited with saving the lives of thousands of our airmen.

Once the war was over, Waller was free at last to strive toward the crowning achievement of his brilliant career. Refining his earlier techniques, he experimented with multi-lens cameras, varying numbers of projects and louvered screens that would absorb distorting reflections and deflect them harmlessly to the rear. Ultimately, he settled on three projectors facing a curved screen seventy-five feet wide and twenty-six feet high. The result was that the audience's peripheral vision was totally engaged, in exactly the same way that a man crossing a city street sees, not only what lies directly before him, but approaching traffic from the left and right. Waller's new process, for the first time in history, took a picture out of its conventional prescribed limits —the frame of a painting, the thirty-five millimeters of a typical film strip—and offered very nearly all that the human eye was capable of encompassing. People in the audience would not be viewers but participants; instead of bringing the outside world to man, the process could take man to the most distant reaches of earth and let him experience for himself what was happening there.

And this process Waller called Cinerama.

Fred Waller realized that if Cinerama was to be graphic enough to do this, to pull the audience right into the picture, it would have to be linked with a totally new kind of sound, one that would wrap itself around the ear as the picture wrapped itself around the eye. It was at this point that Waller turned to Buzz Reeves, whom he had met while working on the Perisphere exhibit.

By that time, Buzz Reeves had already built himself a record as a gifted and creative sound engineer, as well as a resourceful entrepreneur. It didn't take him long to see the potential in Waller's process. He not only agreed to take on the task of developing the multi-dimensional sound that was needed, but he did "buy out the Rockefellers" and all the restless sponsors who had backed Waller to that point. Then he went to work.

What Reeves wanted for Cinerama's sound track was what Waller had given it for a picture—sound that came from all directions, as it does in real life, sound that would move from place to place with the action on the screen, sound so good it would be virtually indistinguishable from the real thing. For two years, working with the best engineers in the business, he designed and built special equipment, keeping what worked and discarding the rest. Eventually he evolved a system of nine microphones, extremely high fidelity amplifiers and the same number of magnetic oxide sound tracks that could be stripped right onto the edge of standard motion picture film. The result was omni-directional sound of near-flawless quality. It had what sound experts call "presence," another way of saying it was as good as being on the spot when the action happened. Later surrealist artist Christopher Young described the combination as "more real than real." Reeves' sound was no mere adjunct to the Cinerama picture—it was a full-fledged partner.

There followed a series of test reels and a procession of movie moguls to the Oyster Bay studio, all of whom gaped at what they saw, absolutely captivated, but too intimidated by Cinerama's radical departure from the tried-and-true to take a chance on it—too costly for presentation in the thousands of neighborhood theaters in which they were interested. I suffered no such inhibitions when our turn came. I took one look and was convinced Cinerama was, quite simply, the most spectacular form of entertainment I had ever seen. "Buzz," I said, "you and Waller have a gold mine."

"I know that," he replied, "but nobody wants to help me cash in on it and I can't do it alone."

I turned to Smitty: "What do you think?"

"Lowell," he said, "why don't you start thinking about the kind of Cinerama film you want to do and leave me here to see if I can work out some arrangement with Reeves?"

When Smitty began talking that way, you could consider the deal locked up. What he worked out was an option that gave us as our end of it a newly formed company called Cinerama Productions Corporation with exclusive rights to the process for one year. We agreed to produce a show and to purchase from Reeves' company, Cinerama, Incorporated, all the equipment theaters would require.

Clearly this was going to take more than small change, at any rate more than any of us carried loose in his pocket. But Smitty didn't regard this as an insuperable problem, and indeed it wasn't. He simply got busy on the telephone and called a few friends, the conversation going something like this: "Hello, Governor Edison, Lowell Thomas and I are going into a new movie process called Cinerama and I've got you down for twenty-five thousand dollars. Send me your check when it's convenient." And such was the style of Smitty's friends, so absolute their confidence in him, that in twenty-four hours he raised $950,000.

Where did Mike Todd figure in all this? Although he had never had anything to do with motion pictures, he was infinitely resourceful and, considering the novelty of our venture, we agreed that a measure of gall might be a most useful asset on our side. So, in exchange for some stock we decided to make Todd our P. T. Barnum.

I was to be the producer, and my first decision was that nothing should be done to take the spotlight away from the wonder of Cinerama itself. I wanted no star performers or spectacular drama to capture the audience's attention. If Charlie Chaplin had offered to do *Hamlet* for us I'd have turned him down. I didn't want people judging Chaplin or rediscovering Shakespeare; in this case, not the play, but Waller's miracle process was the thing. The advent of something as new and important as Cinerama was a major event in the history of entertainment and I was determined to let nothing upstage it.

Toward that end, my choice for director of our first presentation was the grand old man of nonfiction films, Robert L. Flaherty, celebrated for such classics as *Nanook of the North* and *Moana of the South Seas*. And Flaherty was every bit as enthusiastic about the possibilities as we were, but unhappily, just as he was about to go to work, he suffered a heart attack and died. Under pressure to get started, improvising, we re-shot the roller coaster sequence Waller had made as one of his test films, one that would have women screaming in the theater and men white-knuckling the arms of their seats.

Every year there are many glorious festivals in Europe, so Fran and I hurried over in search of spectacles especially suitable for Cinerama's all-encompassing eye. We found them everywhere—in Scotland, the first gathering of the clans in 200 years; in Salzburg, a theatrical music festival; in Spain, a bull fight and a fiesta; in Venice, a panorama on the canals and a water extravaganza; in Milan, the most splendid opera house in the world. Ready to fire all guns, I telephoned New York and sent for Todd, a crew and all our ponderous equipment. Mike handled the all-important problem of getting cooperation. It was Harry Squires, our ace cameraman, who was responsible for the superb footage we came up with, with Mike pulling a master coup at La Scala in Milan.

Never had cameras been permitted inside those sacrosanct halls. And even assuming we could overcome such a formidable obstacle, how much would it cost to film the world's most prestigious opera company, where would we get the lights—and where would we get that kind of money? Enter Mike Todd, blue-eyed, five-feet-eight and 160 pounds of sheer *chutzpah*, requesting an interview with the managing director of the La Scala opera. For the first twenty minutes he talks about the miracle of Cinerama, its spectacular newness, the smashing impact it is going to make on the entertainment world, the millions upon millions who will come, and come again, to be enthralled by it.

La Scala? Yes, well, a marvelous opera company, perhaps the world's finest, and too bad it is so little appreciated in the United States because it is so little known. In New York and Chicago, perhaps Los Angeles, the *cognoscenti* know La Scala's reputation, yes, but they are a mere handful. Whereas the name of Cinerama will soon be on the lips of two hundred million Americans.

I can just see Mike hunching forward at this point, screwing up that marvelously expressive face in sudden thought.

Perhaps a segment of a La Scala opera *would* be a useful thing for the first Cinerama production. And in any case, he would be willing to do it for the sake of spreading the fame of the great opera company. But there were a few things: the opera must be the opulent *Aida;* full provision would have to be made for the Cinerama crew and their equipment; and to make the occasion appropriately important, the audience—how many could La Scala hold? Two thousand?—would have to be specially invited and, of course, dressed in full evening regalia—gowns, white tie, tails.

Stupefied, bewitched, the managing director agreed. Not a word was said about a fee for La Scala—and, indeed, no fee was ever paid, not a cent. And the half hour we shot of *Aida,* with its magnificent scenery and six hundred players, became one of the highlights of our first production. It was a stunningly beautiful sequence, and some of the most stunning shots of all were of that elite, white-tie audience.

We all returned to New York with visions of glory and reels of spectacular material. But once it was edited down to its obvious best, we realized we had only half a show. Todd, although taken aboard as a pitchman, not a director, was more than willing to go out and arrange for the additional sequences we needed. But Mike was now beginning to present us with some problems—when I say "us" I mean Frank Smith, who was handling our finances and nearly all business details, leaving the production end to me. There being few secrets in show business, Todd's creditors, and they were multifarious, hearing of his connection with our Cinerama group, descended on us like locusts in the seventeenth year. Every other phone call was from someone wanting to know when Mike Todd was going to pay up, and our waiting room began to look like a rest home for people trying to collect on the debts he owed them.

Although that was annoying enough to drive genial Smitty up the wall, the real trouble loomed when we began making preparations to float a stock issue in order to raise the capital necessary to equip additional theaters—so far, we were set only at the Broadway Theater in New York—as our contract with Reeves obliged us to do. Literally everybody was raving about Cinerama, and Wall Street was most receptive. But one small hitch developed: Mike Todd's reputation had preceded him—

and consequently us—and at first we could find no reputable brokerage house willing to do business with an outfit of which one Michael Todd was a member.

Some painful days followed, for it had obviously become necessary to negotiate a divorce. This nobody enjoyed. But anyone who felt sorry for Mike Todd underestimated the resourceful entrepreneur. He walked away with a handsome block of Cinerama stock, which skyrocketed immediately after our New York opening, and which he soon used to advance a competitive venture, the Todd A-O wide-screen process. And this led him directly to the fame and fortune of *Around the World in Eighty Days* and his histrionic marriage to Elizabeth Taylor.

After Frank Smith ousted Mike, and after the death of Bob Flaherty, who I had hoped would direct our first show, in my book there was only one other giant in the field of the nonfiction film. His name was Merian C. Cooper and someday they'll be making a movie about *his* life. A World War I fighter pilot with the Lafayette Escadrille, Coop went over to Poland after the Armistice to fly for Paderewski's free forces against the Russians. Shot down and imprisoned in deepest Siberia, he would have been executed except that on the night before the event was scheduled, he walked out of camp and kept walking until he reached China, eventually reduced to eating his shoes while crossing that vast and empty expanse.

Having survived, Coop figured he was now living on borrowed time and resolved, first, to do some good in the world and, second, to enjoy himself. How he succeeded! In 1925 he made the unforgettable film he and his pal Schoedsack called *Grass*, an account of the migrating Bakhtiari tribe of Persia, followed by *Chang, Four Feathers*, and then in 1932 he saved RKO-Radio from bankruptcy by writing and producing *King Kong*, one of the most popular films ever made. Even now, more than four decades later, it is still being put on in theaters right around the world. But it may be that Coop's most satisfying achievement was reclaiming John Ford, a once-great director who had lost himself in the bottle, by hiring him to direct *Stagecoach*. Ford's subsequent successes are now a film world legend, but he would have died a lost and forgotten soul without Coop's faith and helping hand.

During World War II, Coop had been a flying general

with Chennault in Burma and China, and later with Kenney in the Pacific, and now, in the sunset years of a fabulous life, he was unwinding on the West Coast. We had been friends ever since World War I, and when I flew out to Hollywood to see him, before I could say a word his first remark was, "Lowell, I think you have come to save the motion picture industry." This was when half the theaters in America were dark. Why he had such a wild hunch I don't know. Of course, he was wrong, because Cinerama was not a movie in the accepted meaning of the word. It was an entirely new form of screen entertainment—not even a competitor.

But I knew what he meant. In the first postwar years, the movies had enjoyed the greatest boom they'd ever known. But by 1950, the danger flags were flying and theaters were closing down all over the country. Television, the newest entertainment phenomenon, had captured the motion picture audiences and was keeping them glued to the small screen in the living room. Desperate, the studios searched for some way to lure people back into the movie theaters. No one guessed that Cinerama might be their answer—and it wasn't. At any rate Coop flew East with me, saw what we had done in Europe, was just as enthusiastic about it as Bob Flaherty had been, and played a major role in directing more sequences here at home.

On the evening of September 30, 1952, an audience of critics, opinion-makers and celebrities filed into the Broadway Theater north of Times Square for the premiere of our first production, *This Is Cinerama*. It opened with a prologue in which I appeared on a traditional screen. Then the vast curtains drew back to reveal the immensity of the great curving Cinerama screen for the first time. From that instant the audience was ours, and the word of what had come to pass was first-page news around the world. We had launched the "Wide-screen Era."

There was no three-dimensional gimmick. Instead, Cinerama brought the theater and everyone in it directly into the action. *You* were seated in the front car of that soon-to-be-famous roller coaster, diving down into the head-snapping turns and thrown back in your seat when it climbed abruptly. *You* were in the bubble nose of our B-25 bomber as Hollywood's number one stunt man, Paul Mantz, took us hedgehopping over America's natural glories—Niagara Falls, the golden wheat fields of our Midwest breadbasket, the Rocky Mountains, Crater Lake and the Grand Canyon. *You* stood unseen in a bullring in Spain as close to the snorting bull as the toreador. *You* marched amidst a thousand Scottish bagpipers and were an invisible spear carrier in the brilliant La Scala version of *Aida*.

And all the while Buzz Reeves' wondrous innovative sound track was engulfing the audience with five speakers behind the screen and additional speakers on the side and rear walls. Hence, when a motor boat raced across the screen in the dazzling Cypress Gardens sequence you heard the roar of its motor as each of the mikes successively picked up the traveling sound and sent it across your field of vision in perfect synchronization with the speeding boat.

There was no nervous gathering of the backers at Sardi's to await the reviews that momentous first night. We knew from the tumultuous response of the audience—those who were not too emotionally drained and dazed by the experience stood on their seats and cheered—that our triumph was more sweeping than we had ever dared hope. Publisher Arthur Sulzberger rushed up the aisle past me, hurried over to the New York *Times*, and for the first time ever told his editors what they should use as a front-page story. Richard Rodgers, backstage, told me the music surpassed anything he had ever heard, the way it came from all parts of the theater.

Perhaps it would not be inappropriate to quote a few among the hundreds of critical comments that flooded the press in the next week or so:

New York *Herald Tribune*: The world is hailing Cinerama. This radical advance in the science of the cinema industry . . .
deserves the adjectives that are customarily associated with circus press agents—super-colossal, terrific, stupendous.

Kate Cameron, New York *Daily News*: . . . . the like of it has never before been projected on the screen.

Robert Sullivan, Sunday *News*: Practically every place in the world—except maybe Russia which hasn't yet got around to taking credit for it—has heard of Cinerama by this time.

Bosley Crowther, New York *Times*: People sat back in spellbound wonder as the scenic program flowed across the screen. It was really as though most of them were seeing motion pictures for the first time.

Frank Farrell, New York *World-Telegram and Sun*: Cinerama's opening roller coaster sequence packed such realism in its celeb premiere last evening that my bride, NBC's Ted Cott, *Collier's* Ed Anthony and others around me closed their eyes and wished they had brought dramamine.

Rose Pelswick, New York *Journal-American*: The most important step in motion picture history since the advent of sound.

Archer Winsten, New York *Post*: Incomparably more powerful than anything yet viewed on a screen.

George E. Sokolsky, New York *Journal-American*: It could save this industry; it could fill large theaters.

Columnist John S. Van Gilder: Cinerama has knocked Broadway-ites silly! This brand new entertainment form, brought to us by Lowell Thomas, is as amazing as the first motion pictures, talkies, radio or television. Its future seems fabulous. Long double lines of sidewalk ticket buyers are virtually stampeding the Broadway Theater box office day and night.

H. E. C. Bryant, Charlotte (N.C.) *Observer*: To witness Cinerama is worth the cost of a trip to New York and back.

And it was precisely the same when Cinerama opened in Detroit, Los Angeles, San Francisco, London, Paris, Milan, Tokyo, Rio de Janeiro, Melbourne, Sydney and other major cities around the world. Financially, it was a blockbuster, a success unparalleled in the history of entertainment. And this despite the fact that, unlike the average film which shows in perhaps 20,000 theaters, or twice that number, Cinerama, because of the initial large investment required for special screen and sound equipment, showed in fewer than forty.

This Is Cinerama ran on Broadway for two and a half years and broke every known record for income and total audience. The three productions in which I was to be involved, *This Is Cinerama, The Seven Wonders of the World* and *Search for Paradise*, together grossed more than $130 million worldwide, and the first two, breaking records wherever they were shown, are still on the list of *Variety's* "All-time Rental Champs."

The human response, perhaps even more than this accounting of the huge sums it earned, tells something of Cinerama's enormous worldwide impact, its revolutionary effect on the motion picture industry which now went wide-screen almost everywhere in an attempt to make the public believe they also had processes to rival Cinerama. In Thailand, an eager public broke down a wall erected to hold back throngs of ticket buyers. At the Damascus trade fair, crowds rioted to get tickets and the pretentious Soviet exhibit was so eclipsed by Cinerama that it closed its doors.

One night in New York, during the intermission, a man came up to tell me of an experience he had just had. The woman in front of him was wearing a rather large hat. When he asked her to remove it, she muttered, "Later, can't you see I'm in the picture?"

Two airmen back from Korea were sitting together. During our canyon flying sequence one of them said: "I'm leaving. I can't take it!" To which his pal replied, "Don't go now or you will be killed."

It was all downhill after that. We had an incomparable triumph. But this was one of those cases where art ran head on into life, personified in this instance by businessmen, money men and con men. A basic dilemma surfaced when we set out to equip additional theaters for the Cinerama process. According to our contract with Reeves, we had one year to do this, and though the money was pouring in from our New York oil gusher, the amounts now called for were staggering. At least $250,000 for each theater was required to anchor the three projection booths in concrete and to pay for the huge louvered screen and sophisticated stereophonic sound. It was decided that in order to raise the necessary funds, a public stock issue would have to be floated, for which we turned to Wall Street.

Meanwhile, two things happened. First, my colleagues, in a burst of panic, voted to call in a man who had been referred to as "The Pope of Hollywood," Louis B. Mayer, to sit in as president of Cinerama. This was done to impress and reassure the bankers. What it did, in fact, was mire us in a fatal delay. The once-legendary L. B., aging, tired, seemed unable to make up his mind about anything, and while we debated, Rome burned.

Meanwhile Cinerama had had a galvanizing effect on the "majors," the big Hollywood studios which had originally scorned it. Now that they felt their noses rubbed in its tremendous success and could smell all that money in the making, they went scrambling all over the laboratories looking for what they hoped would be a comparable film process.

First the movie-going public was deluged with a plethora of horror films and cheap melodramas shown in something called 3-D, which required the viewer to wear special glasses. Then Twentieth Century-Fox struck pay ore with a process that had been kicking around since its development by the Frenchman Henri Chrétien in 1928. Refurbished and trotted out to meet what studio head Spyros Skouras now saw as a life-and-death threat by Cinerama—which he had personally turned down only two years before—it was rechristened CinemaScope and, with great fanfare, Skouras and Zanuck and David O. Selznick announced that Lloyd C. Douglas' best-selling novel, *The Robe*, would be the first film to be shot with their new marvel.

Never mind that it wasn't really new, or comparable to Cinerama in any significant way. (What it was was another oblong, essentially flat picture, wider than most.) But once *The Robe* hoopla reached Wall Street—and my longtime colleague Spyros made certain it did—our financiers turned and ran, exercising a contract clause that gave them the option to back out in case of "changed circumstances."

Now we were in real trouble. Theater equipment had been ordered and more was called for by our contract with Reeves. Our original group of founders had dwindled—Fred Waller, the gentle, bespectacled genius who started it all, had died before he even knew of his triumph; Mike Todd was busy hustling and working with American Optical on the process to be called Todd A-O; and when we went to Reeves and asked for an extension of time in which to raise the necessary money, his acquisitive instinct prevailed and the answer was no. Arrayed against Smitty, Merian Cooper and me were men of wealth who had gone into Cinerama solely for the investment possibilities, and at this critical juncture, either unwilling to go looking for the additional cash or simply ready to take their already large profits, they opted to sell out.

The buyer was the Stanley-Warner company, and from a purely practical viewpoint, maybe the decision was not all wrong. In making it we all made a lot of money. But the bells began toll-ing for Cinerama then and there. Stanley-Warner was a brassiere manufacturing corporation, plus owners of a major theater chain. But they were not film producers. Their immediate instinct was to use Cinerama to make another *Gone With the Wind,* overlooking the fact that Cinerama with a nonfiction theme had already outgrossed *GWTW,* until then the all-time top money-maker. They wanted a plot. They wanted a love story—boy meets girl à la Hollywood. They didn't really know what Cinerama was all about.

When they went to Hollywood looking for a producer, they got a cold shoulder—every Hollywood studio was thrashing around trying to develop its own wide-screen process. And so, with their theaters going dark one by one, the Stanley-Warner people telephoned me to ask if I would make another Cinerama feature for them—on my own terms. At first they had thought of me as a radio personality and knew nothing of the world tour I had made with my Allenby-Lawrence, Palestine-Arabia production many years before.

This Is Cinerama had been full of familiar scenes shown in a spectacular new way. For the second production, I was eager to take off for faraway places and show something strange and exotic through the Cinerama lenses. Of the ancient Seven Wonders of the World, all but the pyramids had been obliterated either by vandals or by the ravages of time. But now that we had the revelation of Cinerama, why not seek out the seven wonders of the modern world? In fact, I made no effort to limit it to seven —I would leave it to our audiences to make their own list from the riches we hoped to offer. With Pan Am pilot Willie Smith, and our stunt flyer, Paul Mantz, I simply plotted a random, zigzag course around the globe, ready to pick up where the Greeks of antiquity had left off, flying on to wherever the next marvel beckoned us.

One morning in 1955, as dawn broke in the eastern sky, two airplanes revved their engines and took off. They were strange craft indeed. One was a converted World War II B-25 bomber with a huge three-eyed camera in its nose. Flown by daredevil Mantz, it bore a freshly-painted American flag on its side and the words, "Seven Wonders of the World Expedition."

To properly demonstrate the spirit of adventure with which we set out, Mantz flew *under* all the bridges across the East River before climbing into the sky.

The second plane, a chartered Pan American airliner renamed "Cinerama Clipper," was to serve as our traveling base. I had decided that in place of a fixed script, we would follow a kind of leapfrog system, shooting what most appealed to us as the opportunity presented itself. To do this, several different directors were engaged and the Clipper "Cinerama" became each one's home, workshop and studio while he was shooting his particular segment.

First we set a course for South America, where we flew right up to the face of the flat-topped mountain in Venezuela from which the loftiest falls in the world plunges into the valley, the one named for Jimmy Angel, the American bush pilot who discovered it. We also were just in time for the annual carnival in Rio. Then on from the world's most spectacular harbor, across the South Atlantic to film the mysterious Mountains of the Moon, the live volcanoes of equatorial Africa, breathtaking Victoria Falls where the Zambesi forces its way into a narrow canyon, there to explode in misty clouds and endless rainbows. We of course included the magnificent wildlife of Kenya and Tanganyika. On a river teeming with crocodiles and hippopotamuses, our camera crew was edging toward shore to get close-ups of trumpeting elephants when a hippo emerged from under the barge and tore a chunk from the side. The cameras ground on.

North we flew for an aerial visit to Mount Sinai and a tour of the Holy Land such as no previous audience had ever seen— to the accompaniment of a choir of one hundred voices. On and on we went, with the planes preceded by Lowell, Jr., pre-spotting the wonders and excitement of distant lands.

In a valley just south of the great Arabian desert, half a world from New York, we came upon an almost unknown skyscraper city—Shibām, in the Hadramaut. Then we probed deeper into this land of frankincense and myrrh for a visit with a prince of the desert, Sherif Hussein, who staged a camel charge for us with a thousand dromedaries.

All through the filming of the sequence in the Wadi Beihan, a wild and lawless country once ruled by the Queen of Sheba, machine guns kept the Cinerama crew covered from morning to dusk. Still farther north, we filmed the new world changing the old: oil derricks pumping wealth from an ocean of oil beneath the sands—a million dollars a day for Ibn Saud, a modern Arabian Nights king. On to India we went, where we filmed the holy city of Benares on the Ganges, a temple dance and the inevitably fatal fight between a cobra and a mongoose.

The moon was high when we visited the Taj Mahal. Brilliantly it shone, an ethereal vision in white marble. As our crew stood beside the lily pool, I told them the story of Mogul Emperor Shah Jahan and his beautiful queen, how he spent a fortune beyond estimate and half a lifetime erecting this matchless tomb to fill the emptiness of his own soul; and how he had dreamed of building an identical tomb of black marble across the Jumna River; how his throne was seized by his son, who then imprisoned the Emperor nearby, but allowed him to spend the remainder of his days gazing out at the most stunning building in the world.

At the immense Angkor Wat temple in Cambodia, soldiers were again assigned to guard us because just a few miles away, in Vietnam, there was guerrilla fighting.

Our army of supervisors, accountants, shipping clerks and stevedores had their own adventures in keeping the planes going. The camera crews had intricate, all but irreplaceable equipment, and film shipments had to be made according to exacting standards, insulated from the elements and cooled with dry ice. Communications with our base at home were erratic at best, yet crucial. A cameraman in Mantz's plane told of impatiently waiting for reports on some film footage he had shipped back. Had it arrived? Was it okay? Finally a cablegram reached him in the African jungle. "Merry Christmas and a Happy New Year to all," it said.

We filmed the harbor at Naples, Mount Vesuvius and the Leaning Tower of Pisa, reaching Rome for the final ceremonies of the Marian Year. There we conceived a poignant but humorous story of three pilgrims, Giovanni, Maria and their bambino, riding a motor scooter along the Appian Way. They are hoping to receive the Papal blessing at St. Peter's. Always late, they miss the ceremony, the procession of the Pope and the blessing.

On they go to Castel Gandolfo, the Pope's summer residence, arriving just in time, as His Holiness, Pope Pius XII, gives a special benediction.

In Castel Gandolfo, we had our chance to film the famous Swiss Guards in their colorful uniforms, and then the Pope himself. Our crew erected a platform on a level with the balcony from which His Holiness would speak in public audience, the massive Cinerama cameras within a few feet of his face. In pure white robes, on a balcony draped with red velvet tapestry, Pius recited the Latin blessing while our cameras turned. Stepping back into the room, the Pope began chatting with the kneeling crewmen, who were all but speechless.

"How did I do?" he asked in English.

"Great, sir," one of them managed, "just great."

"I'm not so sure," said Pius XII. "Let us do it over once more."

When the two Seven Wonder planes returned to America, more than forty small flags, one for each country we'd visited, had been painted on the B-25's side. As an epilogue, we filmed the familiar wonders of our own land: technological wonders— the Empire State Building, Hoover Dam and an oil well in a Texas front yard, and the wonders of nature—the Grand Canyon, Niagara Falls, ending with a Cineramic whirl through the giant redwoods of Yosemite, to the edges of a cliff and a vision that reveals the glory of these United States.

The Stanley-Warner people continued to play with the idea of using Cinerama as a fiction medium. They had two films made by others, *Cinerama Holiday* by Louis de Rochemont and *South Sea Adventure* by Carl Dudley. Both included fiction sequences for which Cinerama was not the appropriate medium. Cinerama was—and is—ideal for nonfiction because it gives the audience the unique experience of actual participation. For fiction any motion picture screen—small, large or elongated—can tell your story effectively. A year or so later, still baffled, still groping for an answer, Stanley-Warner asked me to do a third Cinerama production, *Search for Paradise*; like the first two, it was a smashing success.

But why nonfiction—even if the subject is great—should attract huge audiences has always been a mystery to nearly everyone in the motion picture business. The whole idea disturbed them; and for this they should not be criticized. After all, if you are working with a fiction subject, you can control nearly every element—the script, the actors, the sets, the locations —a sort of control not possible on a nonfiction picture. In the latter you are dealing with the real world, which is not always accommodating. You cannot pay a hippo to take a bite out of your barge on cue. There seldom is an opportunity to retake a crucial scene. Such uncertainty frightens the money men, and rightly so.

It was also what worried the top brass at Stanley-Warner. In spite of the success of my two productions for them, they did not understand the medium. They were even puzzled by the audiences Cinerama attracted. I heard them say, "Who are these people? We've never seen them before." So before long they too took their profits and sold out.

This time Fred Waller's marvelous process fell into the hands of a colorful international entrepreneur, one Nick Reisini, who did a natural thing. He began thinking of a possibly simpler, speedier way to make money with it. The solution he came up with was to exploit the fame of Cinerama by shelving the process altogether and selling the name, which by now had become famous around the world. He simply took ordinary motion pictures and relabeled them, using the phrase, "Presented by Cinerama." Thus, with one stroke he eliminated what had been our special cost of production and all the elaborate Cinerama equipment. But he also eliminated Cinerama.

Eventually William Forman, owner of perhaps the largest of all theater chains, came to own the process and equipment, but at last reports he too was nonplussed over the problems of relaunching Cinerama plus engaging in further research to eliminate its few faults. He did transfer *This Is Cinerama* to a single projector, single sound track and ordinary screen, and then rereleased it. But this proved to be a pale, watered-down version. It wasn't Cinerama.

So that's the story of the wonderful life and subsequent putting-on-the-shelf of one of the miracles of our time. There it sits in limbo, an entertainment genie, once more waiting to be freed. Obviously it would take a few million dollars to get it going again, but the prospective rewards could be astronomical.

It's a hundred-million-dollar bonanza awaiting an entrepreneur of vision and imagination and a sizable bankroll. Its creative possibilities, to this day, have not been matched. Perhaps it would also need a reincarnation of General Merian Cooper to revive it—and maybe a younger chap whose initials are L. T. and who in his mid-eighties would still like to play a part in one of the really thrilling adventures of our time, the launching of a worldwide revolution—the wide-screen era.

I'm sure some who read my much too brief account of Cinerama will think it a wild exaggeration when I say Cinerama could have been, and perhaps still can be, a billion-dollar entertainment phenomenon. You may ask, why was it allowed to fade away? Why doesn't someone relaunch it? How could it be brought back? What are the problems?

The inventor of it, Fred Waller, is no longer here to give us the benefit of his genius. Hazard Reeves, successful in other electronic fields, now along in years, is retired. Younger men would have to do the relaunching. How much would it cost to do this? I discussed this recently with Buzz Reeves and here was his summary of what would be involved: the unique Waller screen, although far more expensive than normal motion picture screens, he assured me could be made for $25,000 or less. The three projectors, although of course more expensive now than when Reisini abandoned the process and just marketed Cinerama's name and fame, could be installed for $100,000 or so.

After Waller's death, some of his associates went on with their research; Reeves says the three projectors could be concentrated into one and in so doing the process could be made even more satisfactory, with the impression of their being three screens eliminated.

Nearly everyone connected with Cinerama, with the exception of my wizard associate General Merian Cooper and myself, were baffled as to where product would come from. Everyone agreed it was the perfect medium for nonfiction—also, that you quickly would run out of subjects important enough for the vast Cinerama screen, for shows impressive enough to go for long runs of a year or more at each of the major cities of the world. So—what nonfiction subjects are there—subjects to attract both regular moviegoers and also the other half of the population, the nonmoviegoers?

Our first production, *This Is Cinerama*, was a runaway success. The same was true with my *Seven Wonders of the World*. But where do you find nonfiction subjects with such a universal appeal? I had several in mind. For one, I wanted to take a handsome four-masted sailing ship, such as the one Mrs. Merriweather Post Davies once owned, and make the ship the heroine of the show, on a visit to the most interesting and unusual islands in the world. Such a production would keep a director and crew busy for a year or more.

Live volcanoes have a fascination for all human beings. Of these there are a hundred or more in various parts of the world. I would like to see a Cinerama production feature the most interesting of these volcanoes, together with something about the life of the people who live near them, people who know their homes may be wiped out at any moment. There would be plenty of variety in such a production because the major live volcanoes are scattered far and wide, in the South Seas, the Mediterranean, the coast of eastern Siberia, equatorial Africa, the Andes and so on.

Another natural for Cinerama would be *From Cairo to Capetown*, to give audiences some concept of the vast continent of Africa, both above and below the Sahara. Think of the variety of material this could include!

And I have other suggestions. The opportunity is still there. If I were younger I would be only too glad once again to take on Cinerama, a medium that stunned the world when we presented our first *This Is Cinerama* in New York, London and some thirty other great cities—the medium that brought on the worldwide wide-screen revolution.

VI. Search for Paradise

Heat there is but hot 'tis not,
Cold there is, but cold 'tis not.
                —Kashmiri Poem

Once we sold out of Cinerama, Frank Smith and I began looking around for another venture. Toward the end of 1954, Frank's eye fell on what seemed to him a likely prospect, a radio and television station, WROW and WROW–TV, just outside Albany, New York, which had a weak signal and a balance sheet drowning in red ink. Read on and you will discover why I was far better off traveling, broadcasting and writing while Smitty handled our financial affairs.

We gathered in the office of our friend and attorney, Gerald Dickler, who saw at once that the radio station was holding its own, but that the TV station, on an ultra-high-frequency band, was suffering from the competition of another UHF station and the far more serious handicap of a powerful VHF station owned by General Electric. WROW's owners, all good local citizens, were slowly being bled white.

"What are you going to offer them, Smitty," Gerry asked, "ten cents on the dollar?"

"No, not at all," Smitty answered with his Tennessee drawl. "I'm going to offer them a hundred cents on the dollar, and anyone who wants to put some new money in on that basis is welcome to stay with us."

196

Gerry and I sat there waiting for the explanation. It was vintage Frank Smith. He had been studying the WROW situation for some time, he said, and in the course of his studies had found, about ten miles outside of Albany, what is known in the trade as a "white spot"—an area where a new VHF station could be dropped in without impinging on any other station's wavelength. Now, he went on, getting down to cases, if we could win the Federal Communications Commission's blessing to utilize that white spot by exchanging WROW's feeble UHF for a highly desirable VHF, and if we could then switch the station's network affiliation from ABC to CBS, which had much stronger programming and, in its president, Dr. Frank Stanton, a good friend to all of us, why, said Smitty, we'd be off and running.

"Now then," he finished slowly, triumphantly, "do we want those good people of Albany, who have invested so heavily in the U, running down to Washington while the FCC is considering our petition for a V, saying that a bunch of New York sharpies had taken them for a ride?"

We didn't, and they didn't. In fact, many of those good people stayed in with us and all, without exception, testified in our favor. And that was the beginning of Capital Cities Communications, with Frank Smith its president and guiding genius.

He was indeed a remarkable man. Though he often reached his goals by circular routes, his first precept of business was honesty, and time after time I saw him make a virtue of it. In later years, when we began acquiring other stations, he used to say that we could pay a little more than anyone else because we were better managers. But the hard rock foundation of all his business principles was that no deal was a good deal unless everyone walked away from the bargaining table happy.

He started working on the acquisition of WROW in the same straightforward way he had put together our earlier Cinerama deal, by calling some of his friends on the telephone. With my investment the largest single share, we soon had $900,000 to buy out the Albany interests. But it was still a chancy speculation and the way ahead remained far from smooth. The FCC deliberations dragged on—it would take two years before we had a decision—and meanwhile we had to pump fresh money transfusions into our staggering property, which, month by month, was being slowly strangled by General Electric's area-blanketing

V. In that wooded, hilly country, our transmissions were so weak that one autumn, when some listeners telephoned to congratulate us on our new tower, we were obliged to tell them that we hadn't built a new tower at all, that Mother Nature was responsible for their improved reception: the trees had shed their leaves.

Smitty, cutting corners with wild abandon, became an Albany legend. The huge, three-story frame building which housed our studio and transmitter fell in desperate need of a paint job. But since it backed on the Hudson River, Smitty ordered only the street side painted. Our equipment was so antiquated and run-down that when we were finally forced to replace it and offered it free to Rensselaer Polytechnic Institute in neighboring Troy, they politely declined.

In the meantime, all sorts of other intriguing things were happening. With our switch from an ABC to a CBS affiliation just about signed, the owners of the rival UHF station in Albany, which had had the CBS tie-in and was about to lose it, screamed as though they had been thrown into an Arizona cactus patch. The cream of this particular jest was that those owners happened to be the Stanley-Warner company, which had bought us out of Cinerama and for whom I was then shooting *The Seven Wonders of the World* as an independent producer.

"Gerry," wailed Nat Lapkin, Stanley-Warner's executive vice president, "how could Smitty do this to me? We're such good friends."

This did indeed put Dickler in an awkward position, for at that moment, he was in ticklish negotiations with Lapkin on a totally different matter on my behalf. It seems that I had used up the nearly million-dollar budget for *Seven Wonders* and the picture was still only half finished. At the same time that Stanley-Warner was going to court to stop WROW from moving over to CBS, Gerry was asking them for another $750,000 or thereabouts so I could finish *Seven Wonders*. It was, would you say, a delicate situation?

Stanley-Warner sued on the grounds that we had had a prior agreement with CBS when we bought WROW, which, if true, would have been a violation of FCC rules. Since it wasn't true, they lost the case, but some bad blood lingered between us and the negotiations over *Seven Wonders* dragged on without resolution. Came the Lincoln's Birthday holiday of 1955 and

Gerry found himself under pressure on the home front. He had promised his wife a Jamaica vacation and she sensibly considered that more important than Lowell Thomas' contract troubles.

"Are we going or aren't we?" said Ruth Dickler in *that* tone.

"Yes," replied Gerry, who had decided to make a virtue of necessity, "we are going."

Next day, he marched into Nat Lapkin's office and declared, "Nat, you can have half a picture and an action against Lowell if that's what you want. Or you can come up with the additional money and have a completed picture. You decide— I'm going to Jamaica." And he stalked out.

Now Nat Lapkin, though temporarily smarting from his wounds, was essentially a decent and sensible man. Gerry's dramatic little walkout gave him the time he needed to reflect on life's realities and by the time the Dicklers' vacation was ended, the additional money for *Seven Wonders* was ready and waiting. It was a decision Lapkin never regretted: the picture was a grand slam success and Stanley-Warner reaped a handsome return on their investment, not to mention critical kudos for having the artistic integrity to see it through.

I would have reason to be suspicious of the latter. Around the time I completed *Seven Wonders*, a new production of the Negro folk opera, *Porgy and Bess*, starring two newcomers, Leontyne Price and William Warfield, was making a sensational hit in Dallas, Texas. As soon as I saw it, I decided here was one piece of theater that could prove the exception to my belief that only nonfiction worked in Cinerama. For one thing, Rouben Mamoulian's superb set of Catfish Row was naturally laid out in three parts, divided just about the way the Cinerama screen was divided, with the same breaks and even the same angulation. We only needed to photograph the stage production, a relatively quick and inexpensive procedure, to put the audience right inside Catfish Row, with that magnificent George Gershwin score resounding all around them.

I immediately took an option on the rights for $100,000, then Gerry and I went to see Nat Lapkin, who thought the idea superb. On we moved to the office of Si Fabian, president of Stanley-Warner. He appeared to be listening closely as we outlined the plan, emphasizing how Leontyne Price and William

Warfield had captivated Dallas and the Southwestern heartland. Then he tapped his shiny desk with well-manicured fingers, this real estate operator who had apparently learned nothing of films or entertainment in a career devoted to buying up movie theaters, and he said, "Yeah, well who's gonna want to spend two and a half hours looking at a bunch of coons?"

Sickened, Gerry and I walked out. And here is the kicker: after Fabian's time, Stanley-Warner did do a *Porgy and Bess* in Cinerama—and paid the Gershwin family a million dollars for the rights.

During all this time, Smitty was working hard to keep our Capital Cities ship afloat. It was not beneath his dignity to go out and try to sell a little advertising, no easy matter considering our pallid signal and hefty competition. But he was paying a purely social call when he stopped in to see an old friend, Stan Resor, head of the J. Walter Thompson agency. In answer to Resor's polite query about what was new, Smitty allowed as how he and L. T. and a few others had bought a dinky little TV operation in Albany, and the signal wasn't worth a damn, but if they ever pried their V out of the FCC, it would be a new ball game.

"Well, look," said Resor, a true gentleman, "let me give you some business. Let me give you some General Electric spots."

"I'm afraid you can't do that, Stan," responded Smitty. "General Electric is our biggest competitor up there."

"The hell I can't," said Resor, and did. And those spots helped us survive.

Well, not to overdo the suspense, we did finally win our VHF from the FCC and Capital Cities took off. Smitty went after stations in Durham, North Carolina, and Providence, Rhode Island; then we really spread out with acquisitions in Buffalo, Detroit, Los Angeles, Houston and Fort Worth, and a string of newspapers and trade papers, including Fairchild Publications, whose flagship is *Women's Wear Daily*, and later the Kansas City *Star*, one of the leading newspapers of America. We also had won a listing on the New York Stock Exchange, and anyone who stayed with us from the beginning has had many an opportunity for self-congratulation.

It was Smitty, every step of the way up, who ran the operation—Smitty who was so claustrophobic he wouldn't ride in an elevator, and so afraid of flying he sent Gerry Dickler to close all our out-of-town deals—Smitty who had the courage to hang on, and the sheer business acumen to build a major communications company out of a failing radio and TV station in upstate New York.

And it was Smitty who won for Capital Cities exclusive world rights to film (using my personally owned Odyssey Film Company, presided over by my colleague Milton Fruchtman, to do the job) the trial of Adolf Eichmann in Jerusalem. Though our production expenses were heavy, we promised the Israeli government that all profits earned from the use of the film, both in the United States and abroad, would go to charity. There was, however, no reason why we couldn't attempt to recover our $1,500,000 outlay, and Smitty tried to do this by getting the three television networks to share costs on an equal basis in exchange for free use of the trial tapes, which were to be flown back from Jerusalem daily.

The networks refused. Still smarting because they had lost out to Cap Cities in bidding for the rights in the first place, they decided to sit back and make us swallow those $1,500,000 production costs alone. But they had reckoned without Frank Smith, our resident wizard. Calling the networks' news vice-presidents together in Gerry Dickler's office, he said, "Gentlemen, you win. We'll pick up the tab. But I think you'll be interested to know that as soon as we're finished here, I am calling a news conference to announce that inasmuch as the three giants of American television—NBC, CBS and ABC—could not find it within their hearts to share our expenses, Capital Cities, as a public service, is making the film available to them free of charge."

Jim Hagerty looked at Dick Salant who looked at Bill Mc-Andrew who spoke for all of them: "How much do we owe you, Smitty? We give up."

Smitty had had a couple of heart attacks that he told nobody about. But he must have known the score, for he suddenly elevated himself to chairman of the board and installed Tom Murphy as president and chief operating officer of Cap Cities. Then, one day in 1965, he drove down to North Carolina to attend the funeral of a friend. On the way back, he stopped at a motel in Maryland and was hit by another heart attack. That one killed him. Everyone whose path he ever crossed took the loss personally, but Cap Cities rolled right along. Which is just the way Smitty planned it.

Early in 1955, a brief item in the New York *Times* caught my eye: there was to be a coronation in the Himalayan kingdom of Nepal in April, it said. That was about all, but I was instantly intrigued. Like Tibet, that other storybook kingdom it bordered in the farthest reaches of southwestern Asia, Nepal had been a model for James Hilton's Shangri-La in his book, *Lost Horizon*. It was a mysterious, exotic land whose mountain-locked frontiers had long been closed to Westerners. It was, in fact, so secluded from the rest of the world that our government didn't even have a consulate there, let alone an embassy. Yet I suppose for those reasons, from the time Lowell, Jr., and I had traveled to Tibet some years before, Nepal had been high on the list of forbidden places I longed to visit. Furthermore, it struck me that a coronation in that alien and alluring land might make a spectacular subject for Cinerama.

I went to the telephone and put in another call to Loy Henderson, the career diplomat who had been so helpful in the intricate behind-the-scenes negotiations that finally led the Dalai Lama to invite my son Lowell and me to visit Lhasa, the Tibetan capital. And it was a mark of Nepal's remoteness that though Henderson was now right-hand man in Washington to Secretary of State John Foster Dulles, he knew no more about the impending coronation than I did. But he promised to find out.

Indeed he did much better. "Lowell," he said when he called back a day or so later, "how would you like to attend the coronation in Nepal as President Eisenhower's personal ambassador?"

Of course I was elated. All I had really hoped for was Washington's approval and perhaps some help in winning permission from the Nepalese to film the coronation for Cinerama. That, too, would be arranged, Loy Henderson assured me, and I was to proceed with my transportation arrangements.

Probably it would have been bad luck if so ambitious an enterprise got off the ground without a hitch. Two shocks lay in wait for me, the first when, some weeks later in the midst of preparation, I picked up the *Times* and again saw a news item of particular interest to me: President Eisenhower had just appointed the renowned Minnesota surgeon, Dr. Charles Mayo, to represent him as ambassador at the coronation in Kathmandu, Nepal. Not wanting to embarrass Loy Henderson, this time I called Jim Hagerty, the President's press secretary, who a few days later instructed me to go right ahead with my plans; apparently there would be *two* American ambassadors at the coronation. Well, in the end there turned out to be three, for when I flew into Kathmandu I learned that Virginia Bacon, long prominent in the Republican Party, would also be joining us. And this was one time when it did turn out to be the more the merrier.

My second problem was not so easily solved. Our cumbersome equipment, plus a crew twice the size of the usual Hollywood production unit going on location, would need its own plane—a big one. But there turned out to be no plane available for charter. The airlines, then all awaiting delivery of the first jets, were struggling to keep their swelling ranks of passengers flying in older craft and not one—in America or Europe—was disposed to spare a plane for a charter flight.

Unwilling to let this golden opportunity slip out of my hands, I hurried to Washington and went to see the Secretary of the Air Force, Jim Douglas, who, by happy chance, had been one of my students at Princeton thirty-five years before. When I told him my problem and asked for the loan of an Air Force Globemaster, the largest airplane in the world, he smiled and said, "Lowell, I admire your enterprise, but I don't think even the Secretary of the Air Force has the authority to pass Globemasters around to private citizens."

My heart sank.

But Jim Douglas wasn't finished: "Suppose I invite the Chief of Staff and some of the other brass over here. Then I'll leave it to you to convince them that what you have in mind will be in the best interests of the Air Force. Maybe we can work something out."

I didn't have much time to think about how this was going to be accomplished, for a couple of hours later there I was back in Jim Douglas's office, this time surrounded by Air Force generals waiting to hear why they should lend me a giant Globemaster.

I started talking. And as I talked I devised a plot for our Cinerama film—which until then had not only had no plot, but not even enough of an outline for me to hang my hat on, nothing but my urge to film the coronation. Never mind. The U. S. Air Force would be featured in this film, I said, because the story would be about a fighter pilot and his crew chief.

Our fighter pilot, I improvised for my stiff-backed audience, is nearing the end of his term of service. He has been studying various religions, trying to figure out what life is all about. As our film opens, he has half-decided to retire, possibly to enter a Buddhist monastery. But first he plans to visit the Himalayas, to immerse himself in the land and the culture. Then he will make up his mind.

Now his crew chief, a happy-go-lucky extrovert, thinks this is mad, but since he and the pilot have been close pals, insists on going with him on this journey to the unknown. And so they take off. They attend the coronation at Kathmandu—thank God I had this for a peg!—spend long days wandering through the loftiest mountains in the world and, in the end, our fighter pilot decides the Air Force is really the place for him after all. Whereupon our film winds up with his return to America, highlighted by glorious and spectacular flying scenes.

No doubt it was my lucky day. Also I may have been at my most eloquent. At any rate, they gave their approval and I left Washington with a Globemaster and crew, which would take us to Nepal and complete the circle of the earth on the return journey.

That monster airplane was none too big for our needs. Fully assembled, we were twenty-three, from director Otto Lang and veteran Cinerama cameraman Harry Squires and their technical crews, to an accountant who would be required to keep track of expenditures. Then there was our equipment, which included not only the ponderous Cinerama cameras and lights, but all the gear required for a full-fledged Himalayan expedition. For day by day, the story line of our film epic, now officially entitled *Search for Paradise*, was taking shape—and it called for a long, adventurous journey.

It was to be based on man's eternal search for his personal Shangri-La. In the sky-high realm of the Himalayas, our fighter pilot, a major, and his sergeant sidekick would be seeking an ideal place of escape from the machine age. They would prowl the great heights and Buddhism's monastic haunts, imaginations beguiled by the happy valley of Hunza, that secluded Pakistani principality tucked away in the lofty Karakorams, and the Vale of Kashmir, renowned for centuries as a paradise on earth. Then there was the River Indus, with the great rapids of its upper reaches, all unexplored, its torrents pouring down through the Himalayas. The project suggested itself—and just the thought of it was a thrill: why not try to run the virtually unknown gorges of the upper Indus?

And so we decided on an expedition which would begin with the Kathmandu coronation, then move on through the world of the Himalayas, making a Cinerama spectacular. Our heroes would wander through some of the world's most fantastic landscapes, seeking their happy land. In search of Shangri-La, they would personify the endlessly intriguing theme of escape.

We would close on a parallel theme, equally old, of the one who seeks happiness afar only to return and find it in his own backyard, like Maeterlinck's bluebird and Russell Conwell's *Acres of Diamonds*. On that note we would close—our two airmen, having sought heart's delight in the world of the far Himalayas, returning to reenlist in the Air Force, finding greatest contentment at home. The search for Shangri-La would end where it began.

It was a formidable undertaking. Even for a small group traveling lightly it would have been quite an adventure, and we were a large party burdened with extremely bulky equipment, off on a long and arduous journey through the world's highest mountains—a journey destined to be more dangerous than we had anticipated.

To play the parts of our fictional airmen, we needed contrasting types—the traditional straight man and comedian. The story called for a quality familiar in all literature: the visionary, gazing into the sky, and his prosaic friend, prosaically anchored to Mother Earth—the eternal Don Quixote and Sancho Panza; the jet pilot entranced by the lofty solitudes and the spiritualism of an exotic faith; the crew chief, genial and earthy, anxious only about his next square meal. We might have taken two professional actors along to play the parts. Instead, I chose two old skiing pals, Chris Young, surrealist artist and poet, the dreamy introvert who had been my photographer in Europe during World War II, and Jim Parker, just about the jolliest person and certainly one of the most versatile individuals I had ever known. They were a pair for the highest mountains, and they would play our Air Force major and sergeant.

Before our big plane took off from Mitchel Field, Long Island, a small fighter plane flew in from Washington and the pilot handed over a package which he said was to be a gift from the President to the newly-crowned King of Nepal. It turned out to be an autographed photo of President Eisenhower. I wondered what the reaction would be in Kathmandu when the king and his ministers saw what had been sent by the leader of the richest nation on earth. For myself, I had bought a somewhat more expensive gift, a fairly impressive example of classic Steuben glassware. But still, I suspected we had a bit of a problem here.

Our Globemaster took us to Frankfurt, then on to India. But because there was no airfield in Nepal with runways long enough to accommodate so huge a plane, we were obliged to charter several Air India DC-3s to take our equipment on over the lower range of the Himalayas to the Kathmandu Valley. En route, I reported back to my radio audience:

> I'm sending this message from seven thousand feet above the Ganges Plain. We had hoped the King of Nepal, for his coronation, might have made a runway usable by our Globemaster. It would have been something if we could have flown into Kathmandu in the largest airplane of them all. . . . Captain Jang tells me how he himself was the first airman ever to land a plane in Nepal. He made it in a twin Beechcraft, landing on a flat area the king had specially cleared. Since then, a concrete base and asphalt top have been added to the strip. All of which is still not nearly enough to take a Globemaster. Even with no cargo aboard and almost no gas load, its seventy-five tons touching down would tear up asphalt, concrete and all. So now we are hoping that our Air India Dakotas will have enough room to squeak in.

Nepal is a long and narrow country, 525 miles from east to west and an average of one hundred miles wide. A whole series of peaks above 25,000 feet, including Mount Everest, rise within its confines and on its northern border. But we saw little except clouds, towering masses that filled the sky.

Its history is almost as convoluted as its landscape. For more than a century, Nepal had been ruled by a political system that, even for Asia, was bizarre. The king was a mere figurehead, dwelling in the exotic splendor of an Oriental court, but little more than a royal ornament. The supreme power for decades had been exercised by the head of the Rana family, a powerful clan of nobles which had been the ruling faction of the land. The chief of the Ranas was, by hereditary right, the Prime Minister, sovereign in all but title. King Tribhubana, growing restive as a palace nobody, had rebelled and fled to India. Revolts in his behalf broke out within Nepal. The Ranas were overthrown and, in 1951, Tribhubana—with a major assist from India—returned to Kathmandu, a full-fledged sovereign.

He did not long survive his triumph. But when he died, leaving a son as his heir, the young prince was able to make good his claim to the crown. And that was the background for the brief item I'd seen in the *Times*—a coronation in Kathmandu, young King Mahendra to confirm his succession to the throne with age-old formalities.

But this coronation would be more than a spectacular show. Nepal was now a buffer state between independent India and the world of Communism. It was tied by treaty to India, and presumably committed to the democratic ideal. But Red China was in a position to play the usual game of Communist penetration. In the complexities of the East-West conflict, much diplomatic interest was focused on the coronation at Kathmandu. Planned with all the exotic ritual of ancient days, dazzling pageantry with occult symbolism and parades of panoplied elephants, it might turn out to be the last example of legendary splendor in the Orient.

Captain Jang took us up to 10,000 feet and through a narrow pass. Picking his way between the cumulus clouds over the front range of the Himalayas, he came down to circle Kathmandu, its golden-roofed temples shining in the sun. We made it —but just barely.

The primitive airport, with its single landing strip, was a busy place as other planes brought in all the delegations and functionaries connected with the festivities. We were met by a party of Nepalese diplomatic officials: as the ambassador of the American delegation, I rated a formal welcome. Unfortunately, this did not extend to customs clearance, which turned out to be as primitive as everything else. We might have been there for a week with our masses of baggage and Cinerama equipment—more than a hundred pieces in all—but we finally got through by promising the clerk we'd take his picture.

While we were unloading, two planes arrived from China. We were more than slightly embarrassed when we saw the presents the Chinese delegation had brought—rolls of exquisite rugs, superb Chinese screens and several huge Ming vases. I guessed their value in six figures. To match those opulent gifts, our government had sent an autographed photo of President Eisenhower!

An ancient truck and some antique automobiles were waiting for us. The one sent for Ambassador Lowell Thomas had simply been requisitioned from a Rana noble by the Nepal foreign office. It was a snazzy 1929 Buick, recently painted bright yellow, license number forty-six—which meant it was the forty-sixth vehicle carried into Nepal. For—and as I reported back to my radio program this was one for Ripley—every one of the hundred or so autos in Nepal, which had no roads leading in and only a few miles of unpaved trails within the country, had been borne over the Himalayas by sheer manpower. The performance of this astonishing feat required a crew of more than a hundred men, each automobile resting on a platform mounted on bamboo poles sixty or seventy feet long, each row of bearers in its designated position under the load, all chanting a chorus as they jogged along.

Off we went in a rattling motorcade piled high with luggage, bumping over a rocky road meant for carts and burden-bearing elephants, right through the heart of the city and its exotic traffic, stopping occasionally to give an elephant the right of way. I could not help feeling like an Oriental potentate. My first broadcast from this Nepalese Shangri-La included a little color:

> The streets of Kathmandu are made of broken red bricks and gravel and are so narrow and so jammed with people, cows, dogs and chickens, you'd think the automobile drivers would simply mow 'em down. They blow their horns constantly. Five miles per hour is the speed limit, and in Kathmandu the law says

you *must* blow your horn. . . . I counted seventy people in one Chevrolet truck.

How much did it cost to have your car carried to Kathmandu? In the 1950s, oh, about seven hundred dollars. Also, for years all the gasoline had to be carried in—125 pounds of it per man over the precipitous mountain trail—automobiles and the gasoline to run them carried over a trail on which many would not be happy to ride a horse.

Our destination was a palace compound just outside the city. Kathmandu's normal population of 150,000 must have been swelled tenfold for coronation week, and without the initiative of Dr. Tom Gilliard, an eminent American Museum of Natural History ornithologist and Explorers Club colleague, some of us might have wound up sleeping in the lobby of the town's only hotel. But having heard that Tom was off on an expedition to New Guinea, I arranged with him to act as our advance man.

And what a job he did! By the time we arrived, he had taken over the compound of an unfinished shell of a palace, flown to India and, in the best manner of the maharajahs, arranged to have a huge marquee, a dozen tents, beds, chairs, dishes and silverware, flown up from New Delhi. Knowing food would probably be in short supply before the end of the hectic coronation week, he also hired Gaylord, the best-known caterer on the subcontinent, to fly our meals to Shangri-La. Our forty-foot canvas marquee and our tents were promptly dubbed *Cinerama City*, so proclaimed by a long canvas sign.

But of course life in Nepal turned out to be not precisely a stay at your local Hilton or Intercontinental. One day a cloudburst nearly washed our tents away. Otherwise, the facilities for bathing at Cinerama City consisted of four ten-gallon buckets arranged to function as a shower and surrounded by a canvas wall—no top. From an overlooking hill, the natives gazed down on the showerbath proceedings and collapsed laughing.

Our crew, American to the core, never did get used to Asian fare, tough fowl with rice and spicy curry, or equally tough mutton. Their cry, which came to be mockingly familiar, was, "Ain't we got nuttin' but mutton?" When all food supplies finally did run short, they were delighted with the canned spaghetti and meatballs we opened.

Meanwhile, how about all the handsome presents the Chinese had brought from Peking? At the eleventh hour, how could we match them? As for the autographed photo from the President of the United States, well, even my Steuben glass bowl would seem insignificant. I put the problem to Tom Gilliard, and once more he came through. Tom, who happened to be the world's ranking authority on New Guinea's rare bird of paradise, pointed out, first, that since it had been traditional for the King and Queen of Nepal to wear the magnificent paradise plumes, they had been specifically exempted from the worldwide ban on their use when the birds were found to be threatened with extinction; and, second, that as soon as the edict had gone into effect, the United States government had gathered up all the available plumes in our country and turned them over to the American Museum of Natural History in New York, where they now lay stored in a vault, a thousand or more of them. Tom was sure his museum colleagues would be glad to let us have some— if our request came through the State Department.

Off to Washington and to the museum went long wires, requesting a hundred bird of paradise plumes, together with our reasons and a reminder of the urgent press of time. They must have been shipped out on the first plane and, miracles of miracles, they did arrive before the coronation. Whereupon Tom, our director Otto Lang, some volunteers and I stayed up all night making special circular frames out of bamboo, with fifty bird plumes spread around each. Held aloft, each made a glorious sunburst. When all the coronation presents went on display in the palace ballroom, by far the most spectacular was our stunning display of those plumes of the bird of paradise—plus the autographed picture of President Eisenhower!

The routine for the Cinerama crew was to get out at daybreak for picture-making with the bulky three-eyed camera, making preliminary scenes of the street life, palaces and shrines of the once-forbidden city. Meanwhile, I had to perform a round of diplomatic duties, always in ambassadorial tails and topper, inappropriate, if not absurd, in the sweltering heat. On my news program, I reported:

> For the first time in my life I am not playing the part of an observer, a reporter. This makes quite a difference. At an occasion

of state like this one, a diplomat's duties consist of being greeted by officials, being briefed on what is going to happen next, being cautioned always to arrive at functions ahead of time so you will not commit the unpardonable faux pas of entering after the King and Queen have arrived. You sit or stand for hours in the sun in just about the most uncomfortable clothes so far devised by man, and you change them as often as a Paris model. You ride in processions—on elephants. And you are present at every ceremony until the bitter end.

The astrologers of Kathmandu, who have a large say in royal affairs, selected the time of the coronation and predicted the day would be fair. They were right—the morning dawned bright and hot. At Cinerama City, I cooled off under the improvised bucket shower and got into my formal regalia. The roads were already alive. Peasants, mounted and on foot, poured into the city, many of them carrying gleaming Buddhist images, for the Lord Buddha had been born near this place more than 2,500 years before.

It was early when I reached the shrine courtyard where the ceremony was to be held. With Dr. and Mrs. Mayo and Virginia Bacon, I sat in the stands set up for the international delegations and the highest Nepalese nobles. In the middle of the courtyard was the throne, a large divan with metal snakes for a back and topped with a huge, golden-headed cobra. Hindu priests in robes were busy with their preparations. We had been promised royal cooperation for the ceremony, and we got it: The ponderous Cinerama camera was placed right next to the throne, as were the powerful, glaring motion picture lights. Months later, Cinerama audiences would get a much better view of the proceedings than we had from the V.I.P. stands.

A salute of thirty-one guns was reverberating when the royal couple appeared, walking under royal umbrellas, proceeding toward the throne. The king, a frail-looking man who seemed much younger than his thirty-six years, was dressed in a simple suit of white cotton, and, as always, wore dark glasses. The queen wore a crimson sari, her long hair flowing free. Mahendra could have had many wives but preferred monogamy. When his previous queen had died, he simply married her sister.

The astrologers had calculated the exact moment for the act of bestowing the crown, 10:43 A.M., and at that instant, following a series of arcane preliminaries, the rite was performed. A crown, studded with gems worth millions and set by generations of long-dead craftsmen, was placed on King Mahendra's head. Then, with the salute of cannon fire as a signal, the king and queen left the cobra throne and went into the palace. The throng in the stands poured out. The coronation was over.

In the afternoon, there was a parade through the streets of Kathmandu. In the land of elephants, Jumbo played the principal role in the pageant, an apotheosis of all the circus parades that ever brought joy to American small towns. But there were extra, added attractions no American town ever saw—Nepalese military bands, a corps of ancient drummers, incense bearers and flower bearers strewing fragrant petals left and right.

And of course the elephants, some two hundred of them, their swaying howdahs covered with gorgeous trappings of silver and gold. Most conspicuous of all was the royal elephant, the mightiest of his breed, laden with magnificent tapestries atop which rode Their Majesties in a howdah like a golden throne. Many of the elephants carried delegates from foreign countries, most of them in brilliant Oriental costume. The funniest were those of us from the West in our tail coats and top hats. I felt supremely ridiculous—imagine wearing a topper atop an elephant!

The coronation parade gave us a chance to work up another fictional episode for our film—our two fugitives from modern civilization joining in the royal proceedings. Up to the howdah of a kneeling elephant they climbed. Now when a passenger-carrying elephant gets up, it's pretty shaky and we staged a bit of comedy by having the Sarge nearly fall off. Jim Parker, always the droll prankster, did a first-rate job of comic acrobatics. To really give the audience a sense of what it would be like to ride an elephant in the coronation procession of the King of Nepal, we put the Cinerama camera on top of another patient pachyderm. The result was a dizzy, stomach-tightening sway, like the lurching of a ship in a storm, as our two Air Force men went careening through the streets of Kathmandu.

The festivities of the week lived up to the Marco Polo tradition of Oriental splendors. They gave a glowing hint of the traditional magnificence of the past. In the present, I could not help thinking of the Nepalese peasant villages, the toil of coolie

After the accident we are homeward bound across the lofty Tibetan plateau while my bearers chant, "Oh Lord Buddha, lighten our load!"

Dr. Harry Thomas greets us on our return from Tibet.

Sven Hedin, often referred to as the foremost Central Asian traveler of our era.

Hazard E. "Buzz" Reeves.

Fred Waller, inventor of Cinerama.

General Merian C. Cooper, who was of great importance in the production of Cinerama.

BOX OFFICE

With President Eisenhower, one of the many millions who came to see Cinerama—the process that created a screen revolution.

This photograph was taken the day Cap Cities went on the Big Board. It helps to explain why Frank Smith, on my left, was not to be denied.

The priceless bird of paradise sunbursts we presented to the King and Queen of Nepal, at Kathmandu.

Mahendra Bir Bikram Shah Deva, King of Shangri La, wearing his crown of diamonds, emeralds, rubies and the white plume of the Bird of Paradise.

How do you like the outfit? Riding an elephant in the royal procession wearing tails and a top hat! (Photo credit: Otto Lang)

Jim Parker (left), who was drowned in the unexplored rapids of the Indus. On the right, Chris Young, co-star with Jim in *Search for Paradise*.

Father Ross, who for two years conducted Mass while holding a six-gun under his cassock. (Photo credit: Otto Lang)

The man who came to dinner with the cannibals in New Guinea.

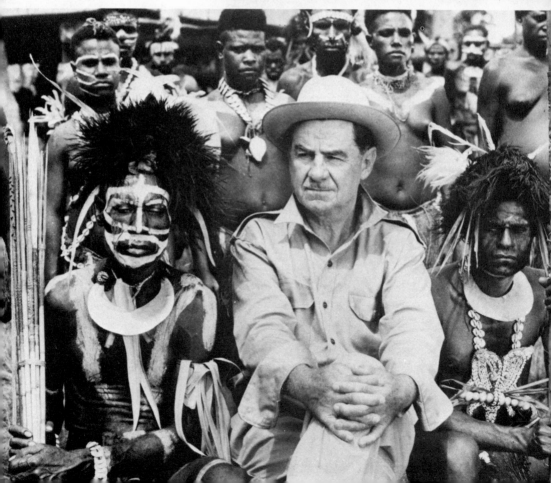

Admiral Tyree in the middle, Governor Luther Hodges on the right. The pole in the background indicates the exact location of the South Pole. The temperature was 45 degrees below zero.

With Admiral Jim Reedy about to take off from Cape Town on the first and only flight ever made across the entire Antarctic, from South Africa to New Zealand and Australia.

With Lowell Thomas, Jr., Bernt Balchen, Sir Hubert Wilkins and veteran explorer Donald Mac-Millan in a plane circling over the North Pole.

His parish included more than five hundred million people.

With Sir Edmund Hillary, Dr. Werner von Braun, Captain Finn Ronne and Dr. Tom Gilliard.

OCCUPANCY BY MORE THAN 204 PERSONS IS DANGEROUS & UNLAWFUL

labor, signified by the age-long rule of the Rana nobles who built a score of palaces to rival Versailles and which had resulted in this golden royal pageant.

Each day during King Mahendra Bir Bikram Shah Deva's coronation week there were elephant processions and glittering ceremonies to film. Usually there was a reviewing stand where the visiting delegations sat. As a procession would go by our Cinerama crew attracted much attention. None of the guests—potentates and diplomats—had ever seen such a huge camera, and our twenty-man crew was in conspicuous contrast to the painted and bespangled elephants and the Nepalese nobles and their ladies in their jewels and bird of paradise plumes.

Occasionally I would leave my seat to go down and make suggestions to the crew. One day, the ambassador from India, Mr. Bhagavan Sahai, said: "How much does it cost to make this Cinerama film?" I thought a moment and replied: "Approximately $20,000 a minute." The next evening, at a banquet, he came up to me and said he hadn't been able to sleep, thinking of those $20,000-a-minute decisions our director and I had been making!

There was a state dinner each evening. These, and all the housing and most of the other problems of taking care of visiting delegations, were handled by a most unusual and talented White Russian, Boris Lissanevitch, a onetime ballet dancer of renown, who had fled from the Bolsheviks. Boris had been the friend of Mahendra's father and during the revolution had landed in prison. Released by the new monarch, he had been given the impossible task of staging most of the coronation events as well as arranging housing and food for the hundreds of V.I.P.'s. Boris turned out to be the most conspicuous personality in Kathmandu, aside from the king and queen.

The final banquet threatened to be a disaster. Boris had ordered a special fish flown in from the Bay of Bengal. Due to some delay in India they all spoiled. Also, thousands of his chickens had been pre-cooked by the blazing sun at an airfield just over the border at Patna, in India. But Boris always managed to improvise and get by.

We had come to the point in our printed program of the week's activities where the schedule read, "Today guests depart,"

a straightforward Nepalese way of saying "the party is over."
Luckily, there was one exception. We were to be permitted to
stay on and finish our work—coronation ceremonies in secondary
cities and odd shots of this and that, as is always the case in
rounding off a film job. Now, with the hurly-burly of the coronation over, we were able to pay some attention to the breathtaking sights of the Kathmandu Valley. A heavy pre-monsoon
storm had cleared the air and there, looming up higher than you
think mountains have any right to rise, were some of the most
impressive of the Himalayan peaks. Off to the west, a hundred
miles away, was one of the most spectacular—Annapurna.

When the time came for us to take our departure, I had
a final interview with King Mahendra and thanked him for the
assistance he had given us. He invited me to return and join him
on a tiger hunt. Then, good-bye to Cinerama City and Kathmandu. We had three planes to transport our large party and
gear, but having advance arrangements to make in India, I left
in the king's own plane, which was flying his royal relatives and
friends to India.

Arriving in New Delhi, I had a shock—word had just been
received that there had been an air crash in Kathmandu, with
many killed. I thought it might be one of our planes taking off from
the primitive flying field and so had a bad few minutes. Then the
details began coming in. Although our group had been on the
airstrip at the time loading up the chartered DC-3 Dakotas, the
plane that crashed was coming in—with a full load of passengers.
Evidently the pilot had been bothered by a crosswind. He landed
on one wheel and before he could get his plane under control
was at the end of the short runway. The plane crashed into a
house, killing the two occupants and eighteen of the passengers.
I did not fully relax until everyone in our party reached New
Delhi.

When it was edited down, the coronation film would give
us a magical hour for our Cinerama production. Now we were on
the quest for material equally exotic and exciting to make up
at least another hour. We began with Kashmir, in that spacious
region to the north of India and Pakistan, where a towering
range of snow-clad summits swings around to enclose a basin of
clear streams, mirror lakes, abundant trees and bright skies. The

climate is temperate and exhilarating, a dramatic contrast to the sweltering plains of India. This is the Vale of Kashmir.

We were warned by several Indian officials, told how the Vale of Kashmir was closed to travelers—tension on the border, which had been true much of the time since the British pulled out. But when I asked for an audience with Nehru's high commissioner for the Vale it was immediately granted. When I arrived at his office I found him seated cross-legged on cushions. He turned out to be the brother of Bhagavan Sahai, our friend the New Delhi ambassador to Nepal. His Excellency Bishnu Sahai put out both arms and gave me a surprise welcome. He said: "Thirty-five years ago I heard you tell about the Allenby-Lawrence campaigns, at Oxford." He quickly arranged for our Cinerama party to fly to his domain, one of the most exciting places in the world.

Kashmir's worldwide fame began with the Mogul emperors of India, who made it their favorite vacation ground. There they built sumptuous palaces and gardens, embellishing a terrestrial paradise to which they took their favorite queens. When the British succeeded to the Mogul power, they fell heir to the allure of the Vale of Kashmir, which became a resort for the proconsuls and grandees of the British Empire and their ladies. Nor was the fame of Kashmir lessened by its chief export, wool—cashmere shawls and sweaters, and Kashmir rugs, as well. For such a faraway place, the name became remarkably familiar in the West.

You might think so fair a land would have a bright history, but in the last half of the nineteenth century, Sir Francis Younghusband, British envoy in those regions, characterized its record this way:

> Kashmir, for many centuries, was a state of perpetual intrigue and assassination; of struggles with brothers, cousins, uncles; of fights for power; of constant fear; of poisoning and bloodshed; of wearying, petty internecine wars.

Our three-eyed camera saw it differently. Srinagar, the capital, is a city of river, lake and canals, something to remind you of Venice. The Jhelum River flows broad and placid through the center to join the Indus far to the south. Dal Lake lies serenely in the midst of the city, artificial waterways on all sides.

There are two magnificent gardens in Srinagar, the Shalimar and Neskat, idyllic mementos of the great Moguls of India. Today the Shalimar is perhaps the best-known garden in the world. Poets have rhapsodized over its beauty for centuries and one, Amy Wooden Finden, who wrote the immortal lines, "Pale hands I love/Beside the Shalimar," demonstrated her sense of romance, perhaps excessively, by committing suicide on the grave of her husband.

In the Vale of Kashmir, the only proper utterance seemed to me to be song, and that thought stayed with me when, subsequently, we put together our Cinerama production. We had the gifted Hollywood composer, Dimitri Tiomkin, write the music, and lyricist Ned Washington the Himalayan rhymes. It was sung for us by Robert Merrill of New York's Metropolitan Opera:

> Shalimar calls me—Shalimar calls me
> Little I care what fate befalls me
> If there is bliss
> It is this—it is this—it is this!

On Dal Lake, that sparkling sheet of water dominating Srinagar, there are communities of houseboats and aquatic taxi-cabs, so inexpensive, as was nearly everything in the Vale of Kashmir, that they too seemed to call for a song, a rollicking calypso on the Kashmiri economy:

> The Shakari boat you can run real cheap
> She don't eat up gasoline like imported jeep
> She don't need no engine and no piston rings
> But if she starts leaking you may need water wings.
>
> Kashmir—Kashmir
> Life is joy—life is minus tear
> Kashmir—Kashmir
> Cut-rate paradise this time of year!
>
> Oh, the boat is house and the house is boat
> If the neighbors are too noisy, just make this note
> You untie the house from the place it stood
> And you float away to a new neighborhood.

Each Dal Lake houseboat has a register in which all guests sign their names. By coincidence we had selected the same one

Harry Chase and I had rented when we were filming the Vale
of Kashmir in 1920. President Theodore Roosevelt's sons, Ted
and Kermit, some time later had told us they also had leased
The Buckingham Palace and had seen our names. They were
loafing there after a strenuous hunting expedition in the Pamirs,
on the trail of the elusive *Ovis poli*, which they told about in
their book *East of the Sun and West of the Moon*. Thirty-five
years later, here we were again aboard the same houseboat.

On Dal Lake, you can live for a song and dream the
legends of old. So, for our little fiction story of two fugitives
from civilization, we worked up an episode with the major and
the sergeant taking up residence in *The Buckingham Palace*,
where they appeared to be living in royal style, as told by Robert
Merrill in song:

> Lowell Thomas found when he reached Kashmir
> That we had a local Buckingham Palace here
> If you care to occupy the royal wing
> For a couple of rupees you can live like a king!
>
> Oh, the Kashmir life is the easy way
> When it's time for you to leave you will want to stay
> Even Lowell Thomas, tho' I may be wrong,
> Will be going native if he stays very long.

But not everything was the subject for a ditty in Srinagar.
We visited the great mosque and saw the immense crowds at
prayer, one single hair from the beard of the prophet Mohammed
attracting pilgrims from far and wide. And these mass prayers
were a sign of the dangerous political and religious conflict over
Kashmir. India had established local self-government with Mos-
lems controlling the regional administration. But Pakistan was
demanding a plebiscite of the people with their huge Moslem
majority, and the conflicting claims made Kashmir an international trouble spot.

Hitherto, we had traveled by airplane, automobile or
truck. Now we set out for a trek into the mountains that ring the
Vale of Kashmir, up into the lofty Himalayas. Where wheels
wouldn't work, we had to go back to the ancient style of travel,
the mountain caravan, on foot or on horseback. And ours was a
caravan a mile long, the twenty-three members of our party and
a small army of native porters carrying supplies and our cameras,

lights and sound equipment. The journey took us through Gulmarg at an altitude of 9,000 feet, commanding a magnificent view
of the Vale of Kashmir.

In the days of the British Raj many Indian Army officers
and civil officials escaping the intense heat of Lahore, Multan,
Peshawar and other cities fled to Kashmir. Their favorite resort
was Gulmarg, where there had been a well-known inn—Nedu's.
We found it still there, but almost a ghost inn. When my CBS
radio engineer, Gene Nicks, and I entered the office we were
greeted by a distinguished-looking Indian who said with much
surprise, "Why, Lowell Thomas, how did you find your way to
Gulmarg?" He was Dr. P. S. Gill, Nehru's cosmic ray scientist.
He told us how he had studied at the University of California in
Los Angeles, then at the University of Chicago under Dr. Arthur
Compton, and he invited us to his cosmic ray laboratory across
the valley, where he had a glorious panorama of the Karakorams
and the Vale of Kashmir.

It had been a pleasant surprise to find that a friend, a
Princeton colleague, had been to the Vale of Kashmir the year
before. Professor Arthur Compton, the physicist who had been
awarded the Nobel Prize in 1927 for his work on X-rays, had been
a graduate student at Princeton forty years before, he as a physicist and I an instructor as well as a student. In 1954 he had been
invited to Gulmarg to dedicate Nehru's prestigious cosmic ray
laboratory in the Karakorams high above the most famous valley
in the world. Now, 1955, the lab was under the direction of
Compton's student, Professor P. S. Gill, who showed me the guest
book, in which Art Compton had written:

> The understanding of Nature is in one way hard and in another
> way easy, for no one can grasp it nor miss it wholly, but from the
> contributions of many there gradually arises a certain grandeur.
> —ARISTOTLE

Invited by Gill to record my own impressions below, I
wrote:

> If Aristotle had seen this mountain top, his remarks about "the
> understanding of Nature" would have been even more eloquent.
> I know of no view to surpass the one from Dr. Gill's front yard.

After we dined with Dr. Gill he brought out a bottle of Scotch. He said he had it hidden from his wife, an orthodox Hindu for whom alcohol was taboo. As we sat there enjoying the awesome scene I forgot about the effect alcohol has on you at such an altitude. Later, as we rode back to Nedu's, Gene and I sang and were in high spirits. But when we arrived at the inn, I caught my foot in a stirrup while dismounting. Fortunately Gene seized my horse's bridle, or it might have been a repeat of my accident six years before on our way home from Tibet.

When Gene and I entered the door of what was left of what had been a plush resort hotel in the days of the British Raj, hunched over a roll-top desk in a corner was an old man who we later learned was a Nedu. When his father owned the leading caravansary in Lahore, the capital of the Punjab, he had two sons. Years later he put one in charge of his Vale of Kashmir hotel in Srinagar, and the second managed this inn high in the Karakorams here at Gulmarg.

His father, as a boy, had been a street urchin in Athens. A British colonel, a cavalry officer who had survived the Charge of the Light Brigade at Sebastopol, took a fancy to him when for some months he had polished the guardsman's tall boots. When the colonel was assigned to a military post in Mesopotamia he took young Nedu along as his batman. Several years later when the colonel left Baghdad for England, the lad, now enamored of the East, left "Mespot" and went on east. After a short time in Karachi he went up-country to Lahore, today the second city in Pakistan. There he prospered and built an imposing hotel, where Harry Chase and I had stayed thirty-five years before.

In Lahore, Nedu of course heard about the glamorous Vale of Kashmir, to which the British sahibs fled to get away from the intense heat of the plains. Nedu visited the Vale and decided to open a hotel where travelers could stay if they were not renting one of the houseboats on Dal Lake. Eventually he found his way into the mountains, to Gulmarg, where some of the British of Kipling's day took their families. There he built another inn, and a rugged, up- and downhill golf course.

Now comes the modern part of the story which, so far as I know, has never been told. At the time of Partition, in 1947, when the British broke up the Hindustan Peninsula, creating the two nations, India and Pakistan, both countries were eager to take over Kashmir and it became a race to see which would get there first.

Although the population of the Vale was maybe 90 percent Moslem, and ethnically should have been a part of Pakistan, the British, with their divide and rule policy, had kept a Hindu ruler there, Maharaja Sir Hari Singh, at one time known in Europe as "the mysterious Mr. A" when he became involved in a series of London scandals.

According to our host at Gulmarg, Pakistan could have won the race. Their toughest fighting troops, Mahsuds, wild, long-haired men from the Northwest Frontier, were ordered to make a dash for Kashmir. Their route took them over the mountains via Gulmarg. When they reached the resort high in the Hima-layas, at Nedu's they found a supply of champagne, wine and whiskey that they couldn't resist. Whereupon the Mahsuds forgot their mission and went on a historic bender. They stayed several days in Gulmarg and drank everything in Nedu's wine cellar. They almost demolished the inn, and even desecrated the An-glican Cathedral and its sacred silver utensils.

This delay enabled Jawaharlal Nehru to fly troops into the Vale, a force large enough to hold the Kashmir airfield and the approaches to the Vale. Ever since then India has been in tight control of this fabulous valley, one of the most spectacular on our planet. For years, including the period when we were doing our filming, there was war along the frontier, but today the Vale of Kashmir once again is a tourist mecca and the place where prosperous Indians spend the hot summer months in houseboats on Dal Lake, or in the mountains at Gulmarg.

From Gulmarg we climbed to Khalanmarg, a village 2,000 feet higher, with an unsurpassed view of Nanga Parbat, the killer mountain, towering high above. There, however, we were not allowed to make pictures. Strict censorship was being enforced because this was right on the border of Pakistan. Here we en-countered a party of Russian cameramen who had been forbidden to photograph anything in the area. Hence the Indian commander had an added reason for refusing us.

Once back at Srinagar, I left our group again to make ad-vance arrangements for the next stage of the journey through the world of the Himalayas. Our destination now was Pakistan, but because of the tense political situation, one couldn't take a plane direct from Indian Kashmir to neighboring Pakistan. I had to go first to Amritsar, the Indian city near the Pakistani frontier, where the thermometer stood at 117. And still I couldn't simply take a plane to Pakistan's nearby Rawalpindi—nothing so simple. The border had to be crossed on foot, after which Gene and I hiked a mile or more across the no-man's-land on either side of the cease-fire line.

Finally, we reached Rawalpindi for a meeting with Colonel Ata-Ullah, soldier, mountaineer of Pakistan, veteran of climbing expeditions in the Western Himalayas and the Karakorams. With the Cinerama crew, we now planned to make our way to the remote principality of Hunza, then on along the Indus for an attempt to explore the gorges of this, one of the world's greatest rivers. Colonel Ata-Ullah agreed to act as mentor and guide for this next adventure.

As you move northward up the Indus, you pass from a great length of flat country into mountains where the river flows through a valley so deep just the sight of it is terrifying. And this valley leads to the principality of Hunza, a seldom-visited area among stupendous peaks that has inspired the few travelers who have made their way there to awed accounts of a lost world, Utopia. There you come upon a medieval realm left over from the Asian past, and a simple, isolated, unspoiled people in a world removed from the twentieth century.

The road to Hunza is difficult enough for wayfarers traveling lightly, but for our Cinerama expedition it was a heart-stopping adventure. At first our caravan followed a trail that clung to cliffsides falling away sheerly, as much as 6,000 feet. It was an old route barely wide enough for just one vehicle—a traffic problem solved by allowing those going up-trail to move only in the morning, down-trail in the afternoon. Happily, our Pakistani drivers seemed skilled in taking the endless hairpin curves, where a false turn could mean a drop of a mile or more, and the journey provided us with a chance to make another Cinerama thriller.

Halfway to Hunza, the trail ends abruptly; proceeding on foot and horseback, even for those familiar with mountains, is tough going. When a pack animal stumbled off the trail, everyone stopped to listen, but the poor creature fell so far no one ever heard it hit the river.

Arriving at Baltit, Hunza's main town, our Cinerama crew was received with formal protocol by the Prime Minister and the Crown Prince, son of the Mir, or ruler, who came with a platter of fruit, the traditional token of Hunza hospitality. At the palace, a modest building in the style of a Swiss chalet, the Mir himself did the welcoming. Then we moved on to a special camp set up in a nearby village.

The valley might have been cleft by some giant sword slashing down through the stupendous range of the Karakorams. High above the rushing river, the cliffs recede and here, on broad shelves of terraced fields, lies the principality of Hunza. The people, the Hunzakuts, number some 25,000, tall and sturdy, wearing flat hats made of white wool, strongly reminiscent of a hat style among American women not many years ago. They claim to be descended from the Greek soldiers of Alexander the Great, who took to the mountains with Persian wives when Alexander marched to India. There is also a tradition that the Mirs are descendants of Alexander himself.

Hunza's reputation as a paradise on earth had been founded largely on economics. Its fields and crops were divided more or less equally. There were no burdens of debts, no capitalists, no moneylenders, no landlords, no class flaunting great wealth. Even the Mir's palace was no more pretentious than many an American suburban home. This blessed state, a paradise without poverty, was celebrated in song by Messrs. Tiomkin and Washington, with Robert Merrill singing:

> Nobody has too little, nobody has too much
> That's how it's planned
> In the happy land
> Of Hunza.
>
> In everything around you
> You see the Maker's touch
> The human race
> Could use a place
> Like Hunza.

Politics at the time was as simple as economics, with Pakistan controlling the foreign relations, if any, but otherwise leaving Hunza to its old ways. The government was patriarchal; the Mir, assisted by a council of elders, ruled in all matters from the regulation of agriculture to the settlement of village disputes. No bureaucracy, no burdensome system of taxation, no law books, no complicated statutes—only the age-old customs of the people.

As crime had long been virtually unknown, there also were no locks on the doors, no police, no prisons, little discontent and seldom any disorder. No soldiers, no military budget, no national ambitions. The political ills of civilization don't exist—or didn't then—in the simple mountaineering community where the Mir held court and dispensed justice like a patriarch of old. He was both judge and jury.

Our Cinerama camera recorded one of these court sessions, held in an open pavilion overlooked by the snowy ranges of the Karakorams. The Mir, Mohammed Jamal Khan, a sturdy middle-aged man with large features, a cropped moustache and proper natural dignity, wore the traditional costume of ornate coat and plumed cap and sat cross-legged on a dais. A shaggy mountaineer in Hunza hat and long coat rose to register a complaint. The Mir listened to the argument, then gave his judgment. That was all, and everyone departed content that justice had been done.

The health of the Hunzakuts is proverbial. Some diseases common in other countries have been unknown. Western physicians visiting the principality have marveled at the absence of maladies that are the scourge of modern civilization. In 1921, an eminent British doctor, Sir Robert McCarrison, made a study of the Hunzakuts and subsequently reported:

> So vibrant was their health that [I] never saw a case of asthenic dyspepsia or gastric or duodenal ulcer, of appendicitis, mucous colitis or cancer. Cases of oversensitivity of the abdomen to nerve impressions, fatigue, anxiety or cold were completely unknown. Indeed, their buoyant abdominal health has, since my return to the West, provided a remarkable contrast with the dyspeptic and colonic lamentations of our highly civilized communities.

Life is vigorous in the out-of-doors and much bodily exercise is inevitable in the mountain country where every farmer climbs to his fields. The Hunzakuts are reared to the saddle; the national game is polo, which is said to have originated in these parts. It is played from childhood, small boys learning on foot with sticks and puck. Every village has its polo field and the rivalry between village teams is intense. There are few rules and no referees, which can lead to lively clashes between steeds and riders. The Mir put on a game for the Cinerama camera, and a strenuous display of horsemanship it was. The Mir himself was the star, making shots that would have looked good in any league, and taking his share of the bumps in rough mix-ups.

The religion of Hunza presents a paradox. The peaceful husbandmen in a valley of Arcadian simplicity are of the Ismaili sect of Islam, which traces back to the Assassins of the Middle Ages, who made murder by dagger an instrument of their theology and politics. But that was centuries ago and today's Ismailis, maintaining their religious unity, are noted as a quiet, orderly people.

Their spiritual leader is the Aga Khan who—another irony —attracted public notice throughout the 1950s by a life of opulence on the Riviera. Whenever he bothered to explain this apparent contradiction, he would say that he didn't want to favor any one community of the Ismailis by dwelling among them—it would excite jealousies. The distant Hunzakuts, for one, never begrudged him this idiosyncrasy, satisfied that it was proper for their spiritual ruler to live well—and far away. And so the Aga Khan became a social figure, prominent in aristocratic circles of London and Paris. His horses won the Derby five times, he married four times and was perhaps more prominently featured in the news than even he would have preferred when his son, Prince Aly, married and divorced movie actress Rita Hayworth. So it was no great surprise that when the Aga Khan died in 1957, it turned out that he had passed over Aly as his choice for a successor and named Aly's son, then a Harvard student. Since then, little has been heard of the new Aga Khan.

In the vast upthrust of highlands north of the Indian subcontinent, there rises the greatest assemblage of rivers on this planet. From endless enormous glaciers, mighty streams pour down in all directions—the Amu-Dar'ya (Oxus), Yangtze, Mekong, Brahmaputra, Salween, Irrawaddy, Ganges and Indus—all distinguished by awesome gorges with swift and turbulent rapids. Originating at the loftiest altitudes, they follow steep courses that send them tumbling and pitching down as they come out of the world's mightiest mountain range to reach the lowlands. And they also have this in common: their sources and upper reaches are little known and have hardly ever been explored.

So here was a new frontier for our Cinerama adventurers —a mountain is conquered by climbing it, a river by running it in a boat.

Could it be done? Could anyone run a river surging through the gorges dividing the Himalayas and the Karakorams? It had never been done, and there was plenty of opinion that it would never be done. Queried, the Royal Geographical Society in London said no. A few years before, two Europeans had lost their lives trying it. And here we were hoping to run the Indus with a Cinerama camera filming one of the wildest of all rivers.

To scout the prospects, I asked Steve Bradley of Winter Park, Colorado, who was familiar with river and mountain conditions in our own Rockies, to fly the Indus gorges in a light plane and make a survey of the speed and roughness of the cataracts. His report was, yes, perhaps our expedition could make a run in modern rubber rafts—maybe. He added that we would need an expert river-running professional to direct preparations and do the piloting through the white water. He suggested Bus Hatch, a veteran river man from Utah who had spent most of his life on our own Colorado.

A phone call to Hatch at Vernal, Utah, brought an enthusiastic response: he was on his way. And soon Bus and his son, Don, were flying west with a large, deflatable raft. Bus Hatch was then fifty-six years old, a grizzled veteran of the Colorado. For years he had made a thriving business of taking adventuresome customers down all our major western rivers. His son, Don, age twenty-seven, was lean and wiry, the father of three children. Although he taught school in Salt Lake City, much of his time was spent on the river; he had been trained from childhood by one of the best in the river trade—his father.

Arriving, the two experts studied the prospects by making a trial trip to the gorges and agreed that running the Indus was feasible. But it would be rough going, far more dangerous than our own Colorado.

The locals at Gilgit thought we were mad: We would never make it, they said. But we meant to try. First, Bus and

Don made a test run with director Otto Lang. It was Otto's way not to ask his crew to try anything he wouldn't do first himself. The raft, twenty-seven feet long, cast off at 9:45 A.M. Otto from the start found himself hanging on for dear life, as the watery fury was thrown at them with full force and the boat often stood on its stern as torrents of water came cascading in. "I have been involved in a number of close skirmishes against elements of nature," he said, "but nothing could compare with the sweeping power of the Indus."

Bus agreed there were several rapids in the Colorado perhaps as powerful, but in Arizona there were always moments of repose, quiet stretches of placid water. Not so the Indus—the speed was constant and drove on relentlessly. Don simply said that the biggest hole he ever fell into and the highest waves he was ever hit by were on the Indus.

Four hours later and far downstream, when it was all over, Otto reported to New York by cable:

> Bus and Don Hatch made the first descent of the Indus gorges
> from a point thirty miles above Skardu. I was merely a wide-eyed
> passenger and have rarely witnessed such a cataclysmic force
> of nature, only comparable to being swept away by an avalanche.

That first run, of course, was only a preliminary to the business of picture-making. The rubber raft now was loaded with our massive equipment and crew. Bus had designed a solid frame for the huge camera and electrical equipment. There were seven selected to run the river, all volunteers, limited by the number of available life jackets. The total burden: some two tons.

The first test went off as we had hoped. The boat was thoroughly tossed about and shipped a lot of water, which had to be bailed, but all hands were satisfied that the Indus gorges could be filmed. The crew made five stops to check equipment and survey the upcoming rapids, and covered twelve miles.

There followed a series of runs while the rest of the expedition proceeded downstream along the bank, to set up camps for the battered and weary river party when they came in. Bad weather held things up for days, but four stages of river running were completed with success. So far everything was okay. The three-eyed camera had shot some of the most spectacular film ever made. In fact the adventure could have been considered complete. Cinerama could have packed up then and there and said good-bye to the Indus. But there remained a lure that tempted the river runners into one more try.

Downstream was Nanga Parbat, the killer mountain, rising on the Himalayan side of the river. The crew had already filmed its snow-clad summit, the sinister peak in all its majesty and beauty. But another day on the river would bring them nearer and give Otto Lang a chance for a more dramatic juxtaposition of perilous water and killer mountain for a pictorial climax—running the Indus gorges right in the shadow of Nanga Parbat.

This western Himalayan giant, rising abruptly and in solitary glory from the valley of the Indus to a height of 26,620 feet, had run up a tragic record. No other peak in the Himalayas, not even awesome Mount Everest, had taken a fraction as many lives, the grim number then standing at thirty-one.

Preparations were made for a final river run before heading for home.

This time Jim Parker begged to go along. He had not made any of the trips thus far, since river running was no part of his acting job as our happy-go-lucky sergeant. But Jim had been caught by the lure of Nanga Parbat and, at his insistence, Otto Lang assigned him to take the place of an injured cameraman in the boat crew. And so the bulky, fully-loaded craft shoved off, preceded by a small boat manned by Don Hatch. Otto Lang tells what happened next:

> No sooner had we hit the main current approaching the first rapid when things began going wrong. One of our motors conked out. Our attention was riveted on the little boat ahead of us, trying to keep a proper shooting angle and holding a good distance between the two. Then, when we'd been under way for hardly more than a minute, all of a sudden our boat hit a tremendous hole and, within a split second, was tossed high up and flipped over like a toy by the angriest wave I ever saw. All I can remember was seeing the bow of the boat, with the camera attached to it, looming high above my head in a torrent of foaming water, before I was pitched out and went under.

Some of the men, trapped underneath, fought their way free. The others thrashed about, desperately fighting for air while trying to reach the overturned boat. Finally, five of them managed to get to it, hanging on for their lives while guiding it to shore where Lang was able to anchor it.

Two men were missing, Pete Passas and Jim Parker. Soon Pete, spotted by Don Hatch, managed to struggle ashore. But there was no sign of Jim Parker. All hoped against hope that he might have made it farther downstream, but he never did. A reward was posted, but the local people shook their heads knowingly—the Indus never gives up a body.

The deadly river as it plunged by the "killer mountain" once again had exacted its price.

VII. High Adventure

Never having had a commercial flop . . . he communicates a kind of gosh-almighty feeling that (1) the world is his oyster, (2) it contains many nicely turned pearls, and (3) they can be shared by anyone who cares to read, watch or hear Lowell Thomas.

—*Newsweek* Magazine

In 1957, *Newsweek* began a cover story about me with a paragraph that sounded like a scenario for the climactic scene of a *Tarzan* movie:

A man with thick, graying hair and a pencil-thin moustache stood, not long ago, before an uncharted section of steaming New Guinea jungle. . . . From the side came the muted whirr of a 35-millimeter movie camera. Before him, a tribe of ocher-painted cannibals watched him closely. Their arrows trembled slightly in taut bows. The interloper stared calmly back. Then one savage blinked, lowered his bow, eased out of the bush and stood quietly by the man's side. The others followed. Once again, in a long career of facing similar dangers, Lowell Thomas had done the undone.

While the above seems much too lurid to me I guess it's essentially the way it happened. But, at the time, I was far too immersed in the spectacle to be conscious of any potential danger. I was aware, though, that I was a long way from home, more than ten thousand miles, to put a number on it, and witness to a Stone Age civilization that, but for one young Australian patrol officer, had never been looked on by the eyes of white men. The group so vividly described by *Newsweek,* for example, had recently dined on a neighboring tribe, which also happened to be the reason we were there. The Aussie patrolman we had come to visit was having a try at persuading them that eating other people was now generally frowned on.

It all began some months before when General Motors, which had become my radio sponsor, asked me to do a television High Adventure series. I had, as the reader who has reached this point in these chronicles knows, managed to stay away from TV, except for the very first television news program before World War II, as well as some specials. I hadn't wanted to be tied to a city studio. This time, not wanting to offend my sponsor by saying no outright, I tried the tack of asking for the impossible: I would do it, I said, if I could do what I wanted to do, the way I wanted to do it, and have an unlimited budget to do it with. But GM finessed me by agreeing, and the "High Adventure" series was born, programs from some of the farthest-flung spots on earth, each one budgeted at $250,000, in those days a record figure. It turned out to be one of the most popular programs ever televised, with an audience of 35,000,000 for each show, which is about three million more than the average for all sixty-minute special TV programs. Proof of the lure of travel and far places was re-established by its place among the top five TV shows in audience appeal, by similar audience response throughout Europe, Asia and Australia, and by the Christopher Award it won for excellence in television programming for family viewing.

The first of the *High Adventure* films was about New Guinea, "The Land That Time Forgot."

New Guinea, "The Land That Time Forgot," is unlike any other area on our planet. Shaped like a dinosaur, New Guinea's 316,000-square-mile mass seems to lurk in the sea above Australia, reaching westward to the underside of the equator, its mountain-spined tail dipping southeast into the Coral Sea. If Greenland is an archipelago, as the scientists now say, then New Guinea is the largest island on earth, and so ribbed with giant mountains that if you were to flatten it all out it would be as large as the U.S.A., or the continent of Australia. A wild, exotic, primitive land, until quite recently it has been one of the least explored parts of the inhabited world, its interior compounded of dense green mystery and turbulent beauty, of impenetrable rain forests, lush valleys and spectacular gorges gouged by some of the world's mightiest rivers. Through its forests swoop a hundred varieties of rare birds with rainbow plumage, including the one most gorgeous of all— the bird of paradise. In its trackless jungles are kangaroos that climb trees, bats with a wingspan of five feet, giant lizards and turtles that weigh hundreds of pounds. Its rivers are alive with crocodiles.

It is also the last major stronghold of Stone Age man. In the valleys of New Guinea's jagged mountain ranges, there are people—hundreds of thousands of them—living exactly as their ancestors lived ten thousand years ago, not knowing of the white man's existence or even suspecting that there is a world beyond the rim of their valley, and speaking hundreds of different languages. Such were New Guinea's credentials for a place on our "High Adventure" series, and so it was that one day in 1957 I found myself flying high over jungle and swampland to a place called Angoram, upriver from Wewak, where our adventure would begin.

I had already come a long way, across the Pacific to Australia, then on to Port Moresby on the southeast coast. En route to Madang across the mountainous spine of New Guinea, we flew over the scene of some of the fiercest fighting of World War II. The remorseless jungle had long since obliterated every trace of it, except the skeletons of Japanese planes on some of the beaches, and at Madang, in the shallow water inside the coral reef, a rusted ship's prow poking skyward as stark evidence of those desperate days when only a few thousand Allied troops and this rugged island stood between the Japanese and Australia.

In steaming Madang, we boarded an ancient tri-motor German Junker—twelve passengers, our expedition gear, and some heavy mining machinery, none of which anyone bothered to tie down or make secure. Our pilots were young Australians who flew by the seat of their pants, without benefit of instruments or radio. They had to be good, for the strip at Angoram, a swath of grass that ran right to the edge of a high embankment overlooking the Sepik River, allowed no margin for error. Although we came to a stop with only a few feet to spare, no one seemed to think anything of it. Later we were to use airstrips in the narrow valleys of New Guinea where the pilot actually had to spiral in.

We were met by Fred Kaad, the district officer who had overall responsibility for the Sepik country, and a couple of hundred nearly naked villagers. From this point, we were to proceed by water aboard a small flotilla which would serve as our base as we made our way up the Sepik, one of the world's larger rivers, and one of the least known. Along its shores there still lived tribes of headhunting cannibals, with natural perils almost as awesome. Angoram was the last outpost of civilization; beyond was the vast area loosely known as "uncontrolled territory."

Before we set out, District Officer Kaad made us a little speech of advice and warning, which we recorded for our program. This is what he said, without the trace of a smile:

> Gentlemen, as you know, the final destination of the party is the May river patrol post, and before you start, I would like to give you a little background to this area so you will know just what you are getting into. The May River area is still one of those regions where people kill one another, eat one another and cut each other's heads off whenever possible. Over the last few months we have had a patrol officer at the May River post and hopefully he is gradually extending his influence and control. But I want you to realize that your safety—and the safety of the patrol officer there—depends to a great extent on your actions.
>
> The second thing is—and I don't think I have to say this—don't look at the women. That is the surest way you will arouse their ire and get yourselves in trouble. The third thing is, when you are talking to someone, don't make any unexpected movement. These people are still very, very primitive and any unexpected action could be misinterpreted with, shall we say, unfortunate results.
>
> Also, you people look rather big. I am sure you would like to get some of that weight off on the way up to the May so you won't be so appealing to the people up there. I hope I see you all back here in a fortnight or three weeks. Thank you.

None of us had much to say for a while after that, and we were glad to busy ourselves with details of the departure. There were forty-five of us, including twenty native members of the New Guinea River Police. Our flagship was a sixty-foot cabin cruiser, the *Tangalooma*, powered by a single diesel engine. The captain and owner was "Spook" Snook, a Tasmanian who for years had prospected for gold in the mountains of New Guinea, and also had salvaged much valuable copper from World War II planes that had crashed or been abandoned. There were two other power boats in our flotilla, two craft of a type found only on the Sepik, thatched-roof huts built over a pair of long dugout canoes. Each was propelled by a single twelve-horsepower outboard; on the platform of one, lounging in a comfortable rattan chair with a rifle across his lap, sat a veteran crocodile hunter, Tom Davidson. He had told me that he and a few other hunters had taken seven thousand crocs out of the Sepik during the previous year, the skins bringing from twenty to fifty dollars each. I suspect that with the new worldwide emphasis on wildlife conservation, business has since fallen off. At any rate, we suspected Tom and his competitors already had gotten most of them. At night we occasionally saw eyes gleaming at us from along the shore. But not many.

For three hundred miles from the wide delta where it empties into the Bismarck Sea, the Sepik is navigable for vessels drawing as much as twelve or thirteen feet. We could go much farther, since none of ours drew more than seven feet. Our chief problem was dodging shifting sandbars, floating islands of vegetation and the countless large trees that came drifting downstream. For safety's sake, we tied up to the bank of a native village each night.

Our arrival was never a surprise. At every village the people came out in their canoes to look us over. At one, where I presume we had passed muster with flying colors, they even offered girls for sale. Word of our coming had reached them via a communications system that surely dates back eons. Pounding on hollowed-out logs, using a code not unlike our Morse telegraph system, these primitive people can boom their messages mile by mile upriver, covering vast distances with a speed that ought to be the envy of our U. S. Postal Service.

In Timbunke, the villagers, who had never seen a motion picture before, were told in advance they would see one that night. It was a thrill for all concerned. We hung a big screen between two palms and ran a power line from a generator on one of the boats. The audience laughed at all the wrong places—

when someone was shot, when the heroine fell off her horse and was carried off by a rushing torrent—but they had a fine time.

And we outlanders were intrigued by the way an assistant district officer did the narration in New Guinea pidgin which could be understood by some of the villagers who had been out to the coast. Pidgin English of several varieties is spoken throughout the South Pacific and all along the China coast. But by far the most picturesque brand of pidgin is spoken in New Guinea, a colorful conglomerate of a dozen Eastern and Western tongues, with a smidgen of German grammar, some Chinese syntax and a lilt all its own. To the newcomer, it sounds like broken English spiced with native words. But this doesn't begin to explain it. Take the word "firefly," one of my favorites. The local expression for something small is *lik lik*. Anything that flies is a *binidang*. In New Guinea pidgin, therefore, if you want to say "firefly," you simply say, "*Lik lik binidang*, he got shoot lamp alongside ass belong him."

We were not welcomed with open arms at every village. The people of Kanganaman, for instance, were clearly sullen and unfriendly and no one was sorry when we turned away from the bank without landing. Spook Snook said the Kanganamanese belonged to the Cargo Cult, believing that all the white man's wonders—anything made of metal, glass or plastic—were devised by the spirits and sent for delivery to them, but the white man, actually a demon, maliciously kept this precious cargo for himself. Someday, Spook predicted, the cultists would go on a rampage and try to massacre every white they could lay hands on. He wasn't smiling, either, when he said this.

I had wanted to visit Kanganaman because it was said to have one of the largest community houses on the Sepik River, a tribal council hall called a *tambaran*, carved with phallic symbols and grotesque figures and hung with human skulls. Spook said the *tambaran* at Kanganaman was about 200 feet long and tall as a four-story building, resting on massive posts with the floor high off the ground. The tradition was that in building a *tambaran*, someone alive, preferably an enemy, was placed in the first giant posthole. Then the pole was ceremoniously dropped on him, thus assuring good fortune for all who took council in the hall.

In time the Sepik led us into the May River, deep in uncontrolled territory. As all hands watched for the patrol-post landing, I heard a good many tales about the courage and ingenuity of Peter O'Sullivan, the young patrol officer who, with only a few native police escorts to help, was assigned to keep the peace between dozens of hostile cannibal tribes. Only a short while before, deep in the bush, stricken with food poisoning and unable to walk, he had spent seven days crawling out on his hands and knees.

He was waiting for us when we landed, blue-eyed and smooth-shaven, and looking more like a university sophomore than the mainstay of law and order in the farthest reaches of New Guinea's treacherous May River district. Nevertheless, there was something most reassuring about his presence. And he was glad to see us, too, for until we arrived no English-speaking people had journeyed that far—as O'Sullivan put it, into a region where even fluency in pidgin was of no help. He said maybe as many as a thousand different languages and dialects were spoken on the island. This was due largely to the endless steep mountains and deep valleys. For untold centuries each valley's inhabitants had been isolated. If they ventured even a few miles from their own area they were in danger of being killed and eaten. Hence the many languages for which New Guinea is famous.

Things were not dull in the May area. They had had a massacre recently, O'Sullivan told us. It seems that a May River tribe had invited a Yellow River tribe to a peace banquet. They settled all their differences, and then at the close of the festivities, the hosts killed and ate the guests, all thirty-two of them, keeping the heads for trophies. Peter then went up to make peace before an all-out war ensued, but only two days before we arrived, a message had come downriver for him from Yellow River. *He* was next on their list. They were going to cut off his head and then eat him.

I don't think he gave it a second thought, although his hand did shake a bit when he raised a glass to toast us. We went with him to have another try at soothing ruffled tempers, and it was then that we filmed the headhunters deciding whether they wanted to cook up a Lee Robinson, or a Lucky Harris, or a Lowell Thomas stew. Nonetheless, our guards were on full alert, on the prowl all night during our stay. We were a sizable group and would make a welcome prize for a raiding party.

"Peter," I said as we sat in his tent one evening, "how do

you explain the urge these people have to behead and eat their enemies?"

He had obviously given the question considerable thought. He mentioned the theory, held by some, that it resulted from the lack of game in these parts, and the resulting meat and protein shortage. But his own belief was that it was simply a tradition, going back thousands of years, tangible evidence of a warrior's skill. "To kill is the first objective of a warrior in this primitive society," he said, "and the head of his victim attests to his triumph. To eat their enemies, these people believe, is to nourish themselves with new strength, and particularly with sexual vigor."

Ever since the earliest missionaries invaded the South Seas there have been endless cannibal anecdotes. Of course our Australian companion regaled us with a few, and at the time my favorite was one told to us as his hand shook when he took a sip of a second *chotapeg*.

At a tribal luncheon, he said, an old chieftain kept repeating something over and over to his son. When Peter, out of mere curiosity, asked what it was all about, the interpreter replied: "Oh, Chief say, 'Son, I've been telling you, you should never speak with some*one* in your mouth!'"

Before we left, we had a chance to see the solution of at least one tribal problem. Peter's May River neighbors had captured a girl from another village. He was able to persuade them to send her back before another war of reprisal started, but the trouble was they didn't know how to do it. So the job was up to Peter.

Did we want to go along? A cautious yes. Peter gave us a briefing, making no attempt to conceal what might happen and emphasizing that we were not to shoot unless we were attacked. "There is a certain risk in that," he said, "but the other risk is the loss of all the hard work I and other patrol officers have done up and down the Sepik."

Taking only the canoes, we set off upriver, the girl sitting rigid with fear in the prow in front of Peter. Before long, we were turning into the landing, not a soul in sight. As we tied up, we were aware of being watched from the dense undergrowth. On Peter's orders, a native policeman helped the girl ashore, both braced for a shower of arrows. A moment later, a villager stepped cautiously from the bush, then another and another. They advanced toward us, spears raised.

Peter O'Sullivan got out of the boat and went forward to talk to them, alone. In the canoe, someone translated for him, which is difficult in New Guinea with its many different languages. With the girl now safely returned, he told them, the government would punish the kidnappers, and there must be no reprisals, no fighting.

One of the natives spoke. Another laughed. The tension was broken, the danger past. One slow, small step had been taken toward peace in the May River valley. A single district patrol officer named Peter O'Sullivan had done what an army probably could not have.

Our New Guinea program was a thriller, but I knew we had only skimmed the surface of that wild, complex, little-known, intriguing land. Five years later, in 1962, I was back with a camera crew to film a spectacular event—seventy-five thousand Stone Age people gathered in the mile-high, 100-mile-long Wahgi Valley for a roistering "big fella sing-sing" and a display of tribal customs as old as time. The gigantic conclave, an agricultural festival sponsored by the Australian district administration, was centered at Mount Hagen in the just-opened Western Highlands. An Australian prospector and explorer, "Mick" Leahy, with one companion, had been the first white man to see this great valley. This had been not many years before our visit. The two Aussies had come upon a rich agricultural area inhabited by a hundred thousand tribesmen who knew nothing at all about any world beyond where they lived. I had visited "Mick" at his cattle station near Lae a few miles inland from the Bismarck Sea. He was hard of hearing as a result of being bopped on the head with a war club by a Wahgi Valley tribesman. A few years after our first encounter with "Mick" Leahy, I had the pleasure, at a New York Waldorf banquet, of presenting this modern Columbus with the much-prized gold medal of the Explorers Club. He had indeed found a new world and, unlike the Admiral of the Seven Seas from Genoa, "Mick" had known where he was going and when he returned to Australia he knew where he had been.

Before we dropped down in a plane at Mount Hagen the tribes had been on the move for weeks, trickles at first, villagers coming from 250 miles away and more, across the ridges and ravines, on all the paths leading to Mount Hagen. The trickles swelled to huge waves of humanity, all arriving full of excitement and anticipation—and fear—for their imaginations could not grasp the enormity of such an event.

Before dawn of opening day, we were awakened by wild chanting and drumbeating as thousands of tribesmen poured onto the huge field prepared for the gathering. Singing, shouting, stomping, they flowed across the open ground in a surging flood of humanity, their faces fierce with tribal markings, bones and boars' tusks thrust through their noses, their bodies glistening with pig grease. All were virtually naked, but their headdresses were the gorgeous plumage from hundreds of rare bird species, worth a fortune. Through it all, Otto Lang, our Hollywood film director, and our cameramen, oblivious of any danger, dashed around as wildly as the Papuans, trying to preserve every incredible scene on film.

As this frenzied pageant spun across the field, the mountain air ringing with primitive chants, the earth actually shaking with the dancers' rhythms, it came to me that few from the world beyond this valley had ever witnessed such a spectacle. Even some of the observers were out of this world. One of them had been dead for months. Smoked by his fellow Lagaip tribesmen, he had been brought there and propped up on a hillside because he'd expressed a wish to attend and his relatives didn't want to disappoint him. Just as impressive and of course far more lively was the representative of the Queen who had been sent out from London. Lord d'Lisle, a World War II air hero and one of the few living airmen to wear the Victoria Cross, was on hand in full regalia almost as resplendent as the costumes of the Papuans with their bird of paradise plumes. Lord d'Lisle and I had been together a few years before when we both were ambassadors at the Kathmandu coronation of King Mahendra in Nepal.

There were two others in our party who attracted much attention. One was "Chips" Rafferty—height six feet, seven inches. Every tribesman gazed up in awe at him. And then there was the "script girl" with our film crew, a stunning young blonde from Salzburg, Austria, our film director's home. Christl, to the New Guinea natives, seemed to be a goddess, and several tribes wanted to make her their queen. However, she had an even more pressing problem—the young Australian bush pilots and patrol officers. One even followed her back to Europe, hoping to persuade her into living with him under the palm trees of wild New Guinea. Instead she married the Salzburg "boy next door."

Added to the color here at Mount Hagen there was a real possibility for trouble. These tribes had been warring for centuries. All bore spears, bows and arrows, razor sharp stone axes. All were keyed to a fever pitch of excitement. And the occasion was rife with the opportunity for "mary stealing"—the kidnapping of marriageable girls—along with other lesser causes of tribal vendettas.

But curiosity overcame belligerence. Many were seeing other tribes close up for the first time. Between dancing and sing-sings, they milled about, ogling one another or gazing entranced at the exhibits, which included superior farm produce, livestock, schoolwork and handicrafts that had been taught to the more advanced tribes by the white man. For any Stone Ager, there was much to marvel at, and much to set him thinking about what he, too, might have or become.

This, in fact, was the basic purpose of the big show. "What we want to do," veteran District Commissioner Tom Ellis told me, "is break down their insularity, let them see how cooperation with the government can expand their lives, bring them law and order, health—and above all, peace."

After World War II, Australia, without a shilling's help from any other nation, had made massive contributions toward moving New Guinea out of the Stone Age and into the twentieth century. In 1946, there were no government schools; by 1969, preparing the people for self-rule, the Aussies, according to my Mount Hagen host, Tasman Hammersley, had established 2,000 primary and secondary schools, as well as a university, with a total of more than 215,000 students enrolled. Tens of thousands of natives were being taught better farming methods. A program for roads was being pushed into the hinterlands. Indonesia, which took over the former Dutch colony on the western half of the island and renamed it Irian-Jaya, had spurred no such progress. But by 1974, Papua, New Guinea, thanks to Australian foresight, had taken responsibility for all its domestic affairs and was governed by a native Papuan government.

It was the magic cry of "Gold!" that lifted the first veil on the mysteries of the interior. Rumors that the alluring metal lay beyond the ranges first began after World War I, and adventurers trekked in. Few ever came out. But one who did, a salty character named Sharkeye Park, had struck it rich, and his discovery started a stampede. To those gold-fevered men, to the government patrol officers who had to go in to control and often rescue them, and to the missionaries who inevitably followed, belongs the credit for opening up the glorious New Guinea highlands.

Sharkeye Park was a seasoned Australian miner of mature years who had been to the Klondike and still had the fever. He had taken off into the land of the Kukukukus, the most cunning, savage and unpredictable of the cannibal tribes, and had to beat off so many attacks, not to mention malaria, that even he was on the point of giving up.

He was called Sharkeye because one eye, made of glass, was always fixed in a cold, dispassionate stare. Concerned that natives, both local tribesmen and his own carriers, would steal his supplies and weapons and leave him defenseless in the wilderness, he took out his glass eye, set it on a log outside his tent and advised all and sundry: "Now eye belong me he lookim all along. Suppose you get up no good, all right, he can lookim you, talk along me. Understand you?"

For some time, the eye fulfilled its purpose. Then one of the more cunning tribesmen reasoned that, as with any other eye, this one had no ability to see backward. Early one morning, as Sharkeye lay weak with malaria, he sneaked around behind the eye and placed one of the grizzled gold-seeker's old fur hats over it, then went off to plan some skullduggery. It was not long, however, before Sharkeye, his ear finely tuned to the sounds of the camp, realized that all was not as it should be. Looking outside his tent, he saw the eye covered up and immediately understood the situation. In a flash, he whipped out his false teeth, placed them beside the eye and threw away the fur hat.

"All right," he barked at the startled natives, "suppose some silly bugger like coverupom eye belong me. All right, teeth belong me, he bite-em hand belong him."

The procedure was thoroughly effective, the rebellion quickly quelled.

Soon after, without warning, the great moment came.

Sharkeye was lying in his tent one day trying to regain enough strength just to get back to civilization when his native boy suddenly burst in clutching a big chunk of gold-encrusted quartz. That was the start of the fabulously rich gold strike on Edie Creek, at Bulolo. The big stampede followed, and with it came the first probings of civilization.

One of those early pioneers was Father William A. Ross, a remarkable Catholic priest who, in 1926, left his home in New York State to save souls in New Guinea. In 1934, only a year after the Wahgi Valley was discovered, Father Ross led an expedition into the area, walking in from Madang, a nightmare trek that took thirty-eight days. He had been there ever since.

He seemed to bear a charmed life. Both priests who accompanied him lost their lives at the hands of Mogei tribesmen, and scores of white men had since been killed in the area. But Father Ross was never harmed. A miniature of a man, barely five feet tall, with a flowing beard, bright gleaming eyes and a joyous spirit, he was in the Wahgi Valley for four years before the first government official arrived.

"In those days, believe me, we weren't saving souls, we were saving ourselves," he says. "I kept a pistol under my cassock and my preachment really came from the heart: 'Love thy neighbor,' I told them. 'Don't hit him with an ax. Don't kill him with a spear. And don't steal his mary.'"

After Ross had devoted long months to bandaging sores, passing out aspirin and quinine and giving first aid to little children who fell into the fire that was at the center of every hut, the Mount Hagen chief asked him, in effect: When is the payoff?

What did the chief mean? Father Ross inquired.

And the answer was that the people were good and worried. Natives give nothing for nothing, and here was a man spending all his time and supplies for the people without asking for pigs or women or anything. So, the chief wanted to know, what *did* he want, anyway?

And Father Ross told him: "Give me your boys to put into a school, to live under our care at the mission station."

"Will you feed them?"

"Yes."

And so the deal was made, and the first school in the

interior of New Guinea was opened in January, 1935.

The knights-errant of this primeval land were the 500 men of the Australian field force directly charged with guiding nearly 2,500,000 natives out of their aboriginal state. Within each one's post borders (some with a sprawl over a thousand miles) he was all things to all the people: the law, the health officer, the agricultural and forestry expert, the map-maker and the marriage counselor. And in the face of endless danger, he had to scrupulously respect the government's insistence on "peaceful penetration."

"Shoot back," quipped one patrol officer. "Sure. But only after they've killed you."

Learning of a pocket of people not yet contacted, a patrol officer would head for the area, accompanied only by a few aides. They'd travel hundreds of miles through swamp and jungle, across rivers and over mountains. Such a trip would last three months or more. Then it was a case of one man facing as many as 10,000—none of whom had ever before laid eyes on a white man. This was how twenty-eight-year-old David Hook described the job to us:

> Going in, you have to be ready to be attacked. If there are no women or children around, you'd better look out. You may have to pull back, try again a day or a week later. But as soon as possible, you summon the village elders and firmly tell them, "Government, he strong-fella too much. But he no like fightim you-fella. He like shake hands. Government, he say you-fella no can killim other fella. Fighting must finish." If they reach for their spears, you use your gun. Preferably you shoot a pig, just to demonstrate the power of the gun. When that's settled you open your box of trade items—steel axes, shells, salt. You show them seeds that will make new crops. Your native medical aide treats their ills. Eventually you work out a set of rules with the elders, rules based not only on Australian law, but on their own codes as well. You appoint their head man as the government's representative. And you pray a lot.

Hook's station at Kopiago, at the time of our visit the most recently opened in the high central range, was a model of what can be done. Though in a territory then still unopened even to missionaries, Hook and his wife Christine had largely put an end to fighting and murders. They had started schools and farms, introduced such crops as corn, peanuts, cabbage, tomatoes, and new varieties of sweet potatoes, and improved the people's protein-poor diet with chickens and better pig stock.

One measure of how far the native population had come in a few years was the people's attitude toward airplanes. In the early 1930s, when the highlands were first being opened up, they were startled and dumbfounded by the big birds. Sometimes they even brought piles of sweet potatoes to put under a plane's nose so it might eat and be pacified. Once, an interested native went peering under the fuselage of a Cessna, then explained with penetrating wisdom to the pilot, "Kanaka, he look-him underneath, him he like savvy this fella. See him no he-man. Him, he-mary."

We were ourselves witness to an illuminating example of how quickly the people adapted to the air age. Father Ross had told us how a tribe, seeing its first plane in 1933, would be panic-stricken by the roar in the sky that came nearer and nearer. Then they saw the mysterious ghost with wings. Would it harm them? Would it swoop down on the people and carry some of them off? They began to scream, running to their huts in utter terror. Anyone who could find a pig immediately killed it and made a peaceful offering to this new ghost. "Boy, how dumb we be then!" one chief confessed to Father Ross. "And how many good pigs belong us we killim for nothing!"

But by 1962, when our DC-3 touched down at the Mount Hagen airport—by then the seventh busiest in the Southern Hemisphere, with as many as fifty flights a day—we saw on one side of the airstrip a grass slope where a hundred or so naked natives stood watching. As our plane swung around, it threw up such a huge cloud of dust that these spectators were completely swallowed by it. Some flung themselves to the ground and held their hands over their heads until we passed. But then they stood up again to watch, waiting peacefully for the next plane.

In 1969, with film experts Jerry and Hila Feil, we were back for a third expedition in New Guinea. Our camera crew accompanied Deputy District Commissioner Robin Barclay into the Nomad River region, on a "patrol into yesterday," hoping to find the Hisu, a tribe that had had absolutely no contact with the white man and, in fact, did not know of his existence. And our second crew headed off to the Western Highlands, 200 miles over the ranges and 1,000 years into the past, to search for a vanishing way of life.

Barclay, a rangy young officer, apologized for not meeting our plane at the Nomad patrol post. "We had some routine business to see to in the interior," he explained. But the "routine business," we learned, had involved a ritual murder, and Barclay had just returned from a dangerous patrol deep into hostile country. An unpacified tribe had raided a neighboring village and killed and eaten a woman they accused of sorcery. Barclay and his men had had to go in for the evidence, which he now held out to us in a bag—a smashed skull and an assortment of bones. "We know who did the killing," he said, "and we'll have to go in again to apprehend them or this whole area will burst into bloody tribal war."

Once the Nomad patrol was under way, I set off to launch the second arm of our expedition. We were to film the Enga, a tribe of some one hundred thousand who live high in the western mountains and have begun, ever so slowly, to emerge from their primitive isolation. They had accepted the jurisdiction of the Australian government and had begun to build a road that would link them to the outside world. But their dress and homes and appearance had not changed in thousands of years. As we were to see, neither had their fatalistic reliance on sorcery and the arts of black magic.

In a remote village, a man lies ill. For the Enga, there is only one explanation—a spirit has been offended. As our cameras turn, the sorcerer is called in and, with his mysterious bundle of sticks and indecipherable incantations, seeks to make contact with the spirits so he may discover which one is angered and why it is causing the man's sickness. Suddenly his eyes roll, his jaw quivers —he has reached the spirits.

Now the bargaining begins. The sorcerer offers a pig in exchange for the man's life. The family watches tensely. But the offer is rejected. It is the ghost of the man's father who is angered, reports the sorcerer. Such a vengeful spirit will not be appeased. The man will die. We offer medical aid, but it is rejected. And as we stand there, the battle is lost. The sorcerer is right: the man dies.

In the morning we move on to another village to film the purification rites that have to do with a boy's entry into manhood. He is taken to a sacred grove where no woman has ever set foot. Ice cold spring water is dashed in his eyes, and he must neither flinch nor cry out. His purity is tested with newly planted ceremonial irises. If they wither, it is a sign that the boy has had relations with a woman and the punishment can be exile or death. At the conclusion of a week of initiation rites, he is dressed in new finery, clothes that have never been touched by woman's hand. Now he is a man—and returns to the village to choose a bride.

Alas, our young man is unlucky. Though he has brought the proper "bride price"—many pigs and shells—to compensate the girl's family for her loss, the girl he has chosen spurns him. In the old days, this might have led to a bloody vendetta. Happily, times have changed. The lad, speechless with shock, leads his pigs away and begins hunting for another prospect.

All this time, I was in radio touch with our other party. They had moved on beyond the friendly villages into the unknown. Their walking was unrelieved, eight hours a day through steaming jungle, improvising log bridges over unmapped rivers and slogging through swamps that were not supposed to be there. Sometimes they were able to trade with the natives for food, but their requirements were heavy—it took some six hundred bananas a day to feed their ninety carriers—and soon they ran short. Once we were able to arrange an air drop, but at the end of a full month on the trail, they were on the verge of turning back.

Then Robin Barclay found another trail. He warned the crew that it might lead nowhere, that it could be a protective device of the Hisu to confuse enemies. But they voted to push on. And eventually they came on a clearing with a longhouse—the village of the Hisu, two civilizations seeing each other for the first time.

Communication was difficult, for these people did not speak any language Barclay or his men had ever heard. But he was able to convey to them that his party was hungry and traded some steel axes for a pig. When he demonstrated the power of his gun by killing the pig, a first step had been made toward leading them out of the Stone Age.

For Robin Barclay and his people, much remained to be done. But for them, it was the end of the search. For the Hisu, it was a beginning.

*　*　*

Ever since those long-ago days before World War I, when I packed a cumbersome Ernemann motion picture camera into Alaska, the Far North has fascinated me and lured me back again and again. I've almost become a commuter to our forty-ninth state over a period of more than six decades. I even presided at the ceremony when Alaska became a state, and the legislature years later voted me an honorary citizen. In the late fifties Lowell, Jr., who started his travels in Alaska in 1940 and later became a full-fledged Alaskan, joined me in taking our "High Adventure" crew north to capture on film the majesty and promise and a few of the hazards of this vast and still little-known land. Even then, young Lowell was no *cheechako* (greenhorn). Today, as lieuten-ant-governor, he has long since shaken the Eastern dust off his boots and committed his family and fortunes to Alaska. I was fortunate in having him as expedition leader for our Far North venture.

One of the first programs was a Panhandle-to-Siberian Coast survey of the Great Land, which is what Alaska means in the Aleut Indian language. In a small plane, we crisscrossed a state big enough to include any six Western European nations, and Lowell, Jr.'s wife, Tay, and my granddaughter, Anne, then not much more than two years old, went along for color and company. But though we filmed everything from the birth of an iceberg to skyscrapers going up in booming Anchorage, it simply was not possible to encompass the state's enormous vigor and variety in a single program. Indeed, so big is it that a familiar barroom riposte to visiting Texans is, "Quit bragging or we'll cut Alaska in two and make Texas third."

All of which provided ample reason for several shows about the north country. And so it was that early in September, 1957, Lowell, Jr., and I gathered together at Elmendorf Air Force Base outside Anchorage four of the world's most distinguished living Arctic explorers, ready to launch an airborne expedition across the top of the world. None of us realized how dramatic it was to be. My companions were:

Admiral Donald B. MacMillan, who had made the historic over-the-ice dash for the North Pole with Peary in 1909, only to be sent back within a few miles of the prize. Since then, although he had made some thirty expeditions to the Arctic in his own vessel, the *Bowdoin*, he hadn't been to the Pole. On this trip, his dream of a lifetime was to come true.

Australian-born Sir Hubert Wilkins had not only pioneered aerial exploration of the Far North, including the important first early flight over the Arctic Ocean all the way from Alaska to Spitsbergen, then later spending months combing the polar sea for a lost Russian airman; he had also, as early as 1931, taken the first submarine, the *Nautilus*, under the ice pack in the Polar Sea.

Air Force Colonel Bernt Balchen, known to explorers and geographers the world over as the first man to pilot a plane over both poles, was also widely acclaimed in Alaska as the wartime organizer and commander of the Tenth Rescue Squadron, which had saved hundreds of downed airmen, military and civilian, on missions all the way across the Arctic in Alaska, the Canadian islands north of North America, as well as in Ellesmereland, Baffinland and Greenland.

Peter Freuchen, another who went with us, had devoted his life to filling in the blank spaces on the map of the Arctic. The New York *Times* had called him "a modern Viking, a character out of Conrad, a giant of a man with a Rabelaisian verve for living . . . one of the world's great explorers."

Peter, a modern Renaissance man, had not only probed the farthest reaches of the polar regions, but at the age of seventy-two somehow he also found time to pursue careers as a newspaperman, author, lecturer and expert whaler. Few mortals could match his genius at storytelling. Traveling north, we had stopped in Washington State for a detour up Mount Rainier, where, over lunch at Paradise Lodge, Peter hypnotized us with the tale of how he had been forced to amputate his own leg. It was during the winter of 1921–22. With the Danish explorer Rasmussen and several Eskimos, young Peter Freuchen had started to cross the top of North America by dogsled, a feat never before achieved. Sent back from the northern tip of Hudson Bay to Greenland for supplies, he encountered severe weather and both his feet froze, one so badly that amputation was unavoidable. "It was," he told us with a bearded grin, "a case of leaving a foot behind or keeping it company with my corpse." So, with the aid of his Eskimo companion, he cut it off, somehow made it back to civilization and wore a peg leg ever after.

But alas, Peter's adventuring days were just about over.

Soon after we reached Elmendorf, as the five of us talked of our imminent take-off for Ice Station Alpha, a floating ice island on which our scientists were probing the secrets of the Arctic, he suddenly spun around and fell unconscious at my feet. I think he must have died in my arms; in any case, he was gone by the time we got him to the base hospital. Now we added a melancholy rite to our itinerary. In keeping with Peter's wish and at the request of his widow, Dagmar, we made arrangements to drop his ashes over the now famous Greenland air base which, years before, he had named Thule.

Word of his death in far-off Alaska created quite a stir in the rest of the world. Walter Cronkite, broadcasting from New York, got through to us live at Elmendorf and asked me for a report:

> Walter, the principal topic of conversation up here today has been the sudden passing of our Viking companion. Around the Explorers Club in New York, with his beard, wooden leg and breezy style, he was easily the most colorful in the company of men who are all colorful. Freuchen had been telling us only yesterday how he first went to Greenland in 1906. It was then that he established a trading post at the head of the heart-shaped bay the Eskimos called Umanak. Peter renamed it Thule, and today, as you know, it is our principal air base in the Far North. So it will be both appropriate and poetic to drop his ashes over Thule. From Anchorage, we will continue our flight into the Arctic with heavy hearts. Our next stop, Fairbanks, then Point Barrow, on to Station Alpha, an ice island near the North Pole and finally Greenland. Tonight I'd like to pay tribute to one of the most picturesque personalities in all Arctic history. For Peter Freuchen it means going home to Greenland, where he spent some forty happy years.

It was to be a thousand-mile flight over the Polar Sea from Point Barrow, northernmost tip of Uncle's Sam domain, to our drifting ice island, now barely three hundred miles from the North Pole. As the "High Adventure" cameras turned, I asked Bernt Balchen how our navigator would be able to find the tiny camp at Ice Station Alpha when, in such close proximity to the magnetic North Pole, our compasses were useless and, below, all you could see was ice for thousands of square miles. "We have a special system for finding our way in the Arctic," he replied, "—

by celestial navigation." We went up to the cockpit to have a look at the navigator "shooting the moon," but somehow that wasn't as comforting as the knowledge that we would eventually be picking up a radio signal from Station Alpha out on the ice and would home in on that.

Three hours north of Alaska, at 9:15 P.M., there was still no night; the sun hovered five degrees above the horizon. It would drop a bit more, then start climbing again. In three months, however, it would vanish altogether and there would be no day. Meanwhile, we had run into a thirty-mile-per-hour head wind. MacMillan, staring out into the sun-streaked sky, kept marveling at the difference between this flight and his bitter journey on the Peary expedition nearly half a century before, dogs and sleds crawling over the pressure ridges and forever circling to find a crossing over the open water leads.

An hour later the weather had closed in and we could see nothing but gray murk. But flying in on Alpha's radio beam, we were soon circling the snow-covered ice strip, safely arrived at one of man's two or three most remote outposts on this planet— to me, a miracle of navigation. Below us were hard-packed snow and seven feet of cake ice. Below that, nothing but ocean. We saw a cluster of Quonset huts, and a group of grinning young men, nearly all with frosted beards. We were told we were drifting an average of three miles a day, though the polar wind could sometimes speed it up to fifteen. But the most amazing thing of all was the question of what eighteen human beings were doing in this desolate place—if you could call it a place—drifting God alone knew where.

The answer would prove to be of considerable significance to the way the world looked at and understood the great Arctic reaches atop our globe. Ice Station Alpha had been established to commemorate the International Geophysical Year—the Russians had three ice stations drifting through the polar seas, too—and specialists in a broad range of scientific disciplines, all volunteers, were taking this unique opportunity to study the natural phenomena of the Far North for longer periods and at closer quarters than anyone had heretofore thought possible.

Some men were studying Arctic Ocean currents, about which there was obviously still a great deal to be learned. Although they had been there nearly four months, they still didn't know precisely where they were or where they were apt to be when the International Geophysical Year ended the following June. Not only was their camp on the ice gradually but irregularly moving north, it was also doing considerable rotating; when they woke up each morning, the first thing they had to do was check their compasses to see in which direction they were going. As an incidental hazard, they could never be sure in which direction their air strip would be facing for incoming planes.

Meteorologists were monitoring balloons sent up to altitudes of thirty miles and more, recording wind, temperature and humidity. When the long polar night closed in, physicists would be studying the colors of the aurora borealis, the spectacular northern lights, with automatic, highly-refined instruments which they hoped would tell them of what sort of energy particles it was composed, a mystery that has long baffled man. Oceanographers were measuring the depth of the ocean floor with the most modern seismic equipment. First they would drill a fourteen-foot hole in their island, then set off a dynamite blast below the ice. The sound waves from each explosion, bouncing off the seabed two or three miles down, accurately measured depth and told them a great deal about the composition of the ocean underlay. They also did borings, using a winch and 20,000 feet of steel cable to haul up a three-foot vertical core from the bottom of the sea. These samples enabled them to look back in time 200,000 years, to a geologic period when the polar area was a tropical region.

Was the island safe? "Well," said Sir Hubert Wilkins, "based on past experience, we know that these ice floes break up quite suddenly and without notice. The cracks might come anywhere, sometimes right under a building, splitting it apart."

And Bernt Balchen, who participated in the establishment of the first ice station in 1951, told how it was crushed in less than half an hour, with the men having to scramble onto adjacent floes. But he also tapped the long box against which we were leaning and said it contained a twenty-man life raft in which we could always take to the open water. A cheering thought.

One night, sitting around in the station mess hut, adrift on our erratic cake of ice, we listened spellbound as Sir Hubert told us of one of his adventures in these parts thirty years before, when he and the legendary Alaskan pilot Ben Eielson had flown out from Barrow in a single engine Stinson for some aerial exploration. In a matter of minutes they were beyond the edge of the mapped area and Wilkins was charting a course into the unknown. When their instruments indicated they were more than six hundred miles from land with nothing below but rough pack ice, the engine began to stutter. Eielson dove steeply to give the propeller more speed, and the engine seemed to take hold.

"She's okay now," he shouted. "We'll keep going."

"No, no," Wilkins called back. "Let's land—we'd better check the engine."

They glided to a landing on the ice and came to a safe stop. Eielson was properly troubled, but Wilkins was exultant, for the two had made history—theirs was the first airplane landing ever made on the Arctic ice!

While Eielson worked on the engine, Wilkins cut a hole through the ice and prepared to take some soundings with his listening devices. Soon they were able to take off, but within two minutes were forced down once more. More repairs, another take-off—but this time they ran into stiff head winds and, still seventy miles from the coast, they ran out of gas. The engine cut out suddenly, as if the switches had been snapped. There wasn't even a sputter from the starved carburetor, only an intense stillness, then the lonely hum of the wind in the wires.

Eielson managed another safe landing, but this time they were really in trouble. Their radio had gone dead and soon a raging blizzard had swept down upon them. For five days and nights they huddled in the cabin while the storm howled. Then they started walking toward land, carrying Wilkins' precious instruments and such food as they had, zigzagging across ice fields and backtracking to make their way around open water leads.

Thirteen days later, with only a pocket compass and the watches hanging around Wilkins' neck to guide them, they reached the coast—coming off the ice within only three miles of their intended destination. Found by some Eskimos and taken to a trader's house, they realized their troubles were not yet over. Eielson's fingers were so badly frozen that only immediate medical aid or an emergency amputation would save his life.

And there was no doctor nearer than Point Barrow, a three-day dog-team journey away.

Wilkins did not have long to think it over. He decided there was nothing to do but fill his pal the flier up with whiskey and do the best he could. Eielson took the plan standing up, though he knew it meant the end of him as a pilot. He had already taken a good belt from the whiskey bottle when they were astonished to hear a plane overhead. It was one of the searchers, blown off course and glad to find a place to land outside the trader's cabin. Within minutes, Eielson was bundled aboard and an hour later was in the tiny hospital at Barrow. There, a surgeon amputated the little finger of his right hand, saving the rest, a miraculous ending to a spectacular adventure.

After two days and nights on the ice, we flew the thousand miles back to Point Barrow, then four hundred fifty more to Fairbanks. There we reassembled our party and gear and, aboard what was then the largest flying machine in the world, the U.S. Air Force Globemaster C-124, we took off on the three-thousand-mile, non-stop journey over the North Pole to Greenland. It was a comfort to know the men of the Tenth Rescue Squadron would be keeping a constant check on our position until we crossed the Pole.

The work of the Tenth was vital. As long as men fly, the law of gravity unexpectedly will bring planes down when those aboard don't want to come down. Shortly before our arrival, one of these giant Globemasters had taken off from Elmendorf with only her eleven-man crew aboard. Forty minutes out, an engine quit, so they turned back—and almost made it. But finally the pilot had to put her down in the icy waters of Cook Inlet. Luckily, the huge plane stayed afloat, her crew scrambling out on top of her. Within minutes, the men of the Tenth Rescue were over them with helicopters, picking the men off one by one. Later, the Globemaster was towed through the ice and reclaimed—two million dollars' worth of airplane saved from an icy grave.

That was an easy one. Most of the time the men of the Tenth were on missions taking them hundreds of miles from their base, covering an area including all of Alaska and a sizable sector of the Arctic Ocean, a total of 2,500,000 square miles. Then there was the matter of civilian pilots, more than a hundred take-offs a day from Merrill Field in Anchorage alone. But for reasons no doubt explained by a stubborn Alaskan streak of independence, not one take-off in ten was marked by a flight plan, a simple indication by the pilot to the authorities of where he meant to go and when he planned to get there. And so the Tenth Air Rescue's job started when families began worrying and called to report a plane overdue, but often couldn't offer even a clue as to where it might be.

More tales of the frozen wastes below us as we drone on toward Greenland . . . Bernt Balchen reminiscing about the chain of air bases he built across the top of the world so planes could be safely ferried to Europe during World War II . . . and of his doughty commander, General "Hap" Arnold who, told that a certain job was impossible, agreed, then said, "But that doesn't mean you can't do it."

Wilkins, telling of his historic trip under the polar ice in the submarine Nautilus, and how he was forced to turn back only 350 miles short of the Pole—by a toothache: "I'd ordered all the men to have their teeth checked before we left, because the most miserable thing to suffer from in cold weather is a toothache. But one of the men didn't go. So he came down with a terrific case of neuralgia and a sympathetic abscess and practically went out of his mind. So we turned back, costing me about $200,000 [a million today] and a chance to reach the Pole."

Crossing the Pole, we all toasted veteran explorer Donald MacMillan, who had been forced to leave Peary within days of the great goal. Now, with Lowell, Jr., at the head of our expedition, he had finally made it to the North Pole—after forty-eight years.

And then we landed at Greenland with a last tribute to Peter Freuchen, the grizzled, giant, gay comrade who had started this journey north with us. Flying his ashes into the brilliantly colored Arctic sky in a helicopter, Lowell, Jr., scattered them, as the valiant explorer always wished, over the little settlement where Freuchen had opened a trading post some fifty years before.

In September, 1963, I was invited to join a team of U.S. Navy flyers gearing up to attempt history's first flight all the way across the bottom of the world, from South Africa over the Antarctic continent to Australasia—a flight that fourteen years later has not been repeated. I wired my acceptance and packed a bag, almost simultaneously. During the preceding twelve months I had paid my first visit to the Ultimate South, having flown from New York to the South Pole and back, with side trips to New Zealand, Australia, India, the Himalayas, Iran and Europe. I also had gone off to New Guinea for the second of three expeditions to the land of the Stone Age people—but I couldn't imagine anything that would have kept me from joining Admiral James R. Reedy and his Cape Town-to-Christchurch flight. The Admiral said they had arranged to take three pilots in his lead plane, and then had decided to drop one and take me in his place. Would I have gone if I'd known that my "inner clock" would break down and I'd have to be hospitalized with what seemed to be a heart attack? Of course.

The government of South Africa had been most cooperative, and to show his appreciation Admiral Reedy asked them to send one of their scientists on what was sure to be a historic flight. An eminent geologist, Professor L. C. King from the University of Natal, made the trans-Antarctic journey aboard our second plane.

To the naval aviators who maintained America's Antarctic research stations at McMurdo Sound and the South Pole, the flight was an experiment in shortening logistical lines. To me, as I remarked to Admiral Reedy as we waited to board our giant Lockheed C-130 Hercules ski-planes, "This is the last great long-distance flight left to be made on this earth connecting two continents." (I was wrong in saying this. Ever since the first world flight, in 1922, airmen had talked of the day when someone would do it the hard way—circle the globe via both Poles. In 1965 I played a small part in helping Fred Austin and Harrison Finch, veteran TWA captains, accomplish this feat. They asked me to go along, and when I was unable to get away they invited Lowell, Jr., himself a pilot of many years' experience. Taking a leave of absence from his duties as a state senator in Alaska, he made the flight with them and we included his account of it in a book we did together, "Great First Flights That Changed History." It was the only time this aerial circuit of the planet via both the North and South Poles has been made.

Commercial flights from Cape Town to Christchurch, until

1962, swung far north through Bombay and Singapore, flying nearly 14,000 miles in thirty-five hours. Our flight—if it worked— would cover 7,100 miles on a straight line in only twenty-two and a half hours. Modern planes had crossed greater distances, but none had ever flown over as many as 4,700 miles of ocean and ice (the distance between Cape Town and McMurdo, our only stop), then on to New Zealand and Australia.

Just before 2:00 P.M. Greenwich mean time, Monday, September 30, we were ready for take-off. I was in the lead plane of two. Each was loaded with 62,000 pounds of fuel, good for about seventeen hours of flying time, but so heavy that the wings drooped and the extra tanks in the hold pressed the lumbering craft almost to the tops of their ski-wheel landing gear. But after a long, long run, Lt. Comdr. Richard G. Dickerson, our number one pilot, called out, "Wheels up!" I looked at my watch: It was precisely 2:00 P.M.

We climbed toward 20,000 feet, the Cape of Good Hope slipping away behind us, our companion C-130 off our tail. We would go higher as we lost weight by burning fuel, but there would be little to see in the opaque iciness outside. Soon the South African frigate *Transvaal* checked in for our first radio contact: she had been sent far into the Antarctic seas to serve as a weather observer and, should it come to that, as search and rescue vessel. Less than three hours later, we flew over the brave little craft, invisible beneath the cloud cover, and then lost contact. We began to climb into our cold weather gear, not because it was cold in the plane but because, as Admiral Reedy put it, "If we have an emergency, we don't want everyone scrambling at the last moment to tie the shoelaces on their thermal boots."

At 8:45 P.M., with a comforting tail wind helping to push us along, we reached our PSR—the Point of Safe Return, as the Navy optimistically puts it, but actually the final moment when we could have turned back and hoped to make it. We were now exactly 2,347 statute miles out from Cape Town. The good news was that McMurdo, far to the south, was coming in loud and clear on the voice radio. They had a message from the Soviet contingent at Mirnyy Station: "Congratulations and best wishes. Facilities available at Mirnyy if you wish to land." The bad news was that the weather at McMurdo was turning sour. At 11:00 P.M., our station at the South Pole reported visibility down to a quarter of a mile in blowing snow, temperature twenty-eight degrees below zero—mild indeed. Said our chief pilot Dick Dickerson wryly: "Typical day at the Pole—hot and dusty."

We crossed the Pole a little past 2:00 A.M. and, soon after, the midnight sun was well up into the sky. The hours passed in the drone of engines and continuing reports of deteriorating weather at McMurdo. But even as we began to think about the possibility of coming down blind, Ground Control at the station reported they had us on their radar. They steered us onto a new heading for the landing approach and our own radar showed us lined up between the rows of gasoline drums marking the runway. And moments after we first saw the snow-covered ground, our skis had made contact and we were rumbling to a stop—just one minute off our flight plan!

Although our layover at McMurdo was short, we had a meal with our Antarctic colleagues. Col. Ronald A. Tinker, the New Zealand commander at their nearby Scott base, in a mellow mood, made a three-hour speech of welcome. He was still speaking when I slipped away to catch a few winks. Others followed my example and our Kiwi friend didn't even notice we had left. Airborne again, we flew on across the wild southern ocean to Christchurch, New Zealand, and I went on to Australia. We had proved that regular flights across the bottom of the world were feasible. Of course this was hardly likely to revolutionize the flight patterns of the world's airlines; there is not that much air traffic between South Africa and Australasia and if ever there is the great supersonic jets will make the trip without need even to stop at McMurdo. But we had shortened the traveling time to our main base on the Antarctic continent and—forever the true impetus in exploration and travel—we had done what had never been done before.

Six weeks later, I stepped off a plane in Detroit, three speeches on my schedule, and that night, at a banquet in honor of George Pierrot, when called upon to speak, I wasn't sure I'd make it through the next twenty minutes. I did, but the people I talked to seemed separated from me by a sheet of plate glass and, when signing autographs, my hand shook so I could barely keep the pen on paper. At midnight I telephoned a doctor and, next thing I knew, I was in the Ford Hospital, with Fran on her way from New York and Lowell, Jr., from Hawaii. It looked, said the reports, like a heart attack.

But it wasn't a heart attack, as the doctors didn't know at the time, but eventually found out. Later it became known as jet lag, most modern of maladies, the utter exhaustion that overtakes the human body when it is carted from time zone to time zone in six-hundred-mile-an-hour jets and dumped into high noon when its inner clock says it should be sleeping. I suppose I had been traveling too far too fast all my life, but now that we were full into the jet age, I had found the perfect instrument to accommodate my wanderlust—and it finally laid me low when I left twenty-nine flight crews behind as I went speeding on and on not knowing what it was doing to me.

Consider: In a matter of months I had twice flown over the South Pole, as well as to Australia, New Guinea, India, Iran and Europe. After an earlier flight across the bottom of the world from Tahiti and New Zealand, I had flown to Australia and deep in the north country to film the wildlife and aborigines. Then on to Kabul, capital of Afghanistan; Samarkand; and Moscow. Next came the flight to Europe, then the length of a continent to South Africa for the first crossing of the entire Antarctic. From Australia I had flown to Europe, caught a jet to New York, changed planes and flew on to Detroit for those three speeches. In that brief span, I had crossed all twenty-four time zones at least twice and blithely gone on with my radio and television routine, while managing some writing and even a few ski trips. As a result, something unusual had happened to me—occasional blackouts and memory losses—but not until my day in Detroit did it actually and finally happen: my badly abused biological clock simply went haywire and I wound up in the hospital.

We still don't know too much about that mysterious inner timer that governs our physiological rhythms. Is it physical or chemical? Is there one, a sort of master clock, or many, with one for each of our major bodily functions? But we do know that, one or many, our biological clocks are not geared to go hurtling through space, indefinitely crossing time zones, without eventually breaking down. That was the lesson I learned in Detroit, as well as some ways in which we can help our biological clocks adjust to abrupt change: sleep when everyone else is sleeping at your destination even if it's noon back home; don't schedule important meetings or hectic sightseeing tours on your arrival date, but take a day or so to get in phase with local time; eat and drink lightly.

Of course nothing will keep me from traveling by any means available—ship, train, elephant or yak—and since jets get there fastest, most of my traveling will continue to be at near or even supersonic speeds. But since the episode in Detroit, I've been heeding the advice telegraphed to me in the hospital there by General Jimmy Doolittle: "Keep up the jet flying, Lowell, but turn off your afterburner!"

VIII. This Is Your Life

Yes, Lowell Thomas, THIS IS YOUR LIFE!
                              —RALPH EDWARDS
The hell it is!
                              —LOWELL THOMAS

From time to time, well-meaning but essentially unin-
formed people have referred to me as another Marco Polo. The
comparison is forced. Marco Polo's classic account of his journey
across the known world from Venice to China remains, to this
day, the greatest travel book ever written. It is a basis for modern
geography. His descriptions of his experiences in the court of
Kublai Khan, and of the vast realms under the Mongol emperor's
sway, were the first ever brought to Europe. His observations of
Oriental society and topography, scorned as wild exaggeration
by most of his contemporaries—in some English schools a tall
story is still known as a Marco Polo—have stood the test of the
centuries and his judgments have been proven sound by modern
scholars. No, if my name is to be linked with Marco Polo's, let it
be in my simple salute from a present-day traveler to the greatest
traveler the world has ever known.

The best evidence is that Marco Polo was born in the year
1254, two hundred and fifty years before the great voyages of
discovery by Columbus, Magellan and Vasco da Gama finally
established the contours of our world. His father and uncle, distinguished merchants of Venice, had already made one journey

to the court of the Great Khan when, in 1270, the seventeen-year-old Marco joined them in the long overland trek to the East that would immortalize all three. Through Persia they traveled, across the great plateau of the Pamirs and over the Gobi Desert, arriving finally at Emperor Kublai Khan's summer palace in Shang-tu in 1275—where nearly 700 years later I made an unscheduled landing aboard a modern flying carpet. The Emperor, grandson of the redoubtable Genghis Khan, was much taken with young Marco and entrusted him with many missions and important posts. For his part, Marco kept meticulous notes about the cities he visited, the customs of the people, their crops and industry. At first hand he saw two engineering marvels unsuspected in the Western world: the Great Wall of China, fifteen hundred miles long; and the Grand Canal, almost as long, the last 600 miles of which were completed by Kublai Khan and which to this day remains the longest waterway ever constructed by man.

More than a quarter of a century would pass before the Polos returned to their native Venice, where they had long since been given up for dead. The riches they brought back in silks and jewels were convincing evidence that they were indeed much alive, but in the eyes of history their most valuable treasure was Marco's notes, which formed the basis for his epic book, *The Travels of Marco Polo*, written in his later years when, for several months, he was confined as a prisoner of war.

Ironically, neither his geographic observations nor his accounts of the marvels he had seen in China were credited in his lifetime—nor for several hundred years after, for that matter. Scholars scoffed when he said that paper currency was widely used in the Orient, or that certain black stones found there could be broken up and used to make fire. Now we have located banknotes of the Ming Dynasty; we know that his black stones were coal. And eventually the map-makers learned that if they followed the descriptions in his book, they could chart the Eastern world with more accuracy and detail than they had ever before been able to do.

I've always felt that the incomparable Marco Polo let us down by not giving us an account of what must have been the most incredible chapter of his fabulous years with Kublai Khan. The Great Khan actually made the young Venetian governor of one large province of China. What an experience for a young European to rule over Xanadu, in Far Cathay!

In the Australian desert, I was involved in a film expedition without the remotest idea how it would all turn out. It was from Lee Robinson, with whom I had been associated on our Sepik River adventure in New Guinea, that I had first heard of the strange disappearance of Harold Bell Lassiter. He was an American-Australian explorer and mining engineer who had been looking for a reef of gold in the heart of the great Central Desert. Lee said this had long been Australia's number one Never Never Land mystery, one he had for years wanted to solve; it would involve an expensive expedition—and could I finance it? According to press reports half a century ago it had been Lassiter who had organized one of the most elaborate expeditions in the annals of Australian exploration. An official on the Governor General's staff had been a member of his party. In the desert their plane crashed, their desert cars broke down and the expedition fell apart. The Governor General's man led the disgruntled group back to Sydney, all except Lassiter, who was last seen heading off into the unknown, on camelback, alone.

He had kept a diary, later found. Was it a fraud? There had been quite a controversy over the Lassiter diary. Some said he had found his gold reef and had somehow gotten enough of it out of the lonely, empty land called the Back of the Beyond to enjoy the good life, without taxes or encumbrances, in the United States—that he had made his way across the waterless Never Never Land and on out via Perth or some other West Australian port. Others said the desert heat had addled his brains, that he was indeed in America, but suffering from the delusion that he was a Mormon bishop. And still others believed that the prospector-explorer, losing his way, had perished of thirst in the unforgiving desert and had been buried beneath the burning sands. The American who had sought gold Down Under obviously had been named for a popular American novelist who was widely read when Lassiter was born: Harold Bell Wright, author of *The Winning of Barbara Worth*, a popular best seller and one of the first novels I had read. Several search parties had failed to find any trace of him—or his gold reef.

As often happens, more than one enterprising promoter had made capital out of it over the years. One was Bob Buck, a onetime English music hall comic who, in later life, became a cattle rancher, a drover and a wanderer in central Australia. Bob made quite a name for himself by announcing that he had found and buried Lassiter's bones. Soon he was traveling around Australia lecturing in cities and towns and giving tent talks for an entrance fee on up-country fairgrounds at stock show time, all about how he had finally solved the riddle of Harold Bell Lassiter's disappearance. Not everybody took Bob Buck seriously. In fact, those who knew a little more about the celebrated case than what had been printed in the newspapers wondered how anyone else could believe his story, since all Buck had for proof was a set of upper dentures that he said came from Lassiter's jaw but that could have been provided by any friendly dentist.

But Bob went on cheerfully spreading the gospel according to Buck and, apparently, making a nice living at it. Once, he told my friend, airline operator Eddie Connellan, he had been paid £500 to lead a wealthy Sydney businessman and his expedition out into the desert to Lassiter's grave. With Bob leading the expedition, off they went in great aimless circles around Ayer's Rock, Australia's most famous natural wonder. He hadn't the foggiest notion where Lassiter's grave was, so Bob finally confessed to Eddie, but £500 was £500.

After three days the man from Sydney began to wonder, not why it was taking so long to find Lassiter's last resting place, but why they hadn't run into any "wild aboriginals." That, decided Bob, was easy enough to arrange. Soon after dark, the expedition was duly attacked by "wild aboriginals" specially hired for the occasion, swooping down on the camp with tin cans, pans, drums—anything that would make a suitably horrifying noise. Then Bob bravely beat them off, firing over their heads with an ancient .303 army rifle and making quite a hero of himself.

End of the expedition! So terrified was the Sydney tycoon of all the sound and fury that he offered Bob another £500 if he got him back to civilization alive. Bob's later comment to Eddie Connellan was worthy of the man: "Well, I figured a man deserves his money's worth." So for the next three nights he had the Abos repeat the "attack," which made his sponsor so happy about his safe return that he invited Bob to his home in Sydney.

This turned into a story, too, Bob later explaining how the luxury of the place made it hard for him to leave. "Hell," he said, "the carpets in the place were so deep a man could get bogged to the fetlocks in them." For a week or so, his charm wore well, his stories were beguiling and he was quite the social attraction for his sponsor's Sydney friends. But after another week or so, it became obvious even to Bob that his company was beginning to pall. Still, as he prudently reasoned it out, a man doesn't leave a plush paddock unless he has to, so he stayed on—and on—until, in the end, his patron had to give him another five hundred to clear out.

Meanwhile, as time went on, the Lassiter legend did indeed become Australia's number one mystery—and nearly thirty years later Lee Robinson lured me back to the Antipodes to have another go at solving it. When I arrived at "The Centre," Alice Springs, an oasis in the great desert that had turned into a thriving settlement, Lee had everything ready for us to set off "into the blue," from the same place and with the same high hopes that had spurred Harold Bell Lassiter three decades before. We had three big G.M. trucks with huge tires for desert and mountain travel, plus a fleet of rugged Land Rovers. Never Never Land pessimists said we were wasting our time, some going so far as to predict we would never never return! The next chapter in the Great Australian Desert Mystery, in their opinion, would be What Happened to Lowell Thomas, his film crew, the scientists Lee had enlisted, and a corps of aborigines.

One member of our party was a tribesman known only as Nosepeg who told how as a child he had been with the aborigines who had buried Lassiter in the desert. In fact, said Nosepeg, he could take us directly to the missing explorer. However, there were some who were not impressed with Nosepeg's story. For one thing, I reasoned, he could have been no more than nine years old when Lassiter died. And for another, the desert, as it unfolded before us, seemed to offer no clues, no landmarks; it was an endless expanse of barren mountains, sand hills and stunted growth, every mile looking precisely like the mile we had just covered.

Water was our main concern—water and the sun. The first

night we came to a ranch, what Aussies of course call a station. Here we camped and filled the water bags on the front of our trucks. Without exception, these oases of human habitation were made possible by underground rivers that ran below—sometimes well below—dried-out surface stream beds, a sort of upside-down river. Once or twice the universal longing for rain was answered with a downpour and flash floods, leaving us sorry we ever mentioned it. As the lean, leather-faced cattle and sheep men put it, the desert was just a lot of damn-all. Shortly before dark we spent an hour chasing emus around Ayer's Rock—the largest single piece of stone in the world, said one of our group, a professor from the University of Sydney. At any rate, it's 1,100 feet high, 6 miles around—a landmark on the otherwise empty land, and "The Centre's" number one tourist attraction. What freak of geology created this red sandstone citadel of stone? What were Lassiter's thoughts as he climbed to the top and looked out over the miles of desert where, somewhere, lay the riches that would triumphantly end his stubborn quest? Now, as we scaled it and stood looking into that vast expanse, I wondered if, after all these years, we could really pry the secret of his disappearance from the silent sands, the empty land where so many before us had lost their lives.

On our way back to Alice we paid a return visit to this Brobdingnagian red boulder. We had taken a huge "fridge" on one of our trucks, to store our film. Having no further use for it, we presented it to the taciturn cattle man who had the only station near Ayer's Rock. Several years later we were told it had made him a prosperous man. He had used it for cool drinks to serve the steady stream of tourists who visit "The Centre," Alice Springs, and go on out to see Australia's top natural wonder.

According to Nosepeg, there was a cave where Lassiter had lived after his expedition broke up. He spoke of bullet holes in a tree trunk marking the defense of the explorer's desert home against hostile aborigines. Lee Robinson was sure that nearby was where Lassiter had spotted his gold reef. After a week of the roughest desert travel I had ever experienced, we came to the area Nosepeg had described. Here we gathered a sampling of rock. Whether we would find Lassiter or not, we hoped an analysis of our specimens would tell us whether this was Lassiter's gold reef, or whether, like so many gold-seekers the world over, driven to some godforsaken place by a delusion, Lassiter's quest had been doomed from the beginning.

That night, alone, I went over my notes from the last pages of Lassiter's diary. His camels had broken away and escaped; he was left marooned, slowly dying of thirst and dysentery. Then the last pitiful words, addressed to his wife: "Goodbye, René, darling wife mine. And don't grieve. Remember you must live for the children now, dear. But it does seem cruel to die out here."

The next morning, without hesitancy or indecision, Nosepeg led us to a place that, to me, was absolutely indistinguishable from any other in the monochromatic desert, a place he had not seen in thirty years. We had not dug far when our pick turned up some bones. Moments later we had a complete skeleton. Our expedition doctor, head of the Alice Springs Hospital, made the Lassiter identification by the skull type and dental characteristics. So the mystery was solved at last, thanks to Nosepeg, a primitive aborigine, and the wizardry of his Stone Age instincts—the same that had led us across trackless desert and uncharted mountains just as a homing pigeon finds its way.

Leaving a simple monument at the gravesite, we started back. The rest of the story is perhaps best told, with inimitable Australian whimsy, by Eddie Connellan, to whom we turned for help with a rather unusual problem:

Lowell Thomas and Lee Robinson, returning from the desert, came to my house and told me they had Lassiter's bones in a box under Lee Robinson's bed in the Alice Springs Hotel. They had, in fact, quite properly put him down in the hotel register: "Harold Bell Lassiter—No Breakfast." They had come to ask what I thought should be done because, after all, they were in possession of the mortal remains of a human being and, as they understood Australian law, it was a criminal offense to open a grave. I urged them to phone the police, who promptly arrested Lee and his film crew. For some months this proved to be something of a handicap to Lee with his film work, for as long as he was under a criminal charge he was unable to leave Australia and go to the United States for the completion of the film on which he had been working with Lowell Thomas. Eventually, though, the whole matter reached a higher authority than the Alice Springs sergeant of police and was quashed.

We reburied Harold Bell Lassiter at Alice Springs and years later, in 1976, thanks to Eddie and Lee, an appropriate large sandstone monument was erected to the memory of the American-Australian explorer whose disappearance had so long baffled those who had sought to solve the mystery. Robinson even tracked down Lassiter's son and grandchildren and had them flown to Alice Springs for the dedication ceremony.

Oh, yes—the analysis of the specimens from Lassiter's "gold reef" showed that while there may have been traces of gold in the area, there was not enough in the claim he'd staked to pay the expense of getting it out. So it had been an empty daydream that Harold Bell Lassiter had followed to his death.

Back in the middle 1960s, when I was involved in making an exploration-adventure series for British television immodestly called *The World of Lowell Thomas*, I was practically a transatlantic commuter. I didn't mind any part of that—I have always been able to get a fair amount of work done on an airplane, and as for being in London, I have spent so much time there, starting with the long run of my illustrated production on Allenby in Palestine and Lawrence in Arabia more than half a century ago, that to Fran and me London had seemed almost like a second home. And it was on one of those working trips for the BBC series that I met the nameless lady I have always remembered as the Admiral's Daughter.

It happened on a Saturday morning, one of those fine October days that make walking in London seem like a great gift. Having passed through Green Park on my way to do some book-browsing at Foyle's, I was strolling briskly along Piccadilly in the vicinity of Fortnum and Mason when a girl fell into step alongside me. At first I was not conscious of her appearance, only the rush of questions she flung at me in a cultured accent: "May I show you London? May I be your guide? You are an American, aren't you? I am something of an expert on London and I'd like to offer my services."

Now I looked. She was heavily made up, and the inured set of her face, the case-hardened expression, betrayed her as a young woman who had seen more than a little of the seamier side of life. Yet she was clearly not an ordinary Piccadilly prostitute.

I told her that I was not a stranger to London, and, politely, that I had no need of a guide. But the encounter was not over—far from it.

"From your hat," she said, matching my stride, "I assume you must be a Texan."

I said I was not, that I lived in New York.

"And you have visited London before?"

"Yes, many times, and even had a home here."

Suddenly she stopped dead and, with a strong hand on my arm, forced me to swing around and face her. "You're Lowell Thomas, aren't you?"

But she gave me no chance to speak. She said, "May I kiss you?" And before I could reply, she did!—loudly and wetly on the cheek. Then she plunged on to say that it was I who had introduced her to her number one hero, Lawrence of Arabia. She explained how, as a child, she had read my Lawrence book, and never shaken off his spell. She added that her impulsive kiss was just to express her gratitude "for bringing Lawrence to the attention of the world."

In confusion, I muttered something in non-brilliant response, and tried to move on.

But the lady was not finished with me. "You've traveled a great deal, haven't you? You've seen and written so much! And your broadcasts and television programs are known all over the world. I too am a journalist and perhaps you could help me find work."

At this point, I was doing a crablike shuffle, vainly trying to get away from her clutch, conscious of pedestrians circling us, pausing to take a good hard look. But her grip was like iron and the torrent of words she had loosed showed no sign of abating. Now I was being treated to her life story.

She was the daughter of a distinguished admiral in the British navy and had traveled widely with her father. They had been to America several times. Then her luck soured. Her father died and, soon after the war, she married a German, "a real Prussian," as she put it, who had mistreated and even abused her. In the end, unequipped for anything else, she had been forced to earn her own livelihood "in this undignified way, in the streets," as a tourist guide—and so on.

I was touched, but also most anxious to get on my way to Foyle's. When she pleaded with me to tell her more about

Lawrence, her idol and hero, and I said I was sorry but I hadn't the time, she suddenly began to berate me in tones—and terms—that seemed to put the hubbub of the traffic into the distant background. People now stopped to watch and I was agonizingly conscious of a gathering crowd, even a few from across Piccadilly at the entrance to Sackville Street. Looking around in desperation, I saw that we were in front of the tall iron fence at St. James's Church and pulled her inside the courtyard. But this didn't slow her down, and only whetted the crowd's appetite for more pyrotechnics. They pressed close to the iron grill, listening as the girl's complaints against me rose to a frenzied shriek. And so, finally, I did the only thing left to me—I ran for it. And as I went bursting through the crowd and out into the street—having decided it didn't make much difference whether I caught a cruising cab or was run down by one—a lady on the sidewalk who had witnessed the whole episode, obviously an American, wagged a finger at me and called out, "Lowell Thomas, *this* is your life!"

And so my two most embarrassing moments were, fittingly, linked.

The other one, referred to with such delighted malice by the American lady in London, was a long time germinating. Sometime in 1958, my old friend and fellow Coloradoan, Eddie Eagan, onetime amateur heavyweight champion, then New York's Boxing Commissioner, asked me to fly out to Manassa, Colorado, to take part in a big shindig honoring the old Manassa Mauler, Jack Dempsey, in his hometown. Ralph Edwards, the impresario of television's top tearjerker, *This Is Your Life*, had arranged to bring his camera crew there and to use Dempsey as the guest star of his popular TV show. This, of course, was to be a secret until Edwards' thunderous pronouncement before the cameras: "Jack Dempsey, this is your life!" There was one other thing, Eddie ahem-ed: Edwards had agreed to do his show in Manassa on condition that he, Eddie Eagan, would get me to appear on one of the subsequent *This Is Your Life* programs.

Poor Eddie, I had to disappoint him on both counts. A long-ago commitment would make it impossible for me to be in Colorado for Dempsey Day; and as for appearing on *This Is Your Life*, I couldn't think of anything more likely to scare the daylights out of someone who, like me, didn't particularly relish parading his personal life in public. I had never seen one of Ralph Edwards' emotional extravaganzas from start to finish— when you are trying to keep half a dozen balls in the air at the same time, as I always seemed to be doing, television-watching is a rarely-indulged-in luxury—but I had caught enough of it when Fran had it on to understand the formula: long-lost relatives and old schoolmates from afar suddenly appearing to stun the featured guest; people falling into each other's arms; copious weeping. Often genuinely touching, and frequently more than a little maudlin.

Relieved to have shaken Eddie off, I could hardly refuse when he asked me to be toastmaster at President Eisenhower's annual People-to-People sports banquet. I said sure, and, since the event was a year away, promptly forgot about it. Then one day in early September, 1959, my infallible secretary, Electra, casually said, "Don't forget that you're toastmaster at the Astor banquet on the thirtieth." And so the trap was sprung.

This annual People-to-People sports gala, thanks to Eddie Eagan, had become one of the top events of the autumn season, with almost as dazzling a roster of celebrities on hand as are likely ever to assemble in one place. This year it was scheduled for the main ballroom at the Astor, one of those New York land-marks that has since fallen to the wrecker's ball. The room was so huge, the largest in the city, that Eddie Eagan was able to arrange two head tables, each half a block long. At the higher one, against the wall, were some fifty or sixty United Nations ambassadors. One step down, on the second dais, was a long line of champions: Jack Dempsey, Gene Tunney, Joe Louis, Rocky Marciano and Sugar Ray Robinson from the world of boxing; the immortal track star Jesse Owens; tennis champion Althea Gibson; Olympic ice-skating star Dick Button; and among those representing baseball and football, Mickey Mantle and Vince Lombardi, and many more.

As always, I missed the cocktail session, being involved with my evening broadcast at that hour. By the time I arrived, the crowd had already moved into the ballroom, and I took my place behind the podium with Aly Khan, then the U.N. ambas-sador from Pakistan, on my left, and India's handsome, sardonic Krishna Menon on my right. I hadn't the slightest suspicion of danger. I chatted with the dignitaries, waited until the coffee had been served and the waiters disappeared, then rose, banged my gavel and was about to proceed with the customary head table introductions.

Suddenly there was some sort of commotion at the main entrance to the room. Incredibly, someone was standing there talking in a loud voice. Then, even more incredibly, the spotlight shifted to draw the audience's attention to the intruder. And he seemed to be talking to me!

"I beg your pardon for interrupting the proceedings, Lowell, but Colonel Eagan has asked me to start things off tonight with something never attempted before at such a splendid banquet. He has asked me to take over with our *This Is Your Life* program. But, Lowell, I am the only one in the room who knows whose life we are going to dramatize. Now let's just run our spotlight along the head table."

I didn't know whether to laugh or to protest. I couldn't believe this was happening. *This Is Your Life* at the People-to-People sports dinner? Yet there was dapper Ralph Edwards, grinning all over his face as he closed on the head table with the TV cameras rolling in right behind him.

"No, Jack Dempsey, we are not doing your life tonight— you were our guest last summer in Colorado."

The spotlight flicked along the table. "No, not you, Mickey Mantle," Edwards intoned, and the spotlight moved on. "No, not Dick Button," and again the spotlight moved, and again and again, until, all at once, it was focused on me, and Ralph Edwards was standing at my side and calling loudly enough for the people dancing on the Astor Roof to hear: "Yes, Lowell Thomas, *this is your life!*"

I didn't know what to do, but words came out absolutely unbidden. "The hell it is," I said, and started to leave. Then I had an inspiration, turned back to the microphone and said, "Why not Eddie Eagan? He's a great picturesque American—he's the one you want." After all, Eddie had outdone any Horatio Alger hero. A poor boy, he had graduated with honors from Yale and Harvard and had been a Rhodes scholar at Oxford. Then, as an amateur boxer, he, with the Marquis of Douglas and Clydesdale (later known as the Duke of Hamilton), had toured the world taking on "all comers."

Ah, but Ralph Edwards wasn't having any of that. Eddie,

who was almost as fit as he had been as a champion amateur heavyweight boxer, grabbed me by one arm; Ralph Edwards took the other, with Gene Tunney giving him an assist and, together, they propelled me up to the big Astor stage. There Edwards opened the huge tome that was part of his act and began reading the story of my life aloud. After a line or two, to which I paid no attention since I was still seeking some avenue of escape, he introduced one of my high school teachers in Colorado, Mabel Barbee Lee. As soon as she appeared from the wings, I cut off Edwards' flow of syrup, jostled him aside and made a little speech about this wonderful and talented lady who I had finally, after years of trying, persuaded to write a book about her gold camp experiences. She had just completed it, a best seller called *Cripple Creek Days*, and I used Ralph Edwards' time to give it a good plug.

This was not precisely what he had in mind. But he recovered and introduced my sister, who was lurking offstage with a microphone.

"Father insisted that you learn every rock and mineral in those mountains."

"I also knew every saloon in Cripple Creek," I burst out.

Edwards was turning pale under his makeup. He rushed Fran onstage and began sentimentalizing our courtship. Fran leaned over to whisper something in my ear, which I promptly shared with the audience: "Want to know what she said? She said, 'Must I kiss you in front of all these people?'"

Next came my longtime friend and colleague, roly-poly, razor-sharp Prosper Buranelli. He recited a bit of gibberish someone must have written for him, then turned to me with a sardonic grin and said, "Are you awfully mad, L.T.?"

"Prosper," I replied, "you've had too much to drink."

"Too much? Hah! I haven't had near enough. Come on— let's get the hell out of here!"

"No!" Ralph Edwards practically shrieked into twenty million television sets. "I mean, we never have anything to drink on this set, only coffee."

By this time, as Russel Crouse once put it, everything was out of focus but the camera. People missed cues, commercial spots went by without any commercials and Edwards seemed to have abandoned himself to utter ruination. As for me, on the spot, I worked out this device for preserving at least part of my private life: I did it by not permitting any of the people Edwards had flown in for the purpose of revealing a juicy biographical morsel to say much more than, "Good evening." This I did by taking over the microphone and talking about *them.*

Bertha Vester suddenly materialized. Edwards had flown her all the way from Jerusalem to tell how we had met there during World War I and how since those days I had helped her a little with her humanitarian work with mothers and children, and I took the opportunity to tell of the remarkable career she had had in the Holy Land. I described her as a super Florence Nightingale, which she was. It was the same when Edwards brought on Count Felix von Luckner, whose heroics in the first war I had told about in two books, and whom, with his stunning wife, Ingeborg, I had managed to save from the clutches of the Russians in the second. Then it was General Terry Allen, commander of the crack Timber Wolf Division of World War II. When General Allen began telling how his men had made me an honorary member of their division after I'd managed to reach their frontline position, I interrupted to remind him of the night of revelry that followed.

The program ran overtime and Ralph Edwards, mournfully predicting that his career in television was finished, had to be helped from the ballroom. Next day, front page stories from coast to coast told what I had done to the "This Is Your Life" show. That night, on my own broadcast, I felt obliged to explain, "If I seemed a bit sardonic, it was because I was utterly startled."

Then the ratings came in—an all-time high for "This Is Your Life"—and Edwards' gloom turned to jubilation. "Lowell Thomas was the best thing that ever happened to us," he announced ecstatically. "I'm going to submit that show to the TV academy as the best comedy of the season."

On the evening of November 22, 1965, in the Grand Ballroom of the Waldorf-Astoria, I was the object of some further public notice, and this time there wasn't much I could do about it. Being then in my thirty-sixth year as a radio news person, I had set all sorts of media longevity records, which I have never considered any great credit to me—I simply started early and lived long. But some of my friends at the Explorers Club, the Dutch Treat Club and the Marco Polo Club thought otherwise. They threw quite a bash for me at the Waldorf and, it being a cold night, some twelve hundred poor souls came to take shelter in the Grand Ballroom.

They had plenty of celebrities to hear and meet. Walter Cronkite was master of ceremonies, Arthur Godfrey was in charge of entertainment; Governor Nelson Rockefeller and former Governor Thomas E. Dewey, among others, made speeches. One of the high points of the evening came with the reading of messages from the three living American presidents, Harry Truman, Dwight D. Eisenhower and the then-current occupant of the White House, Lyndon B. Johnson. Said former President Truman:

> I am genuinely sorry that I can't be with you tonight to pay my respects and esteem to the Methuselah of radio broadcasts. He deserves all he will get from his emulators tonight!

Then, unable to resist the temptation to toss a little barb at such a neatly bunched target, Mr. Truman added:

> I only have the kindest feeling for him—but then I was never much for seeking approval or adulation from you gentlemen of the press—and I might add that, while he never helped me much, he rarely, if ever, hurt me.

General Eisenhower's message, taped, came booming in over the loudspeakers:

> This is "Ike" Eisenhower wishing you many more years of successful speaking and writing and exploring. Of course, on the last point, you have seen just about everything in the world that is worth seeing. Your zest for new places and your vigor in reaching them suggest one possibility—your enrollment as an astronaut. Should you need a recommendation don't fail to call on me.

And L.B.J. rounded out my discomfiture by saying:

> Long before jet airliners had shrunk the world, Lowell Thomas had it in his pocket. He is one of those persons who has been everywhere—twice. I am happy to join your group tonight in honoring a man whose influence on tens of millions of listeners and readers cannot be measured.

Now I cite all the foregoing as a vivid instance of the brevity of an hour in the sun—*sic transit gloria*. Only a few months later, I was addressing the convention of the National Association of Broadcasters in Chicago when, without warning, word reached us that President Johnson was on his way to make a major policy speech before us. Of course the President doesn't need an invitation to address a group, any group—and who wouldn't want to hear the President in person?—but we also understood that so prestigious an assemblage as the nation's broadcasters must have been an irresistibly seductive audience for so publicity-conscious a man as L.B.J.—and on the morning following his historic announcement that he had had it, and would not run again.

All that still left me with the problem of what to do about my own speech. "Being interrupted by the President of the United States," I told my fellow broadcasters, "must be about the same thing as having a four-thousand-pound elephant lie down in front of you."

Naturally I broke off as soon as President Johnson arrived. He was introduced, he spoke—at length and without apology or even reference to having usurped my spot, which thoroughly shattered the thread of my remarks—then he hurried off in the usual swarm of Secret Service agents. So I cleared my throat, went back up to the rostrum, now shielded by the bulletproof glass left behind by the visiting dignitary, and remarked, "As I was saying when I was interrupted . . ."

When I was a boy in Colorado, a school year stretched into an eternity as we waited for summer. Now the years pass in a flash, and there's still so much to see and do. I was on the move throughout the 1960s, accompanying the first flight ever made across the Antarctic from Africa to Australasia—from Cape Town to McMurdo Sound, then on to New Zealand and home via Tashkent, Samarkand and Moscow. I visited Prime Minister Nehru in India, and the Dalai Lama, now exiled from his native Tibet, at his Dharmsala retreat high in the Himalayas. Early in 1964, I was doing a daily broadcast from the Winter Olympics in Innsbruck, Austria, and by the end of that year I was off on still another trip around the world, this time via East Africa,

Arabia, Malaysia, the Far East and Alaska. Before the decade was out, I had journeyed up the Nile, visited Jerusalem and the fabulously wealthy oil sheikdoms on the Persian Gulf and attended a royal wedding in Nepal—nearly always with a camera crew in tow.

Was I satisfied? No. Was there any place on the face of this earth I hadn't seen? Yes—Siberia, a land long sealed off by Russia's Communist rulers and, to me, as tantalizing as Afghanistan and Tibet had been before I succeeded in breaching the barriers and exploring those forbidden kingdoms.

Would I ever get to Siberia? The answer, in June, 1970, was yes—all thanks to an imaginative, enterprising entrepreneur named Charles Willis, the man who had practically created Alaska Airlines. For years, Charlie had been working on a dream of his own—a commercial flight from North America to Siberia— and when, at long last, permission came through, he invited me to bring a camera crew along on the historic first flight.

Siberia. The name that, over the centuries, has meant so many different things to so many different people, is made up of two Tatar words—*sib* (sleep) and *ir* (land)—that give us the haunting promise: Siberia, the Sleeping Land. Dostoyevsky saw it differently. Arrested for political activity and exiled to Siberia, the giant of Russian literature wrote a novel about the bitter hardships of life in the frozen wastes called *The House of the Dead.* This was Czarist Siberia, a bleak and endless expanse where those who conspired against the government could be sent without hope of escape, without, in fact, ever knowing what might happen to them. Dostoyevsky, victim of a cruel hoax, was marched out as if for execution—and then told he had been reprieved.

For centuries Siberia has been a symbol of misery and mystery, a sinister, secret land where uncounted millions have vanished without a trace. From before the time of Peter the Great until after the death of Stalin, political dissenters and hardened criminals have worked there as slaves—dragging their chains, hacking out roads, digging salt mines—until starvation or frozen death mercifully delivered them.

Czarist Siberia was also popularized by writers as the ice-locked wasteland between the Urals and the Pacific. We pictured a vast, frigid wilderness where temperatures dropped to minus ninety degrees and stayed there until spring, where the lordly Russian noble, clad in glossy furs, reclined indolently in a sleigh while his driver cracked a whip over the horses and a pack of howling wolves bounded after in pursuit. It was the land of wild-eyed Cossacks galloping over the tundra, indulging their passion for freedom by smashing through settlements and towns and leaving death and devastation in their wake.

None of these images is wholly inaccurate. But in 1905, when the 4,350-mile Trans-Siberian Railroad was completed after thirteen years of the most intensive effort, the Sleeping Land began to waken. With a firm land link between European Russia and Vladivostok, Siberia was open at last to colonization and economic development. Today the cold and the tundra are still there, as are the prison camps and the Trans-Siberian Railroad—although the jet plane has relegated it to a romantic relic—but now there are also commissars, industrialists, engineers, scientists and workers by the tens of millions. Frontier cities have grown out of the frozen wilderness in a single generation, and old ones are booming. Mills, factories, dams, power plants and airports that weren't even on the planning boards before World War II are realities now.

But they have all hardly made a dent in the breathtaking enormity of what is Asiatic Russia. All by itself it could be the largest nation in the world, 5,000,000 square miles of steppes, tundra, mountains and lakes—and that's a lot of real estate to fill. And this immensity, a great sweep of land rolling on seemingly forever, is Siberia's most striking characteristic. Bigger than the United States and Mexico together, it stretches from the frozen top of the world to south-central Asia and covers nine time zones, from Europe to the Pacific. Although it is "next door" to Alaska—in mid-Bering Strait, at the Diomede Islands, the two are only three miles apart—we were forced to fly 4,100 miles before we reached the mainland, going from Anchorage to the city of Khabarovsk in eastern Siberia. From Khabarovsk to Moscow, it is another 4,000 miles.

But as we were to see on this eye-opening trip, the Soviets are determined not to let either distance or hardship keep them from turning Siberia into the new Russian heartland. The development of this enormous territory, one-tenth of the earth's total land mass, is the Communists' top economic goal, with a higher priority for men, money and machines through the 1970s than the Soviet space program.

The great push began during World War II and has already yielded astounding results. Siberia now produces half of all the U.S.S.R.'s steel, cast iron, coal and gold; and it may be that as much as 40 percent of all the world's mineral wealth and power potential is still buried in this virtually untapped, sub-zero treasure house. Thousands of geologists are at work there now, and new discoveries are being made daily. In just a few short years, sixty different oil fields have been found, one small section alone has oil reserves comparable to Alaska's North Slope, and natural gas reserves are reportedly bigger than those in the United States.

There is more coal waiting to be mined in Siberia than in all the rest of the world put together—in many places, local residents simply cut it from cellar walls to heat their wooden houses. Iron ore is almost as abundant. One-third of all the timber in the world is there. And flowing through the almost virgin forest that covers three-fourths of Siberia are 53,000 miles of rivers. Just two of them, the Yenisey and the Lena, pack more potential for electric power than all the rivers of the United States put together.

The shroud of silence that for centuries shut this fabulous land away from the world is now being partially lifted, and not for sentimental reasons. In a major policy changeabout, the Kremlin has conceded that hard currency—dollars, marks, yen— is more important than its cherished secrecy and has permitted tourism to become big business in the Soviet Union—including vast Siberia. More than a hundred Soviet cities, several in Siberia, are now open to foreign visitors. "Last year we had something like two million tourists," I was told by Leonid Khodorkov, first vice president of Intourist, the government agency in charge of all foreign travel in the U.S.S.R. "We are encouraging more of them to visit Siberia."

Of course there are still huge areas of this distant land that cannot be seen by outsiders. The Soviets do much of their atomic testing in Siberia, and it is the home of major air bases and several dozen missile-launching sites. Vladivostok, a closed arsenal so secret that even few Russians are allowed to go there, is headquarters for the Soviet Pacific fleet.

Its huge empty spaces make Siberia a tempting target for China and its population of nearly one billion people. The two giant Communist powers uneasily share a 4,500-mile-long border, and at least forty Soviet divisions are stationed east of the Urals. In Khabarovsk, only 35 miles from the Chinese frontier, one is constantly aware that the Russians have taken to heart the warning of Charles de Gaulle: "The Chinese will eventually expel you from Siberia."

How did Russia, which borders Poland and Romania in the west, penetrate so far eastward? Vladivostok is a fourth of the way around the world from Moscow. And the answer is that the Russians, like the Americans, have a saga of transcontinental migration. They, too, expanded to the Pacific; while we were moving westward to California, they were working their way eastward into the Maritime Territory of Siberia, and for many of the same reasons: empty land, economic opportunity, a chance for a new start.

Now, with an exuberant spirit not unlike that of our Westerners, Siberians refer to their land and many of its phenomena as the biggest or the best in the world. We visited one of their proudest achievements, the giant Bratsk Dam, deep in central Siberia. Built over a period of seven years at a cost of $760,000,000, it has an installed capacity of 4,500,000 kilowatts, more than twice that of Grand Coulee, America's largest dam. To build it took more than 16,000 workers, many of them criminals who thereby earned cuts in their sentences. Most, however, were Young Communist League members challenged to perform their "national duty."

The hardships were incredible, with construction continuing right through the savage winters. Most workers lived in tents and the temperature, dropping to sixty-five degrees below zero, froze faces, burst eardrums and welded bare skin to any metal surface. Normal vodka froze, so a one hundred ninety proof product was provided, which was consumed with relish—but also used as an anti-freeze for motor vehicles.

Completed in 1964, the Bratsk Dam is a stupendous achievement. The lake created is 2,000 square miles in area, the

"Prosper, you've had too much to drink."
"Too much? Hah! I haven't had near enough. Come on—let's get the hell out of here!"

Interrupted by L.B.J. when I was addressing the *National Association of Broadcasters.*

While Bishop Herbert Welch and Arthur Flemming were performing at Ohio Wesleyan, Chancellor Herbert J. Burgstahler, Herbert Hoover and I fell sound asleep—but that was twenty-eight years ago, and we have been forgiven.

Dr. Harold Taylor, then President of Sarah Lawrence, suggested these photos should be captioned: "Keeping abreast of the news." The two lovelies are Colette Ramsay and Jayne Mansfield.

In Assam on a search for a man-eating tiger.

At my eightieth birthday celebration with Captain Eddie Rickenbacker (right) and Dr. Frank Stinchfield, who performed orthopedic miracles for me in 1949 after the accident in the Himalayas.

With explorer Oral Roberts on Mt. McKinley.

Bertha Vester, a modern Florence Nightingale whose humanitarian work spanned some seven decades.

Tay and L.T., Jr., with us at the Lahaina, Maui, ceremony before we set forth on our fifty-thousand-mile honeymoon trip.

The rose-red city of Aqaba which we revisited on our honeymoon.

Jordan's King Hussein, a man of wit as well as courage. Nine attempts have been made on his life. Thirteen years ago when I told an audience they should see the Jordan River, he said, "Better hurry up, or it won't be there."

With Dick Durrance in British Columbia (above).

John Gow, who is following me, became a ski instructor and mountain guide after losing both feet. (SIMON HOYLE)

With Marianna at the University of Vermont for another degree, June, 1977.

At the June, 1977, Dartmouth commencement with Melvyn Douglas, Helen Gahagan Douglas, President John Kemeny, William E. Buchanan, Dr. David Davis, Ray Kroc and Earl Blaik.

third largest man-made lake in the world. Highly automated, the huge hydroelectric facility can be run by only five engineers and maintenance men on each shift. Using its power are a giant aluminum mill and a pulp paper and cellulose plant employing 8,000 people. Chemical complexes and other power-hungry industries are being constructed as fast as 50,000 Bratsk workers can build them.

Bratsk itself, once a motley construction camp, has become a boom town of more than a quarter of a million people, linked to the rest of the country by a rail line, new roads and commercial air routes, with 15,000 new residents arriving each year. Like Siberia generally, it is an attractive magnet for Soviet young people, who see it as a place of opportunity and adventure. "We have gone east the way you Americans went west," one of the residents told me. Marriage and birth rates are the highest in the U.S.S.R., and so is the divorce rate. And I was glad to observe that hemlines, as elsewhere in emancipated Siberia, were considerably higher than what is acceptable in Moscow.

The sense of challenge and excitement is evident in Bratsk. "We can get ahead on our merits here," said one young supervisor of a paper factory. "There are no older bosses standing in our way. We're writing our own book."

Only the natural wonders of Siberia are more spectacular than the new works of man. Lake Baykal, for example, with three hundred rivers flowing into it and only one, the angry Angara, flowing out, is the deepest inland body of water in the world. More than a mile deep, close to 400 miles long and 50 wide, Baykal is believed to contain a fifth of all the earth's fresh water reserves, about as much as is held by all of America's Great Lakes. It is one of the world's scenic wonders, having some 1,800 varieties of flora and fauna—including the freshwater seal—two-thirds of them found nowhere else on earth.

Unique in all the U.S.S.R. is a forty-mile paved road to Baykal from Irkutsk, a modern city of half a million. In 1960, in anticipation of a four-hour visit by President Eisenhower, this road was hacked out and paved in a few weeks' time. Then the Russians shot down our U-2 spy plane, Khrushchev had a public fit over it and the visit was cancelled. But for some obscurely Russian reason, the name of the road remained unchanged: the President Eisenhower Highway.

In their constant battle with the weather, Soviet builders are applying innovative—but incredibly costly—measures. At one diamond-mining town sixty miles north of the Arctic Circle, all the buildings are connected by heated tunnels, enabling the 5,000 inhabitants to live and work for weeks at a time without going outdoors. Also on the drawing boards is a plan for an entire city in northern Siberia, to be roofed over with plastic and glass, where thousands will live in comfortable artificially controlled temperatures.

But perhaps the most imaginative Soviet effort in Siberia is a reality, Akademgorodok, known in the West as the Science City. Of all the thousands of Russians who move to Siberia each year, none are more highly favored than the scientists and technical specialists who are remaking this prodigious land, and of these none are showered with more special privileges than those who are assigned to Akademgorodok, near the Ob River dam in southwestern Siberia. Headquarters for the Siberian Division of the Soviet Academy of Sciences and focal point for many of the U.S.S.R.'s brightest brains—1,200 of them with at least the equivalent of an American doctoral degree—the Science City is a hotbed of dreams for Siberian development. And this is one place where dreams come true.

Pursuing their research in modern buildings facing broad, well-lighted avenues, Akademgorodok's scientists live in garden apartments and handsomely landscaped one-family homes, virtually unheard of elsewhere in the nation. Their children play in beautifully equipped parks and playgrounds and on the wide beaches of a lake created by the Ob River dam. In the summer, the lake is filled with privately owned power boats and sailing yachts. Ballet, opera and theater troupes come regularly from Moscow and Leningrad.

The intellectual freedom in Akademgorodok is astonishing. In the town's bookshops, works by novelists condemned elsewhere in the country are openly displayed. Local libraries contain such forbidden periodicals as the *Wall Street Journal* and the New York *Times*. When Russia invaded Czechoslovakia, slogans condemning the action appeared on the walls of many buildings in the city, but there was never any official crackdown.

Indeed, Akademgorodok illustrates a fact that I found generally true of all Siberia, that the farther one gets from the

Kremlin, the freer and more friendly to Americans most Soviets become. People laugh in the streets of Akademgorodok, and in cities like Irkutsk, Tomsk, Bratsk and Khabarovsk as they seldom do in Moscow. In this city of science, so far from the bureaucracy of Soviet life, so alive with freedom of thought and expression, it is easy to forget the problems that plague Siberia and to think only of its magnificent promise. The people of Akademgorodok know they are privileged, but believe that their standard of life will eventually be shared by all Soviet citizens.

"We are tomorrow," said one young doctor. "Now the politicians will have to catch up to us."

In June, 1974, for reasons known only to themselves, the members of the National Press Club in Washington, the most prestigious fraternity of news gatherers and reporters in the country, honored me with a testimonial dinner. I thanked them in a brief talk and said I was proud to be among them. "All my life I have felt that I was a reporter, not, as some would have it, a journalist. A journalist is a newspaperman out of work."

Right after the dinner, I took off on a trip to Alaska. It was nearly my last port of call. In Juneau, the state capital, I checked into the Baranof Hotel, the sturdy old nine-story landmark, as I always did there, and went about my business. But one night, I woke out of the sound sleep that overtakes most of us by the small hours of morning, and I was struggling for breath. My room was full of smoke. The electricity was off and all I could make out in the pitch darkness were the luminous hands on my watch—2:30 A.M.

I felt along the wall until I came to the open window. From there I saw smoke pouring out of the building from a floor below and billowing up into the windows of my floor, the ninth. I shut the window. So far so good. But then what? I groped around until I found my pants, put them on and felt my way to the door. But the hall was just as dark and full of smoke as my room, and of course with the power cut off the elevators wouldn't be running. Choking, unable to see, I inched my way along the corridor wall until, finally, I reached a stairway at the far end. Had I turned the other way, I later learned, I'd have run right into the fire.

Barefoot, I worked my way down the eight flights of

steps and into the main lobby. It was chaos—firemen, most of the three hundred hotel guests—many of them Alaska state legislators—and reporters. One person had been killed, several others injured. A state senator, an old Navy man who knew something about knots, had used his bedsheets to lower himself to the ground, escaping with only a broken leg. Fire department ladders provided escape routes for those on the lower floors, and the rest of us had fought the smoke and darkness to make it down on our own. Apparently I was the last one out.

And as I stood there wondering whether to tuck my pajama top into my pants or just let it hang out, a bright young television reporter, microphone in hand, said: "Lowell Thomas! How did you manage to get down here?"

"I walked down the steps," I said.

"And can you tell us your thoughts and feelings as you were making your way down?"

"Well, I decided that if this ever happens to me again I'm going to grab for my shoes instead of my pants."

When you have lived as long as I have, you have to be braced year by year, for the loss of friends and contemporaries. For me, this grim reality first hit home, forcibly and much too soon, the night Prosper Buranelli died. He was the single most fascinating human being I ever knew, and though we were closely associated for nearly thirty-five years, I didn't ever spend a dull moment in his company. He never finished grade school, but I saw him back a Nobel Prize-winner into an intellectual corner, checkmate a chess champion and engross two American presidents with his witty, wide-ranging conversation. Herbert Hoover often said that Prosper was his favorite fishing companion, and F.D.R. would have lured him away from me to work in the White House had not Prosper lived by an old-fashioned virtue known as loyalty.

We first got together back in 1926, when I had exuberantly signed with Doubleday to do six books without having committed a single word to paper. When Capt. J. B. L. Noel of the first Mount Everest expedition told me about this marvelous little man who had the gift of organization and could write like a streak, I invited him to spend a weekend at Quaker Hill. It was a literary marriage made in heaven. Prosper and I were a team from then on; he became my friend and alter ego, working with me on books, radio broadcasts, Fox-Movietone News scripts, as well as TV and Cinerama. In his spare time, he ghosted autobiographies for the likes of Hollywood composer Dimitri Tiomkin, bomb squad detective Mike Fiaschetti and heavyweight champion Gene Tunney. Nelson Rockefeller borrowed him to help with what Nelson always said was his first important speech. And when the *Saturday Evening Post* asked Tunney, who had a public image as a good, clean-living athlete, for some articles on the importance and techniques of body-building and conditioning, he turned again to Pros. The result was a successful, highly convincing series on the evils of smoking and drinking, a splendid collaboration by two men who enjoyed both.

The fact is that Prosper's most vigorous form of exercise was laughing. And although he occasionally accompanied us on ski jaunts to Colorado, Utah or the High Sierra, he then spent his time in the handiest bar of the nearest town. Afterward he would berate me with something like: "You show so little enthusiasm for the finer things in life that I have to drink for both of us."

Then came the night of June 18, 1960. I was just back from an expedition to the South Pole and my Quaker Hill neighbors had given me a welcome home party and dinner. When the festivities were over a few of the guests went back home with Fran and me—Prosper; former Governor Dewey and his wife, Frances; Janet and Ed Murrow; and Ruth and Norman Vincent Peale. It was a fairly high-powered and diverse group, as you can see, but as usual it was Prosper who held center stage, keeping us all, by turns, hypnotized and roaring with laughter with his sparkling talk. And then, shortly after midnight, in that circle of warm friendship, as he would have wished it, he suffered a massive heart attack and died.

Now Prosper had never gone to church as an adult, his reasoning being that he had had an overdose of religion as a boy in the role of acolyte. But I knew how he admired the Catholic Church for its art and music, how he relished good conversation with members of the clergy, especially Jesuits, and I was hoping his funeral could be held in New York's St. Patrick's Cathedral. When I was informed that this was not possible because he never attended Mass, I did something the likes of which I had never done before. I leaned—hard. I got word to Cardinal Spellman about how Prosper, over the years, had done as much as any single individual in the United States to portray the Church and its Pope in a sympathetic, inspiring light through our radio and newsreel projects; how he played a vital part in the making of the climactic sequence of our Cinerama production, *The Seven Wonders of the World*—the filming of a magnificent papal ceremony at St. Peter's in Rome.

Soon I heard from the Cardinal's office: the original decision had been reversed; Prosper could be buried from St. Patrick's, after all. And a spectacular funeral it was. As a farewell salute to my colleague and dear friend, I rounded up a contingent of nearly a hundred eminent Americans as honorary pallbearers, including former President Hoover, several governors, a number of onetime cabinet officers, top sports personalities, radio and TV tycoons, publishers, authors, editors, soap opera stars—and two saloonkeepers. Prosper must have been laughing all the way to the pearly gates.

The years sped on by. No one could really take Prosper's place, just as no one could take Frank Smith's place, but life goes on and somehow one manages to keep pace with it.

Then Fran became ill. She just seemed to recede before my eyes, and though she lived on for a long time, life changed. It was as if someone had dimmed the lights in the big house on Quaker Hill; there were no more glittering dinner parties or impromptu gatherings, no more distinguished guests dropping by for the weekend. We did make a few more trips together. Fran wanted to see the wildlife in Africa while there was still time, so we went on a long safari in Kenya and Tanganyika; then we went on around the world, to visit her favorite haunts in Europe, around South America and to the lofty heights of the Bolivia Altiplano. Electra nearly always went along. Without her most of our later journeys would have been impossible, especially our final travels in Europe, to Alaska, to Iceland and in the grand swing around South America.

When Fran became almost completely helpless, the zest went out of my own travels, for I begrudged the days I spent away from her; each trip was diminished by not being able to share it with her on my return. I took to spending more time in reflection, memory. Later, going through her things, each old letter I came across, each gift she'd bought during our long-ago wanderings because "someone will like this," could bring her straight back to me, just as she had then been. Particularly vivid were the pages of impressions she sometimes jotted down. Once, after a dinner at the White House in honor of the King and Queen of Nepal, she wrote:

> An aide in full dress helped me out of the car. Another took me up the steps, another to the door, another to a desk where another took L.T.'s invitation. Then an officer said, "Mrs. Lowell Thomas, behind me is the main door to the dining room. You can see on this diagram where you are sitting. Your dinner partners are Dr. Charles Mayo and Mr. Stebbins, U.S. ambassador to Nepal." All these aides were young and shiny with brass ropes around their shoulders, but I never saw such regimentation. I thought we'd all have to be fingerprinted before we got in.
>
> At 8:00 P.M., the President appeared with the Queen on his arm. Mamie came in with the King. They stood in the doorway and the line filed past them. When it was our turn, Ike called Tommy "Lowell" and Mamie said, "I remember when we visited you at Pawling." I had a friendly chat with her. Liz Arden was good for her. She looks wonderful. Her hair is now a bronze red, the same horrid bangs, but the back was very pretty with a turned-under bob, a sort of pageboy.
>
> It was a cozy little dinner for ninety-eight. Dr. Mayo said to me, "Turn your plate over—I'd like to know what kind of china this is." I said, "I will if you'll pinch the grapes to see if they are real." I did and he did; the china was Lenox and the grapes were real.
>
> Next morning Tommy played golf at Burning Tree. As his foursome was coming in, Ike was going out. "Lowell," he said, "I never had a harder job to do than last night's. I could not get anything but a yes or no from the Queen, and she speaks better English than the King."

That's how I remember her—full of good humor, never awed at the rarefied circles into which fate occasionally thrust us, but still filled with her always observant sense of wonder. Others remember her that way, too—everyone who was lucky enough to know her. Not long ago, I found some ruled yellow paper on which, decades ago, Mary Davis, our longtime secretary in New York, had begun a sort of journal, given up and, years later, sent me the pages:

> I capitulated to Mrs. Thomas on our first meeting, a lovely, gracious lady of inordinate kindness and humor. After twenty years of knowing her, my capitulation is still complete.
>
> Mr. Thomas, the indefatigable worker, was wont to swamp her home at times with office staff and office chores. But Mrs. Thomas always bore up patiently and gave warmth and understanding to us all. Nothing really got her down. Maybe it was the servants' day off and L.T. had arrived home unheralded with two of the staff and a group of friends. Completely at ease, Mrs. Thomas would go down to the kitchen and prepare a delicious meal for all of us, and afterward we'd sit around the big kitchen table that looked out on the sloping green lawns. Then I'd help her make up the beds before starting the day's dictation with the master of the house.
>
> Nothing ever fazed her or destroyed her calm, whether visiting royalty or just "us help." To her goes my admiration as the sort of life partner most really successful men have by their sides, from their early struggles to the peak of achievement.

Toward the last, I restricted my wanderings to the absolutely essential. Regretfully, I turned down a nomination by President Nixon to become a member of a United Nations commission that would have required me to spend a great deal of time abroad. In the afternoons, I sat in Fran's room reading to her, though never certain whether she could hear me. Then on a winter day in early 1975, February the sixteenth, peacefully, as though very tired and glad to go, she slipped away from us. We had been married fifty-eight years.

On April 30, 1976, I went to my old hometown, Cripple Creek, Colorado, and announced at a news conference that I would be making my last regular news broadcast on May 14th, two weeks away and some 16,800 days after it all began, some forty-six years of "Lowell Thomas and the News." No earth-shaking event propelled this decision, no sudden flash of insight. However, it did seem a good time to start on all those projects I'd always tucked into a corner of my mind with a promise to myself that I'd get to them one of these days. By that time, my program had been on the air without a break for far longer than any other program of any kind in the history of radio and, according to those who keep track of such things, my voice had been heard by more people than any other since mankind first learned to communicate.

Was I retiring, then? a reporter asked me.

I told him that depended on what he meant by retirement. I was leaving my CBS radio program, yes, but I already was in the midst of a syndicated television series, "Lowell Thomas Remembers," reminiscing about the great events of the past as they were shown on the screen in the most dramatic news film we could find. At last count, I had made some seventy or eighty of these shows, with plans mapped out for another two years to follow.

I had recently become a director of the Golden Cycle Corporation, an enterprise that has begun again to operate the long-silent gold mines of the Cripple Creek district where I had worked as a boy. I wanted to be more active in that operation, as well as in Capital Cities Communications, which now controlled six television and thirteen radio stations, as well as a whole string of newspapers and magazines, including the Kansas City *Star/Times*, the Fort Worth *Star-Telegram*, the Oakland *Press* (Pontiac, Michigan), *Women's Wear Daily* and others. I was also completing these memoirs and, at last, the biography of our number one national hero, Jimmy Doolittle, which I had started nearly five decades earlier. And who knows, I might even have another whirl with Cinerama. No, I told the reporter, to say I was retiring might be a bit misleading.

It could, however, be considered a pause for reflection as I entered my eighty-fifth year.

I had never been long absorbed by possessions. Naturally, as a lifelong nomad I had, now and then, picked up something unusual. For example, a rare, almost priceless Pungi chest, exquisitely carved and completely covered with heavy gold leaf from a Buddhist monastery at Mandalay far up the Irrawaddy in Burma—a spectacular chest in which the monks kept their sacred scrolls. I have some 200 hats, and can't explain why. Also, one of my Quaker Hill neighbors, who was an importer of furniture from palaces in the British Isles, in a burst of friendly folly, saw fit to give me the desk once owned by the Duke of Wellington. Oh, yes, and the astronauts sent me a large, superb picture of our planet as seen from the moon.

There was a brief period when I kept track of the honorary degrees that came my way. This all came about as a result of my friendship with Dr. William Mather Lewis, then president of Lafayette University in Easton, Pennsylvania. Without bragging, simply conveying an odd bit of information, Dr. Lewis told me he had accumulated twenty-eight honorary degrees and believed it was a record. Since I was then nearly alone in the field of broadcast journalism, and had been for some time, this had attracted the notice of college presidents and trustees, and I myself was acquiring a number of new degrees every year. So I thought, why not a race, just for fun, with the eloquent Dr. Lewis? Maybe Bob Ripley would feature it in one of his cartoons. Eventually he did. Then my balloon was punctured. One day former President Hoover took me to the top floor of his tall Hoover Library Tower at Palo Alto, California, where on the wall were more honorary degrees than I could count. I estimated there were at least a hundred of them, from American and European universities. Whereupon I retired from my race, and from then on, when I gave a commencement address, I usually asked that the degree be given to a friend who deserved a Ph.D. but didn't have one. I did this for eight or ten educators, clergymen and explorers—yes, and three times for my father, who had already had a full quota but who enjoyed going with me to these sometimes inspiring ceremonies.

Deserved or otherwise, degrees still keep coming my way—four this year—and I've given up keeping track of them. People and places—those are my real interests.

Sixty years ago, when I was with Allenby and Lawrence in the days when they were driving the Turks out of Palestine and Arabia, I met a remarkable woman in Jerusalem. Her name was Bertha Vester and she had been brought to the Holy Land by her parents when she was three years old. They had come seeking solace after losing four children in a tragic accident at sea, and then an infant son to scarlet fever; they stayed to render a lifetime of service to their fellow men. Bertha, the only surviving child, raised in this spirit of benevolence, reorganized and ran the Turkish hospitals in the Holy City, continued under Allenby and later organized a clinic for needy mothers and children of all faiths and races. It was financed by her American Colony Charities Association and, through a long and distinguished history, was headed by such notables as Dr. John Finley, editor of the New York *Times*, Rev. Harry Emerson Fosdick, Dr. and Mrs. Norman Vincent Peale, Dr. Edward Elson, chaplain of the U.S. Senate, and several American diplomats. I had been a somewhat inactive member of the board of directors for many years, but when Bertha asked me to succeed the Peales as president, I couldn't refuse.

The years pass and the scene shifts. In Ohio, a generous, wealthy man, Fred Coppock, apparently with nothing better to do with some of his money, decides to present an Ohio Historical Museum with a special wing to enable me to share the museum with General Mad Anthony Wayne and Annie Oakley. This within a few miles of where I was born. The year was 1967, when I was no more ready to be immortalized than I am now, but how do you say no to a man who invites you to the dedication of your own museum? So I went. Afterward, I fell into conversation with a striking-looking young woman named Marianna Munn, who had been born only a few miles from my own birthplace—the two events, of course, somewhat widely separated in time. She asked my advice about where and how she could make a personal contribution, however small, to world peace, and I suggested that perennial tinderbox, the Middle East. Well, in a short time she was involved in our Jerusalem project, serving as executive director of the American Colony Charities Association, raising funds to help the mothers and children of the Holy Land. Over the next ten years, using me as a front man, she did quite an effective job of it, against great odds, due to the guerrilla fighting as well as the all-out wars between the Israelis and their neighbors.

Finally, though, we both decided this work ought to pass on to other hands. So we went out to Oklahoma to see if we could persuade Oral Roberts to take on the presidency, with a tie between his impressive university and the American Colony humanitarian work in Jerusalem. I knew I had the right man when he demonstrated his salesmanship by talking *me* into going up to Alaska with *him* to participate in a TV spectacular he was shooting there. Then Marianna and I decided we would go to Jerusalem and pass on the reins in person. And, by the way, I said to her, as though it was a brand-new idea, although I had grown extremely fond of her in the years since Fran's death, "Why don't we get married and make a honeymoon trip out of it?"

Happily for me, the lady said yes, and we began plotting the course for a honeymoon trip that would eventually take us 50,000 miles and last some four months. It would have been even longer if I'd stuck to my original idea of having the wedding on Pitcairn Island, that remote Pacific home of the *Bounty* mutineers' descendants, or under Buckminster Fuller's geodesic dome that houses our contingent of scientists at the South Pole. But when I phoned the Alaska Lieutenant Governor's office to break the news to Lowell, Jr., he said that if Marianna and I would be married on the Hawaiian island of Maui, where he and Tay had a get-away-from-it-all home, they would be able to come and stand up for us.

So the arrangements were made, mostly by my longtime friend, retired four-star Air Force General Hunter Harris, who reserved the lovely little chapel at Lahaina and fixed it with Bishop Harry Kennedy to perform the ceremony. At the eleventh hour we had sent out a few invitations, not really expecting anybody to come, considering the distances involved. But seventeen of our friends turned up, from as far afield as Colorado, Idaho, Alaska, New York, Connecticut and Alabama, and one who couldn't make it wired: "Marriage and the President's Medal of Freedom in one week—what a paradox!"

For that's precisely what happened: On the day after the wedding, on January 6th, I was summoned to the White House by President Ford to receive the Medal of Freedom, the highest honor that can be conferred on a civilian. And so, leaving my bride in Hawaii with the wedding guests, I hurried off to Washington, and the honeymoon didn't begin until the following week. Once it did, though, it was just about nonstop.

We started west across the Pacific, headed for the Marianas, in that vast expanse of ocean dotted with the hundreds and hundreds of islands collectively known as Micronesia. During World War II, the exotic names representing specks of coral in a 3,500,000-square-mile sweep—Guam, Wake, Kwajalein, Saipan—flared in headlines and impressed themselves on the national consciousness, and I had been to many of them. Then came peace and, to a new generation of Americans, the stepping stones of islands our soldiers had painfully fought for as they advanced toward the Japanese homeland slipped into legend, occasionally visited in a war movie with John Wayne on the late show.

But the war, like the successive rule of the Spaniards, the Germans and the Japanese, is now all part of Micronesia's storied past. Administered by the United States as a trust territory until they are ready for independence, the two thousand islands and their 100,000 native people are resourcefully blending their Pacific culture with realities of the last quarter of the twentieth century.

Our first port of call for a one-week stop was Truk in the Carolines, a forty-mile-wide lagoon surrounded by a protective coral reef and consisting of eleven major islands and scores of smaller ones. With its natural anchorage and strategic location, Truk had been a bastion of the Japanese Imperial Navy, "the Gibraltar of the Pacific"—until the morning of February 16, 1944. That was the day the U.S. Navy, under Admiral Marc Mitchner, launched an air attack against Truk which lasted two days and a night and sent some sixty (the people of Truk say ninety) Japanese naval vessels, tankers and cargo ships to the bottom of the lagoon.

Today, that act of wartime fury has produced one of the seven wonders of the underseas world. For the sunken fleet of Truk Lagoon has become the greatest concentration of man-made reefs on earth, collecting over these thirty years a mass of marine growth that has attracted uncounted species of fish to the crystal-clear waters of this lake in the Pacific Ocean, and creating a dream area for deep-sea divers.

On we flew to Guam, largest and most populous of the Marianas. Two days after Pearl Harbor, this main base of the U.S. fleet fell to the Japanese, and two-and-a-half years later we took it back in a bloody battle. Now, strangely, it is the single most popular resort favored by Japanese honeymoon couples. We didn't stay long. We had just heard of an island nation, smallest in the world to be admitted to the United Nations, called Nauru, the "Friendly Island," whose inhabitants, per capita, were said to be the wealthiest on earth. Our traveling companion on that leg of the journey was King Taufaahau of Tonga, who had at least two intriguing claims to fame: his mother, the former

Queen Salote, had been one of the stars of Queen Elizabeth's coronation; and King Taufaahau, at three hundred eighty-five pounds, down from four hundred fifty, was surely the weightiest ruler in the world.

The eight-square-mile island of Nauru, population 4,300, lies just south of the equator and is virtually one big pile of phosphate. Result: its per capita wealth is an annual $20,000 for every man, woman and child, with money left over to build a skyscraper in Sydney and there to deposit a $500,000 trust fund for each inhabitant against the time, around the end of this century, when their phosphate finally runs out.

Only a few Nauruans work—who can blame them?—and they have imported some 4,000 Gilbert Islanders to do their chores. Meanwhile, they spend their time driving around their ten miles of paved road in their 2,000-odd automobiles, which, as you can imagine, makes for some monumental traffic jams. They are also avid skin divers and, having suffered a number of decompression accidents, they took enough out of petty cash to send to the United States for a special decompression chamber. The only trouble was that no one on the island knew how to work it, so that when the president's son got into trouble in the deep and shot to the surface suffering the dread bends, paralyzed from the neck down and in danger of death, the Nauruans' lifesaving decompression chamber seemed useless. Then someone had the idea of telephoning an expert in California. For the next three-and-a-half hours, Bob Schelke of Riverside, California, talked an *ad hoc* rescue committee through the necessary procedures and so staved off disaster. Later he visited Nauru and was so overwhelmed with hospitality that he had to fly back to California to recuperate.

We reached the Asian mainland at Hong Kong, that teeming crossroads on the South China Sea, where an American industrialist, John Galbreath (who also owns the Pittsburgh Pirates and Derby-winning racehorses) was tackling the chronic housing shortage in a typically American way: Working with Mobil Oil, he was building a subdivision that would provide houses for 300,000 people, an instant major city. On to India we flew, via Bangkok, then to the Himalayas where at Kathmandu, in the Kingdom of Nepal, we stayed with the American ambassador, a beautiful and dynamic young lady, Marquita Moseley Maytag, whose father had been my pilot more than half a century before, on the first flight around the world. This resourceful friend arranged for a single-engine plane to fly us up to mighty Mount Everest, tallest peak on our planet, which in the late thirties had been seen from the air for the first time by the Duke of Hamilton and two companions as they shot a film which I edited and narrated for them.

Even in this day when commercial jets crisscross the earth's four corners, not many Western travelers find their way to the remote fastnesses of Central Asia. But when we landed in Afghanistan, it was a third visit for me. Half a century before, using the crude and heavy photographic equipment of the time and driving over desert where there were no roads, I had been the first Westerner to enter the forbidden land and make a film of its cities, mountains and people, including Amanullah, the Amir. I have wondered if it could be argued that my visit cost Amanullah his throne? He had permitted me to come because he hoped to open his remote and isolated land to the world, and this alone angered the traditionalists in high places. But when he followed up his invitation to me by taking his wife on a European tour where she was photographed in rather daring décolleté, his enemies flooded Afghanistan with thousands of copies of the picture, cleverly cropped so she would appear to be in the nude, and Amanullah was finished. He lost his throne and spent the rest of a long life in exile in Italy. Now, as we flew over the Khyber Pass, gateway to Afghanistan and the well-trod invasion route from Central Asia to India, one could see, as none of its conquerors ever had, a twisting, twenty-six-mile-long ribbon of road high in the mountains.

From Kabul, the capital, and Bamiyan, a former capital eighty miles to the northwest, we went on to Tashkent, in Turkestan, capital of the Soviet Republic of Uzbekistan and fifth-largest city in the U.S.S.R., and then to Samarkand, which once lay astride the Great Silk Road to Cathay and was one of the major capitals of the ancient world. Samarkand, one of the earth's oldest cities, already was a metropolis when conquered by Alexander the Great in 329 B.C. A thousand years later it was destroyed by Genghis Khan, but rose again, rebelling against its subjugators or absorbing them, and finally achieving its ultimate splendor as the capital of Tamerlane's empire in the fourteenth century.

Tamerlane, also called Timur-the-Lame, was a Mongol who claimed descent from Genghis Khan, and whose deeds of cruelty remain notorious in all history. From his capital at Samarkand, he invaded Persia, Russia and the Levant, and in India he piled a hundred thousand skulls on the battlefield at Panipat, near Delhi. In Asia Minor he annihilated the Ottoman Turks. But this ex-bandit, who by the year 1402 had reconstituted the empire of Genghis Khan with merciless, unremitting attacks on enemies and innocents alike, was also a visionary and a builder. He called the best artists and thinkers to his capital, Samarkand, and today its architecture, serene mosques and tiled domes of a blue color never since reproduced, remains a testament to his nobler self.

In 1868, Samarkand became a part of the Russian empire and in the early 1940s, Soviet archeologists were busy excavating the ancient Timurian tombs, heedless of Tamerlane's curse, which promised the scourge of war to any who defiled his bones. On June 21, 1941, they made their way into his tomb and learned, among other historically fascinating things, that Tamerlane, or Timur, had indeed been lame because of a shortened right leg. And on June 22, the Nazis invaded the Soviet Union.

In Iran, where the Shah had invited us to be married at Persepolis, ancient capital of Darius the Great of Persia, both Marianna and I came down with a bug and were temporarily out of action. By the time we reached Jordan, however, we had recovered, for which we were particularly grateful, as we were to be the guests of King Hussein. Again memories came flooding back: twenty years before Hussein was born, I had known and ridden with his kinsmen who, under the inspired leadership of his great uncle Emir Feisal and T. E. Lawrence, were revolting against the Turkish rule.

Once in those long-ago days, I traveled by camel caravan from the head of the Gulf of Aqaba to Petra, "a rose-red city half as old as time," a journey of three days and nights. This time, in a fast car on a modern highway, we made the trip in a few short hours from the Jordanian capital at Amman. But little of the ancient city itself had changed in the more than half-century since my earlier visit—still to be seen were the unbelievably wild configuration of the hills, the brilliant colors, the well-preserved temples and tombs that date back to the time of the Nabataeans, a vanished race that ruled the country as far north as Damascus five centuries before the birth of Christ. Oh, yes, we did find that an American archeologist, Dr. Phillip Hammond, had further uncovered the amphitheater and several palaces.

And so finally we crossed the Allenby Bridge into Israel and made our way to Jerusalem. Bertha Vester had died in 1968 at the age of ninety, but her great spirit lived on in the clinic she had founded so many years before, and in the dedication of her daughters, who had taken up her work. Marianna and I bid them a warm personal farewell, confident that this new generation would, with the help of nurses, interns and doctors from Oral Roberts University, continue to give life to Bertha Vester's dream.

From London we flew home on the Concorde. We did this primarily because my life has spanned the Age of Aviation—and then some. I was eleven years old when the Wright brothers first lifted a heavier-than-air machine off the ground at Kitty Hawk. Since then I have flown in virtually every kind of aircraft, and some who know about such things say I may have spent more time aloft than any passenger in history. And so it seemed singularly appropriate for us to be flying in commercial aviation's first supersonic jet, a slim, sleek bird of a plane that halved the time between Europe and America. As this is written, controversy surrounds the Concorde, but its progress cannot long be denied; in another decade or so, second generation Concordes, supersonic jets of many nations, will be flying the air routes of all the world —including Kennedy Airport.

Our honeymoon trip was not yet over, not quite. With my eighty-fifth birthday coming up, Marianna and I flew north to do something a little different to commemorate the occasion. That is, we flew out to the Canadian Rockies for some high-mountain Alpine skiing.

Long ago, I discovered that wherever I go I encounter someone who has a great story to tell. No doubt every roving newsman could make the same statement. Maybe, without knowing it, I've developed an instinct for finding stories with that extra dimension of excitement and meaning. And so it happened to me on my eighty-fifth birthday in the Canadian Rockies.

My original intention had been, once again, to get the special thrill of going by helicopter to glaciers where few if any others had ever been. Glaciologist Mal Miller of the University of Idaho, with whom in other years I had spent many days on a great icefield in Alaska, told me he thought there could be a thousand nameless glaciers in the vast area between southern British Columbia and Lake Atlin in the Yukon Territory. Several years ago, I had gone into these mountains by helicopter with Jim McConkey, a young Canadian and one of the most spectacular skiers I have ever known. This time Jim said weather conditions in the glacier country were unpredictable, and urged me to put it off from April until May. So at the last moment, I decided to round up a few friends, fly to Calgary and check on snow conditions in the Selkirk Mountains near Banff. This turned out to be a fortunate decision.

The Selkirks were still covered with many feet of snow, and we celebrated my eighty-fifth at two areas, Norquay and Sunshine, where I had never previously been. Among my companions were Dick Durrance and his wife, two famous American skiers, Dick having been our first winter Olympic star. Our party also included the Jack Simplots from Boise, Jack being one of the most rugged skiers I have ever tried to follow. We also had with us Tom Watson, Jr., of IBM, and Ivor Petrak, both of whom had skied all over the world. And there were the Milton Fruchtmans —Milton had long been associated with me in producing motion pictures for the screen and TV—who now make their home at Banff.

With us most of the time on this ski holiday in the Selkirks was John Gow, a tall, blond, curly-haired, always-smiling young man who was introduced to us as the assistant manager at Sunshine. I was particularly impressed with his ability to ski down those mountains with a perfect parallel technique, almost as though he was skiing on a single ski. It wasn't until I had been with him for a day that I discovered he had two artificial legs.

From John Gow himself and some of his companions at Sunshine I heard the story. Almost exactly eight years earlier, on another April day in 1969, he had been cruising above the mountains in a Cessna 140, with his pal Bernie Royle. John, although only twenty-two, already had qualified as a certified ski instructor, and as a professional mountain guide. The two were scouting for possible places to put up cabins, to be used by cross-country skiers in the winter, and by hikers during summer and autumn.

We have all heard of how a downdraft can play havoc with a small plane. It can even be a problem for great airliners, and is one of the reasons passengers are always urged to keep their seat belts fastened. In this case the little Cessna encountered such a downdraft that in seconds it was dropping at top speed into a forest. John Gow was thrown from the plane a hundred feet or more from the wreckage. When he recovered consciousness and looked around, he saw the apparent hopelessness of the situation. He had serious head and face injuries and could barely walk. His pal, Bernie Royle, had been killed instantly.

The story of what happened to John Gow from then on is almost incredible. He passed out again. In the days that followed he lost consciousness several times as he attempted to make his way through the deep snow to an area where he knew there had been a rough road for men working in the forest. Being without food was the least of his problems. The snow was so deep it filled his boots and, in the end, they froze solid and caused him to lose one leg almost to the knee and the other to the ankle. How he managed to survive a week of struggling, at times crawling through the snow, is hard to understand. Eventually he met a man of the forestry service who helped him to the nearest habitation, and from there they took him to a hospital in Calgary. He had lost a great deal of blood, his face was a mess, and then there was the gangrene problem. During the more than three months he was in the Calgary hospital, the surgeons operated on him some ten times, finally amputating one leg, then part of the other.

During his hospital stay, young John of course wondered and worried about what all of this would mean to his career as a mountaineer. He figured at the least that his skiing days were over, and how would he ever be able to climb mountains again? However, he was a young man of unusual determination. A maker of artificial limbs in Calgary spent some time in the hospital with him and a day came when he was allowed to leave—whereupon he headed for one of his favorite spots in the Selkirks, High Horizons, a camp to which he took climbers in the summer.

When he returned to the hospital a few days later, to the amazement of the doctors he was able to make his way unaided along the corridor, a feat they thought impossible. He accomplished this by endless hours of practicing over the long weekend.

Several months later, still a cripple, he was back at Sunshine. Without telling anyone what he had in mind, he got out some ski gear belonging to a friend—that was his disguise. Then he managed to strap on skis and boots and went up on a short tow, not knowing whether he would be able to ski down. But, he shoved off—and made it. When he reached the bottom of the hill, tears were streaming from his eyes. He could ski. As the days and weeks went by, he took some tremendous spills—once, looking back, he saw his boot and foot in the distance. But he never gave up. And unbelievably, only a few years later, in 1974, he traveled to Europe, to Val-d'Isère and Courchevel, where he entered a tournament for handicapped skiers.

Those who were running the events in the Alps arranged race courses identical to the way it is done at the Olympics. John Gow, sometimes moving at speeds of up to sixty miles an hour, won first in all four events, downhill, slalom, giant slalom and combined, coming away with four gold medals. His colleagues told me that today he is one of only four Canadians who have a ski instructor's rating as well as a mountain guide license. In fact, in 1971, only two years after the plane crash in the snowy Selkirks, he was elected president of the Association of Canadian Mountain Guides.

Yes, everywhere I go, in all parts of the world, I hear stories of men and women who do the impossible. Every skier in North America ought to make at least one trip to Sunshine just to meet this charming, inspiring young man who didn't give up when all the odds were against him.

After our ski jaunt, we headed back east again, to Memphis, Tennessee, where Jimmy Doolittle's Tokyo raiders were having their thirty-fifth reunion and had invited me to attend. There had originally been eighty of these valiant airmen, first to carry the war to the Japanese homeland when they flew their Mitchell B-25 bombers off the heaving deck of the carrier *Hornet* and bombed Tokyo early in 1942. Seventy-three survived the raid, ten were later killed in action, and at this, their thirty-fifth reunion—which, incidentally, happened to be on General Jimmy's eightieth birthday—thirty-five raiders turned up in Memphis to make it a special celebration.

From time to time in these pages I have referred to my father, and his influence on my life. But I haven't given nearly enough credit to my mother. Although the former was the one who insisted on giving me early training in elocution, he himself had done almost no public speaking. As for his voice, it was not unusual and at times rather high pitched. On the other hand, my mother, in church, could be heard above all the other voices. This was true of some other members of her Wagner family. Whether my sister Pherbia and I inherited Wagnerian voices from her, I don't know. But my sister had a deep, resonant, mellow voice, almost as striking for a speaker as was Marian Anderson's voice for singing. So, I may owe much of my success to my mother.

My father was unusually sensitive, always getting involved in arguments, and ready to discuss any subject for hours on end. His sensitive streak must have caused him much agony. Instead of making more than one or two close friends among the doctors in our turbulent mining camp, his pals for the most part were clergymen of all faiths, Jesuit scholars, mining engineers of special ability, educators and others of unusual talent who were drawn to what was then boasted of as "The World's Greatest Gold Camp." Only a wife as patient as my mother could have survived all those years with a husband who was interested in every subject under the sun, and eager to discuss any one of them, which he could do in detail effectively because of his vast, encyclopedic store of knowledge.

Perhaps I inherited much from my quiet mother with the unusual singing voice, who had for her lifelong companion a husband whose major gift may have been his unique ability to teach. What he did in my case was to open endless doors that otherwise would have been closed. I too became an instructor for several thousand embryo lawyers, and later had most of the Princeton student body as my speech pupils. However, I never did have any desire to remain for more than a year or two on any college or university faculty. Even as a trustee of some six or more institutions, I usually was a few thousand miles away when board meetings were held.

When F.D.R. became President, his First Lady soon found

she was expected to appear frequently in public, often to respond to some speaker. Although she had no trouble with conversation, as a public speaker she had a problem, a lisp, an impediment which bothered her greatly. When she came to me, her Dutchess County neighbor, asking if I could help her, I told her I had been away from the instruction side of public speaking for so many years that I felt she needed the advice of someone active in the field. I phoned Dale Carnegie about this and he said Mrs. Roosevelt should consult a specialist in elocution, an expert at remedying speech defects. He recommended Elizabeth von Hesse. For years Eleanor Roosevelt did work with Mrs. von Hesse, and, as we know, Mrs. F.D.R. became an effective speaker.

Several times in his nationally syndicated column Drew Pearson had made the statement that I had been Thomas E. Dewey's speech coach. This was not true. I had only given the governor one suggestion in all the years that we were close friends. At the Republican Cow Palace Convention in San Francisco, the year President Eisenhower was nominated, Governor Dewey, as titular head of the party, was scheduled to speak on the crucial third night of the convention, a Thursday. That morning I called him on the phone and said: "Tom, so far there hasn't been a single effective speech made at this convention. The delegates and visitors are wondering if there is any Republican who really can make a speech." I went on to add how I had noticed over the years that he was far more effective when he spoke without a manuscript, without even a note. Then his personality came through, and he was indeed one of the most eloquent men in America. He laughed and said: "What can I do about it? The speech already is in type and advance copies have gone out to the press."

Of course I should have brought up the subject three or four days earlier. At any rate, I discovered later that Governor Dewey did spend the rest of the day practicing before a Tele-PrompTer, and when he went before the convention in the evening he had his speech so thoroughly in mind that he didn't have to look either at his manuscript or at the TelePrompTer—and he electrified the crowd.

Several years later, at a banquet in Washington, Averell Harriman and I were the speakers, with Drew Pearson as toastmaster. This gave me an opportunity I had long been waiting for.

In my opening remarks I mentioned that Pearson had twice announced in his column that I had been Governor Dewey's coach. "Drew," I said, "you were one hundred percent inaccurate, which leads me to wonder whether other things in your column belong in the fiction category?" When Pearson responded, he made no reference to what I had said, but Governor Harriman did appease the toastmaster by saying that everything Drew had ever printed about him was correct! Which may explain why Averell Harriman survived longer as a roving ambassador than anyone in our history.

In 1892, when I was born, the Duryea brothers built the first gasoline-powered automobile in America. Now there are more cars in the average shopping center parking lot than there were in the world then. When I began broadcasting the news—and for some time thereafter—I had the only regularly scheduled news program on the air. Now there is an anchor man and television news staff in every American city with more than 50,000 people, plus more than 10,000 others handling radio news. We fly to Europe in three hours, communicate by earth satellite and watch, live, as men walk on the moon. So times have changed since 1892. It has, in fact, been the most incredible span in the long story of mankind—from the era of the covered wagon to the nuclear age.

Not long ago, in a reminiscence I wrote for the *Reader's Digest* about my father, who had been born during Ulysses S. Grant's administration and died in 1952, I said that he, too, had lived through a time of astonishing intellectual and scientific advances and, living his life to the fullest, he had kept abreast of it all. If my son can say as much about me, I'll be satisfied.

And so we come to the end of these ramblings. I promised at the outset not to preach, pontificate or prescribe for the world's ills. I wanted to talk about the luck I've had, the people I came to know and the far places to which I have traveled. And having done that, I'll sign off with my customary, "So long until tomorrow."

As the Spanish proverb says,
"He who would bring home the
wealth of the Indies must carry
the wealth of the Indies with
him." So it is in traveling: a
man must carry knowledge
with him, if he would bring
home knowledge.

—SAMUEL JOHNSON

(My father put it this way,
"When you travel you bring
back what you take with you!")